PRAISE FOR THE FOUR PRIORITIES

The Four Priorities is a fantastic tool that I've used for years with the people I disciple. I've found that many Christians don't make disciples because they don't know how, but *The Four Priorities* takes the guesswork out of it. Each chapter tees up great discussions to help a follower of Jesus Christ learn to become an effective disciple maker. You will not believe how much your life and relationship with the Lord will be enriched through the process!

LARRY O'DONNELL, III, FORMER PRESIDENT AND CEO OF WASTE MANAGEMENT, INC. AND FIRST "UNDERCOVER BOSS" ON THE HIT TELEVISION SERIES. AUTHOR OF *MANAGEMENT WASTE – FIVE REVOLUTIONARY TACTICS OF GAME CHANGING LEADERS,* AUSTIN, TEXAS

[*The Four Priorities*] is a great road map for the discipleship journey. Simple, practical, relational, transferable. We use it. Highly recommend it.

RICHARD ELLIS, SENIOR PASTOR, REUNION CHURCH, DALLAS, TEXAS

The saying, "The teacher appears when the student is ready" is so true, but I have found that it is a *must* that the teacher be able to articulate clearly, simply, and with a great application the path to discipling disciple-makers. I have found no greater resource than *The Four Priorities*. Not just for the new believer in preparation to becoming a disciple-maker, but even for this Pastor, it continues to challenge me both day and night every time I teach it. This truth births greater passion every time it's taught for me and every time I see the lightbulbs come on for the new believer.

PHIL WADE, PASTOR OF NORTHSIDE CHURCH, ROME, GEORGIA

Prestonwood has been blessed by the teaching and exhortation of John Tolson. His Discipleship Summit and *The Four Priorities* discipleship material are significant tools in equipping men to be leaders in today's society. John is a gifted and passionate communicator who speaks straight to the heart of what it means to be a disciple of Jesus.

DR. JACK GRAHAM, SENIOR PASTOR, PRESTONWOOD BAPTIST CHURCH, DALLAS, TEXAS

The Four Priorities is one of the most transformative books available to the church today. It's helped me understand my purpose as a believer (to go and make disciples) and given a new direction and focus to my foundation, Unite Mississippi. Our goal is to disciple every person in our state in the next ten years and we have a strategic plan to achieve that goal through discipling and replicating. *The Four Priorities* has had an incredible impact on my life and I highly recommend it.

CHIP MISKELLY, FOUNDER OF UNITE MISSISSIPPI, JACKSON, MISSISSIPPI

After being discipled by Dr. Tolson using *The Four Priorities*, there was clear evidence this would be a source of growth for me and others I care about. My wife and I went through *The Four Priorities* the following year, and now my oldest son and I are reading it. What a gift to see the work of God IN and THROUGH this book. Its packed full of scripture - a key element for success!

MICHAEL SANTIAGO, RED RIVER TEXAS METRO DIRECTOR FOR THE FELLOWSHIP OF CHRISTIAN ATHLETES, DALLAS, TEXAS

As a newlywed wife, new mom, full time strategy leader, and a seminary student; *The Four Priorities* couldn't have come at a better time in my life. Dr. Tolson provides an accessible framework with practical tools. Discipleship has helped me see the God-given gifts that help me grow in every aspect of my life. This incredible experience led me to lean in spiritually when I felt the most overwhelmed.

RACHEL LEWIS, MBTS, DALLAS THEOLOGICAL SEMINARY, DALLAS, TEXAS

In a single volume, *The Four Priorities* is a marvelous tool for making disciples who will in turn make other disciples. This book is a wonderful framework and guide for helping men and women follow Jesus more intentionally, critically examine their own personal lives, grow into treating the world around them as Jesus would, and reach the world for Him.

CARL COUCH, MD, MMA, DALLAS, TEXAS

The Four Priorities study is truly a great experience to help disciple others, and this book makes it very easy to help in that endeavor. Each time I go through it with someone, I myself grow closer in my own personal relationship with Christ. Lastly, it has made a profound impact when my wife and I both lead another couple through the study. We have grown closer together as a result of doing this together.

BLAKE CECIL, DISCIPLE-MAKER, DALLAS, TEXAS

The Four Priorities is such a valuable tool. I believe John and Larry were inspired by the Holy Spirit when they wrote this book. *The Four Priorities* takes what Jesus commanded us to do and gives us, in layman terms, how to not only align our priorities with Jesus' but, fulfill the Great Commission as well. As you go through this book you will experience this promise and the power of the Holy Spirit guiding you, whether you are going through it for the first time or have lead others through it multiple times.

HUNTER WILLIAMS, DISCIPLE-MAKER, DALLAS, TEXAS

Jesus' last command to his disciples should be our first concern...to Reach & Teach. *The Four Priorities* is an essential tool to equip a Christian to accomplish Jesus' goal. Most Christians do not disciple because they don't have a plan...a guide. In my experience with *The Four Priorities*, this is a well-written plan that works. I have observed hundreds of men grow in their personal relationship with God, their families and other relationships and then have the passion to teach *The Four Priorities* to other men...that's reproduction...that's good!

BOB SCHUEMANN, THE GATHERING, PALM BEACH COUNTY, FLORIDA

The Four Priorities is the best disciple-making tool for the busy mom. As a working mom and wife with a toddler at home, it's not always easy finding time to disciple others. But I am fully invested in doing what Jesus called us to do – make disciples who will make disciples – and so I use *The Four Priorities*. Each chapter is concise, full of practical application of scripture, with plenty of discussion points to generate meaningful, life-changing conversation. It's the best resource available on the market today!

MICHELLE SCHROEDER, DISCIPLE-MAKER, DALLAS, TEXAS

THE FOUR PRIORITIES

LIFE IS TOO SHORT TO GET IT WRONG

DR. JOHN TOLSON AND **LARRY KREIDER**

THE FOUR PRIORITIES, 4TH EDITION
Copyright © 2021 by The Tolson Group, Inc.

Published by The Tolson Group
Contact The Tolson Group at thetolsongroup.com.

All rights reserved. Written permission must be secured from the publisher to use or reproduce any part of this book, except for brief quotations in critical review or articles.

Content updated with the assistance of Mark W. Gaither, Dallas, Texas; and Michelle H. Earney, Dallas, Texas

Cover and Interior Design by Roark Creative, roarkcreative.com

Unless otherwise noted, all Scripture is taken from the HOLY BIBLE, NEW INTERNATIONAL VERSION®. Copyright © 1973, 1978, 1984 Biblica. Used by permission of Zondervan. All rights reserved.

Scripture quotations marked (HCSB) are taken from the Holman Christian Standard Bible®, Copyright © 1999, 2000, 2002, 2003, 2009 by Holman Bible Publishers. Used by permission. Holman Christian Standard Bible®, Holman CSB®, and HCSB® are federally registered trademarks of Holman Bible Publishers.

Scripture quotations marked (NKJV) are taken from the New King James Version®. Copyright © 1982 by Thomas Nelson, Inc. Used by permission. All rights reserved.

Scripture quotations marked (Phillips) are from J. B. Phillips, "The New Testament in Modern English", 1962 edition, published by HarperCollins.

Scripture quotations marked (MSG) are taken from *The Message*. Copyright © 1993, 1994, 1995, 1996, 2000, 2001, 2002. Used by permission of NavPress Publishing Group.

Scripture quotations marked (NLT) are taken from the Holy Bible, New Living Translation, copyright © 1996, 2004, 2007 by Tyndale House Foundation. Used by permission of Tyndale House Publishers, Inc., Carol Stream, Illinois 60188. All rights reserved.

ISBN-978-0-9838035-6-0

Printed in the United States of America

CONTENTS

Acknowledgements V
Introduction IX

PRIORITY ONE: A Personal, Progressive Commitment to Jesus Christ

Overview 3
Chapter 1: Who is Jesus? 5
Chapter 2: What's the Big Picture? 17
Chapter 3: What is the Christian Life? (Part 1) 27
Chapter 4: What is the Christian Life? (Part 2) 37
Chapter 5: Our Response to the Grace of God (Obedience) 45
Chapter 6: Relating with the Almighty 55
Chapter 7: Why Do I Need to Give? 67

PRIORITY TWO: A Personal, Progressive Commitment to Yourself

Overview 79
Chapter 8: Physical Assets – Caring for the Temple 81
Chapter 9: Physical Assets – Sexual Control 91
Chapter 10: Mental Assets – The Importance of Influences 101
Chapter 11: Emotional Assets – Griping or Gratitude 111
Chapter 12: Emotional Assets – Bitterness or Forgiveness 119
Chapter 13: Emotional Assets – Depression or Joy 127
Chapter 14: Social Assets – You and Your Relationships 137

PRIORITY THREE: A Personal, Progressive Commitment to Relationships

Overview 149
Chapter 15: Making Your Marriage Sizzle (Part 1) 153
Chapter 16: Making Your Marriage Sizzle (Part 2) 163
Chapter 17: The Parenting Gift of Protection 171
Chapter 18: The Parenting Gift of Identity 179
Chapter 19: The Parenting Gift of Confidence 185
Chapter 20: Small Groups – From Isolation to Connection 193
Chapter 21: Church – Your Body 201

PRIORITY FOUR:
A Personal, Progressive Commitment to the Work of Christ in the World

Overview 211
Chapter 22: A Worldview 213
Chapter 23: The Need for Evangelism 221
Chapter 24: Methods of Evangelism 227
Chapter 25: Your Culture and Your Calling 237
Chapter 26: Work 245
Chapter 27: Caring for Those Who Hurt 253
Chapter 28: Become a Disciple-Maker 259

RESOURCE APPENDIX

How to Begin a Relationship with Jesus Christ 273
How to Make a Difference for Christ Using this Book 277
How to Study the Bible 281
Using the Inductive Bible Study Method 283
Bible Study Tools 287
Preparing a Prayer Notebook 289
Recommended Reading 291
About the Authors
    Dr. John Tolson 292
    Larry Kreider 293
Footnotes 295

ACKNOWLEDGEMENTS

Life is made up of the sum of the events and people who come and go and leave a marker by which you evaluate the past and chart the course for the future.

There are many people who helped craft, contribute, encourage, and strengthen the development of *The Four Priorities*. The first three editions of this would not have happened without the financial contributions from Braxton Green and Bob Stine. The oversight of Dave Veerman and The Livingstone Corporation was invaluable. The contributing writings from Greg Asimakoupoulos were essential. Dr. Finn Amble provided both the insight and words for chapter 8. Joanne Reilly Budzinski generously and tirelessly transcribed John Tolson's Sunday School lectures and Kathy Pierson joyfully word processed every page of this book. The basic concepts for three of the four priorities were introduced to John Tolson in 1970 by Chuck Miller and became the guiding paradigm for the Christian life.

Through the relentless encouragement of a dear friend, Craig Mateer, who said, *"Find that one thing that defines you and give your life to it"*, the Four Priorities has become the hallmark of the Christ-centered discipleship that defines this ministry.

We are deeply grateful for the ongoing encouragement of those people who heard the original lessons of the Four Priorities taught over the past 30 years and have become disciples-making-disciples. Likewise, our family members who not only knew how important this message was, but also lived it out as an example of its effectiveness in their daily lives. John's first wife, Ruth Anne, championed the vision. After she went to be with the Lord, John's wife, Punky, has continued to encourage and partner in the work of this ministry.

The Four Priorities second edition has been translated into Spanish and Portuguese thanks in no small part to the generous gift from Tandy and Lee Roy Mitchell and the Mitchell Foundation.

With this third edition of *The Four Priorities*, we are thankful to Mark Gaither, writer extraordinaire who championed the effort to streamline the chapters; Roark Creative for their creative talents with the new cover and interior design; Pastor Richard Ellis and Reunion Church, who provided in valuable insight as a church committed to make disciples using *The Four Priorities*; the BASICS Class at Highland Park Presbyterian Church in Dallas, Texas, and disciple-makers from the Gathering of Men luncheons for their encouragement and feedback from using the first three editions of *The Four Priorities*; and the Board of Directors and staff at The Tolson Group and The Gathering USA for their support of this fourth edition.

Most especially, we owe a tremendous debt of gratitude to Michelle Earney, Project Manager for The Tolson Group who tirelessly oversaw the third edition from beginning to end. Not only did Michelle manage the project, but also with a heart for making disciples of Jesus she read and reread every word with discernment and love, making suggestions and developing ideas with the "new believer" in mind. Her invaluable contribution has made this third edition of *The Four Priorities* absolutely outstanding.

John and Larry can teach this material with confidence because their families attest by their lives that it is true. John's wife, Punky, and his children, Christin and Luke; Larry's wife, Susan, and two children, Brett and Erica, have formed a team of encouragement without which this project would not have been possible.

Last and most importantly, we thank our Lord and Savior Jesus Christ whose Great Commission to *"Go…and make disciples…"* has been passionately burned into our hearts and lives, and is the foundation of this ministry. For His glory we continue the eternal work of making disciples for Jesus Christ!

The material you're about to read may dramatically alter the way you live your life.

Proceed at your own risk! You have everything to gain if you continue; everything to lose if you don't.

This is not a Bible study. This is not another spiritual task to check off your list.

This a new way to live your life!

EXTRA CREDIT: SCAN THE QR CODE!
At the beginning of each chapter, you'll find a code that looks like this ⟶

Open the camera app on your smart phone and hold the camera over this image. Follow the prompts to be taken to a video where the author, Dr. John Tolson, shares more encouragement and insight for each chapter.

The information in the videos is supplemental to what you will find in this book, therefore, we hope you will take the time to watch each video before or after you read the corresponding chapter. And if you are going through The Four Priorities with another person or in a group, we encourage everyone to watch!

QUESTION: WHAT DO YOU WANT YOUR LIFE TO COUNT FOR?
We get only one shot at life on this planet. Unfortunately, as most people near the end of their one-and-only life they find they've missed it some way, and they take a final breath filled with excuses and regrets.

Life is too short to get it wrong! The God who made and loves you has also called and equipped you to live the Great Adventure, changing the planet one disciple at a time. If you embark on this adventure, you will be filled with joy knowing you are creating an eternal legacy. And that's really what we all want, isn't it?

Therefore, as you turn the page and begin these twenty-eight life-changing weeks, I urge you to consider the question: At the end of your days, *what do you want your life to count for?*

Now, let's begin with that end in mind.

INTRODUCTION: GETTING STARTED

Time is the scarcest resource and unless it is managed nothing else can be managed. —Peter F. Drucker

Scan here to watch the video!

Take a walk through your local cemetery, choose a grave marker, and study it carefully. Etched into the granite or marble is the name of someone who now lies six feet beneath where you stand, someone who once lived and breathed as you do now. The memorial also records the person's first and last days on earth, two dates separated by a short line. This dash, perhaps no longer than half an inch, represents everything the individual said and did on earth. It's a fitting reminder that life is short—far too short to get it wrong.

Tragically, however, many people do get it wrong. They live out their days with sincere intentions of making the most of the time God gives them, earnestly planning to make a lasting impact for Christ . . . someday. But as Allen Saunders wrote, "Life is what happens to us while we are making other plans."[1] Before they know it, half a lifetime has passed and a crisis ensues. Some people make the necessary changes, get priorities straight, and begin living the life God always intended for them. Many, however, do not.

Someday, you will have a grave marker bearing your name and two dates separated by a dash. Hopefully, that's a long time from now. Today, however, you have an opportunity to decide what that dash will represent. This critical decision begins by asking four introspective questions:

- Does my relationship with God affect my daily existence, or do I acknowledge His presence primarily on Sundays and in emergencies?
- Am I committed to continual growth and development in every dimension of my life, or do I merely exist day to day, following the path of least discomfort?
- Do I cultivate meaningful relationships with others, or do I maintain superficial contact with people I like to keep from feeling lonely?
- Do I intend to create a lasting impact on my community and in the lives of individuals, or am I more concerned with my own comfort and prosperity?

All that Jesus talked about in the Bible helps us answer those four questions, each corresponding to a specific priority He expects His followers to maintain in order to live a life that has the greatest, lasting impact for Him. When Jesus was asked, "'Teacher, which is the greatest commandment in the Law?' Jesus replied: 'Love the Lord your God with all your heart and with all your soul and with all your mind.' This is the first and greatest commandment. And the second is like it: 'Love your neighbor as yourself'" (Matthew 22:37-39). This scripture, together with many of Jesus' teachings, form the foundation of the Four Priorities. They are:

PRIORITY 1:
A PERSONAL, PROGRESSIVE COMMITMENT TO JESUS CHRIST
"'Love the Lord your God with all your heart and with all your soul and with all your mind.' This is the first and greatest commandment" (Matthew 22:37–38).

PRIORITY 2:
A PERSONAL, PROGRESSIVE COMMITMENT TO YOURSELF
"Love your neighbor as yourself" (Matthew 22:39). *You are only able to love your neighbor to the degree you are able to love yourself; you are only able to love yourself to the degree you understand God's love for you.*

PRIORITY 3:
A PERSONAL, PROGRESSIVE COMMITMENT TO RELATIONSHIPS
"Love your neighbor..." (Matthew 22:39)
"A new command I give you: Love one another. As I have loved you, so you must love one another. By this all men will know that you are my disciples, if you love one another" (John 13:34-35).

PRIORITY 4:
A PERSONAL, PROGRESSIVE COMMITMENT TO THE WORK OF CHRIST IN THE WORLD
"When he saw the crowds, he had compassion on them, because they were harassed and helpless, like sheep without a shepherd. Then he said to his disciples, 'The harvest is plentiful but the workers are few. Ask the Lord of the harvest, therefore, to send out workers into his harvest field'" (Matthew 9:36–38).

If all four priorities are implemented, your life will be revolutionized and you can be sure that your "dash" will reflect a life of highest impact. In this book, we intend to explore these priorities, discover the biblical principles within, apply them to daily life, and then pass on what we have learned to others.

PASS IT ON
Before Jesus ascended to Heaven, He gave his followers one last command. "Then Jesus came to them and said, 'All authority in heaven and on earth has been given to me. Therefore go and make disciples of all nations, baptizing them in the name of the Father and of the Son and of the Holy Spirit, and

teaching them to obey everything I have commanded you. And surely I am with you always, to the very end of the age'" (Matthew 28:18–20). We know from Jesus' other teachings that living the Four Priorities will align our lives with what He deems a life well spent. But, what is a disciple and what does he mean by "make disciples"?

Before we go and "make disciples" let's first look at what it means to be a disciple of Jesus. We must acknowledge three critical components of discipleship: learning, following, and reproducing. Picture these three components of Christian[2] growth as three sails on a boat. As the wind of God's Spirit catches these three sails, a person's life begins to experience the spiritual adventure God intends, and he or she begins to leave a wake that will impact others (John 17:18,20). These three sails are the three elements of discipleship.

A DISCIPLE IS A LEARNER

Matthew 11:28–29 records Jesus saying, "Come to me, all you who are weary and burdened, and I will give you rest. Take my yoke upon you and learn from me." In the first century, teachers used the image of a yoke to illustrate a student's submission to teaching. To take on a teacher's yoke is to demonstrate the essential quality of "teachability." A willing student never says, "I know it all."

Learning takes place when one individual becomes a student (disciple) of another. "Every person has specific needs that must be targeted by a trusted mentor who has taken the time and put forth the effort to develop a meaningful one-to-one relationship," writes Bill Hull.[3] Much of discipleship is caught rather than taught, learned in the midst of life rather than in a classroom. We all need someone to help us become the persons God wants us to be so that we'll be able to do what He wants us to do. Based on the kind of regular interaction you have with one or more individuals, ask yourself what kind of changes are taking place in your life and how are you being pushed to resemble Jesus more each day. And that includes passing on to others what has been life-changing in your life (Colossians 1:6).

True learning, biblically speaking, only takes place when one's life is transformed...*when it changes the way you live.*

A DISCIPLE IS A FOLLOWER

A disciple is one who follows and imitates the life and teachings of another person. For the Christian, that means following another who, in turn, follows Jesus and obeys what He taught. Paul wrote to the believers in Corinth, "Follow my example, as I follow the example of Christ" (1 Corinthians 11:1). Paul never claimed to be perfect. He was, however, consistent in the way he followed Jesus. We can become model disciples as well. To have the kind of impact that God desires, we need to make sure we are following Christ consistently.

Much of discipleship is caught rather than taught, learned in the midst of life rather than in a classroom.

True learning, biblically speaking, only takes place when one's life is transformed.

If you think you have to be a perfect model, think again. The Lord knows we are imperfect. Our job is to point others to Him and we can do that even as we fail, repent, receive forgiveness, and resume our pursuit of Christ. Remember our friend Peter who dared to walk on the water? He had his share of failure, too. Even so, Jesus didn't disqualify him. The Lord said to His willing follower, "I have prayed for you, Simon, that your faith may not fail. And when you have turned back, *strengthen your brothers*" (Luke 22:32 italics added). Strengthen your brothers on the basis of your failure, your weakness, and what you learned from God's abundant mercy.

A DISCIPLE IS A REPRODUCER

Reproducing disciples involves taking what the Lord has invested into our lives and passing along those truths to others. The essence of being a disciple is to be a dispenser of truth, not simply a depository of divine data. Too many Christians consume information without letting wisdom change them; consequently, they become stagnate pools of useless knowledge. One study indicates merely twenty percent of all Christians consistently tell others about Jesus Christ.[4] Fewer still actively disciple new believers. This study also reveals ninety-five percent of those who claim to follow Jesus have never led one other person to the Lord.[5]

How tragic! Christ has already set in place a strategy for maximum impact. But His followers must be willing to allow the Holy Spirit to work through them in order to fulfill Christ's mandate, "Go and make disciples of all nations, baptizing them in the name of the Father and of the Son and of the Holy Spirit, and teaching them to obey everything I have commanded you" (Matthew 28:19–20).

So, how do you "make disciples"?

First, tell others about Him. Tell them your story, how Jesus has loved you and changed your life, and how He'll do the same for them. *You don't have to wait until you finish this book to do that!* **You can tell people TODAY about what Jesus has done in your life.**

Second, walk alongside them in their new faith journey (disciple them) and help equip them to become a learner, follower, and reproducer for Jesus Christ. Just as young children need strong parents, family and caretakers to rear them, so do young believers need mature and wise believers helping them grow in their faith. Whether you are a young or mature believer (and age has nothing to do with it!) as long as you walk this earth you should seek out others to invest in you as well as to pour yourself out.

REMEMBER!

The Four Priorities is a tool to use in reproductive discipleship: discipling people to disciple others who will disciple others (2 Timothy 2:2). As we build a growing network of Christ-followers, our goal is to help others learn the Four Priorities and live them out. The priorities should become the filter through which we plan our calendars, spend our money, and live our lives. Once you complete this book with a disciple, encourage them to reproduce and begin discipling someone else with *The Four Priorities*, and then you begin with someone new as well!

Believe it or not, a person can actually become a Christian without ever becoming a disciple. In fact, we see this all the time! With all that we know from Jesus' teachings and commands, I pray that this is not the case for you. I encourage you to make a maximum impact with your life: become a learner, follower, and reproducer for Jesus Christ by using the Four Priorities to realign your thoughts, priorities and relationships. And don't stop there... teach (disciple) someone else to do the same!

Now, "Go! And make disciples!"[6]

NOW GO AND MAKE DISCIPLES!

For more tips on how to best use *The Four Priorities* in your discipleship relationships, see "How to Make a Difference for Christ Using this Book" in the Appendix.

PRIORITY ONE

1

"'LOVE THE LORD YOUR GOD WITH ALL YOUR HEART AND WITH ALL YOUR SOUL AND WITH ALL YOUR MIND.' THIS IS THE FIRST AND GREATEST COMMANDMENT."

MATTHEW 22:37–38

A PERSONAL, PROGRESSIVE COMMITMENT TO JESUS CHRIST

OVERVIEW

Jesus acknowledged that we have basic needs that must be met, such as food, water, clothing, and shelter. He did not, however, see these as a priority. He assured His followers that the Father would see to their needs so that we would be free to pursue another, more critical need: our growing relationship with God. He said,

> So do not worry, saying, "What shall we eat?" or "What shall we drink?" or "What shall we wear?" For the pagans run after all these things, and your heavenly Father knows that you need them. But seek first his kingdom and his righteousness, and all these things will be given to you as well. (Matthew 6:31–33)

To "seek his kingdom" is to cultivate a personal, progressive commitment to our King, Jesus Christ. To understand what Priority One is all about, take a close look at each word.

PERSONAL

The phrase "personal relationship" used to be redundant. Not today. We live in the age of email, Twitter, Facebook, and text messaging, a world of constant communication without meaningful connection. To be in "personal" relationship assumes one-on-one involvement. We not only communicate, we join one another in shared interaction. Too many people maintain a virtual relationship with Jesus Christ, using church and religious activities as a means of contact without ever experiencing the joy of firsthand connection with God. While other people can contribute to your understanding of what it means to be a disciple, nothing can replace your own, personal relationship with Christ.

PROGRESSIVE

Relationships develop over time. Relationships grow. A decision to embrace the Son of God as your savior doesn't mark the finish line of your spiritual journey; it's only the beginning! While Jesus Christ knows you better than you know yourself, getting to know Him takes time. It's a process, a journey of discovery that will sustain you throughout this lifetime and bring eternal joy in the life to come.

COMMITMENT

Like all worthwhile relationships, your relationship with Jesus Christ calls for commitment, your personal investment in cultivating closeness with Him. The process of walking with Jesus involves an ongoing surrender to what you discover He desires of you. Simply put, it is a day-by-day, moment-by-moment decision to commit all that you understand of yourself to all that you understand of Christ.

JESUS CHRIST

The object of your faith is not a set of rules or a prescribed ritual or even a revolutionary philosophy. We trust in a Person. We believe in, and dedicate ourselves to, the living Lord, who came to earth, lived, taught, performed miracles, died, came back from the grave, and ascended into heaven, and offers new life to all who seek Him.

The process of walking with Jesus is a day-by-day, moment-by-moment decision to surrender all that you understand of yourself to all that you understand of Christ.

CHAPTER 1: WHO IS JESUS?

Scan here to watch the video!

JESUS IS THE MASTER OF HISTORY

History. Now there's a word that calls to mind frightful memories of high school, a subject you may have been all too glad to leave behind. But there is more to that word. Look at it closely. The term "history" looks like a combination of the two words, "his" and "story."

When we look at the impact Jesus made on our world, that's exactly what history means. It really is *His story*. The life of Jesus Christ literally divides the timeline of history into two eras: B.C. and A.D.[1] No other individual has impacted the world or altered history like Jesus, the first-century rabbi from Nazareth. While attempting to explain His identity to one of His followers, Jesus said, "Anyone who has seen me has seen the Father" (John 14:9). In modern terms, He said, "If you're looking at Me, you're looking at God." His voice held no hesitation. He made the statement boldly without pride or shame. In much the same way, Jesus attested to His divine origin when scrutinized by a skeptical crowd. Looking them confidently in the eyes, Jesus drew an unmistakable correlation between Himself and the divine name for the Creator. He said, "Before Abraham was born, I am!" (John 8:58).

In addition to asserting that He was alive before history began, Jesus also announced that He would be on the scene when history reached its culmination. "They will see the Son of Man coming on the clouds of the sky, with power and great glory. And he will send his angels with a loud trumpet call, and they will gather his elect from the four winds, from one end of the heavens to the other" (Matthew 24:30–31). But that isn't all. Jesus drew crowds wherever He went and taught truths they had never heard before. Oh yes, they were accustomed to the teachings of the Mosaic Law, laws that had been handed down from Moses and read regularly in the temple. They had benefited from the traditions taught by rabbis that were based on the Old Testament. But they had never heard anything quite like what fell from Jesus' lips. Unlike most rabbis, Jesus didn't footnote His comments or punctuate His messages with others' quotes. Rather, "The people were amazed at His teaching, because He taught them as one who had authority, not as the teachers of the law" (Mark 1:22).

Jesus left no doubt that He was indeed the Master of History, but as you leaf through the pages of the New Testament, you also see that Jesus was the Master of many things. Let's look at some of them. These insights are condensed from the sermon, "The Absolute Power of Jesus Our Lord," given by Chuck Swindoll.

The phrase "I AM" in Hebrew is closely related to God's personal name, Jehovah or Yahweh... It suggests the timelessness of God, the very foundation of all existence.[2]

—Sylvia Gunter, *Prayer Portions*

MASTER OF QUALITY

Take the occasion of Jesus' first public miracle recorded in John chapter 2. At that celebrated wedding in Cana, Jesus miraculously transformed water into wine that tasted far better than the previous batch. And speaking of water, just two chapters later Jesus encounters a woman at a well in Samaria. He promises her living water that can't be drawn from a bucket on a rope. In fact, He claims that the water He alone can give her will be of such remarkable quality whoever drinks of it will never thirst again (John 4:7–14). What Jesus touches, He transforms. Where do you need His touch in your life?

MASTER OF DISTANCE

Yes, Jesus is the master of history and of quality. But He is also the Master of Distance. Time and space limit our ability, but Jesus was not so curtailed. His power extended beyond where His feet were planted. This remarkable characteristic is illustrated in John's gospel. The son of a royal dignitary was on his deathbed. Nothing could be done to save the boy's life. When the father learns that Jesus has been spotted near to where he lived, hope flickers in his heart. Tracking Jesus down in the town of Cana, the man begs the itinerant teacher to return with him to Capernaum. But Jesus, sensing the man's desperation, simply tells him to head home. Without going to where the boy is, Jesus heals him (John 4:43–54). You can never be too far away from the life and power of Jesus and His ability to touch your life.

MASTER OF TIME

In John 5 we see Jesus proving that He has every right to be called the Master of Time. When He sees an invalid sitting beside the pool near the Sheep Gate in old Jerusalem, Jesus' heart goes out to the guy. It doesn't matter that this fellow has been pushed to the margins of society for thirty-eight years. In one moment, Jesus erases the wasted years and empowers the man to take up his mat and walk (John 5:1–9). No matter how long you have been away from Jesus, He will still draw near.

MASTER OF QUANTITY

John portrays Jesus as the Master of Quantity as well. In other words, He was not limited to the cause and effect laws of the natural order. When a crowd follows Jesus into the wilderness to hear Him teach, He is concerned that they may be hungry and need to be fed. He takes a young boy's lunch of five little loaves of bread and two small fish and miraculously multiplies them so that a crowd in excess of five thousand people is able to eat (John 6:5–13). Jesus wants to take your life, whatever little you have, and multiply it.

MASTER OF NATURE

In John 6 we again see Jesus as nothing less than the Master of Nature. Following the miraculous feeding of the crowd, the Teacher proved that

He had power over the forces of nature and the laws of gravity. While the disciples battle the winds and waves of a stormy sea and strain every muscle to make forward progress, Jesus walks toward them effortlessly as if the water is pavement (John 6:16–21). He who calmed the storm wants to live with you—and in you—to bring peace in the midst of the challenges of life.

MASTER OF CIRCUMSTANCES

The ninth chapter of John shows Jesus as the Master of Circumstances. He supernaturally gives sight to a man who was born blind. When questioned by His critics as to why the blindness had occurred to begin with, Jesus doesn't blink an eye. He makes it clear the man's predicament isn't his fault or his parents, instead, Jesus insists, it is so that the work of God might be displayed. Jesus is fully in control of the circumstances (John 9:1–5). No matter what your circumstances have been or are, He can act and work in you.

MASTER OF LIFE AND DEATH

According to what we see in John chapter 11, Jesus is also the Master of Life and Death. When Jesus' friend Lazarus succumbs to a life-threatening illness, Jesus weeps. He feels human emotions at their rawest. He empathizes with the indescribable sorrow felt by those who love the man. But Jesus proves He has power over the grave. After enough days had passed (so that there was no question that Lazarus was dead and not just in a coma), Jesus stands at the entrance to His friend's tomb and calls for Lazarus to come out. To the amazement of all those standing around, that is exactly what Lazarus does (John 11:17–44)! Jesus wants to give you life, too, now and for eternity.[3]

ONE UNIQUE LIFE

One of Jesus' closest followers, the apostle John, described the life and ministry of Jesus in the New Testament book, the *Gospel of John*. Throughout that narrative, Jesus leaves His fingerprints on every dimension of life. If a crime scene investigator were to dust for those prints, he or she would be forced to conclude that they are fingerprints of Deity. In Jesus we see an utterly unique human being; a one-of-a-kind man. Of all those about whom historians have filled parchments and pages, no one can be found just like Jesus.

Jesus' birth was unique. Unlike any other person in history, His mother became pregnant without ever having sexual intercourse (Luke 1:26–35).

His life was unique. Unlike any other person in history, He lived a morally unblemished life. What is more, His response to those who were spiritually flawed was remarkable. Consider the reflections of His mother, Mary, who had observed Him doing that which was right each and every day of His existence on earth. Rightly did she say to the stewards at a wedding, "Do whatever He tells you" (John 2:5).

Jesus' death was unique as well. While countless individuals throughout history have been cruelly tortured and unjustly executed, Jesus alone suffered sacrificially, willingly taking on Himself the sins of the world (Romans 3:23–26). And, unlike any other human who ever lived, Jesus rose from the dead to begin a new kind of life. The Bible tells of other people who were merely resuscitated; they lived and breathed again after death, only to die again later. *Jesus' resurrection was unique.* He rose from the dead with a new kind of physical body—one that cannot suffer the affliction of disease, injury, privation, deformity, decay, or death.

> **WHAT IS "SIN"?**
>
> Several words in the Bible are used to describe it. One word represents it as a lapse, a slip, a blunder. Another pictures it as the failure to hit the mark, as when shooting at a target. Yet another shows it to be an inward badness, a disposition which falls short of what is good. One word makes sin the trespass of a boundary. Another reveals it as lawlessness, and another as an act which violates justice.
>
> These groups of words imply the existence of a moral standard. It is either an ideal which we fail to reach, or a law which we break.
>
> The Bible accepts the fact that all men have different standards. But all men have broken the law they know and fallen short of their own standard.
>
> What is our ethical code? Whatever it is, we have not succeeded in observing it. We all stand self-condemned.[4]
>
> –John Stott, *Basic Christianity*

Go ahead and check out the other three Gospels in the Bible of Matthew, Mark, and Luke. As you read them you will discover that this One, who claimed to be God, was unlike any other man who has ever lived. And it was this one-of-a-kind individual who focused His unique power toward people in need. The story of Jesus is a story of a Man with supernatural qualities who spent His years on this earth transforming human lives. He transformed people twenty centuries ago, and He continues to transform people today.

Look at the disciples. Those twelve men had no extraordinary qualities: some commercial fishermen, a tax-collection agent, a few blue-collar tradesmen—that's all, just plain folks, average Joes. But they didn't remain average for long. After three years of shadowing the Savior, eleven of the twelve became leaders of a movement that would rock the Roman world. Simon Peter is a classic example. So is the woman Jesus encountered at the well in Samaria. Although burned by previous relationships and living with a man (without benefit of marriage), this spiritually thirsty woman found forgiveness and new purpose in life after a midday conversation with Jesus, the One who offered her *living water* (John 4:1–42). And don't forget about the prostitute who was nearly stoned to death at high noon. When Jesus wrote in the sand, He wrote a new chapter in her life (John 8:1–11). He did the same for a self-righteous crusader from Tarsus by the name of Saul. Because of Jesus' ability to transform his life, two thirds of the New Testament was written by this convinced follower (Acts 9:1–22).

Did any other religious leader transform sinners into saints? No. Buddha didn't. Confucius couldn't. No other religious leader can claim to change the hearts of people to become righteous. Only Jesus can transform the hearts of people who have surrendered to His overtures of grace. It was true in the first century. It continues to be true today.

Jesus left no doubt that He was indeed the Master of History *and* the Savior of the World. When Jesus entered our realm of space and time, He changed everything. Literally *everything!* To understand exactly *how* Jesus changed the world, we need to go back to the beginning—all the way back to the very first moments of creation.

THE END OF THE BEGINNING

Once upon a time a man and a woman vacationed in a tropical forest without a care in the world. It was a dream excursion. The weather was perfect. The animals that roamed the foliage were wild yet tame. The food was delicious, plentiful, and free. All the couple had to do was follow the lead of their travel guide. He promised to take care of all their needs. He asked only that they keep their distance from one specific plant. In the vast orchard with thousands

---

WHAT IS GRACE?

Merit, the opposite of grace, is defined as that which is earned or deserved. Grace, on the other hand, is the *unmerited favor of God*.[5]

We can never know the fullness of grace. Grace literally means *that which we do not have to earn*. It has two great senses always: it comes without charge, and it comes when we are helpless. Grace does not merely help the man who helps himself—that is not the gospel. The gospel is that God helps the man who cannot help himself.[6]

Therefore, grace is that which God does for mankind through His Son, which mankind cannot earn, does not deserve, and will never merit. It is God's unmerited favor in spite of the response of humanity. It is summed up in the name, person, and work of the Lord Jesus Christ.[7]

Excerpted from RC Sproul, *Essential Truths of the Christian Faith*; A.B. Simpson, *Days of Heaven on Earth*; and Charles R. Swindoll, *Growing Deep*

of trees to enjoy, one, solitary, off-limits plant seemed insignificant.

One day they encountered a disgruntled former employee. He claimed the guide merely wanted to keep the fruit—and the insight it gave—to himself. The prospect of a new experience proved too intriguing to ignore, so they dismissed their host's request, walked past the "no trespassing" sign, and helped themselves. But surveillance cameras captured their disobedience. As a result, they were escorted out of the forest and prohibited from ever returning. What is more, their rebellious decision changed everything for all of humankind.

You may have recognized the story of Adam and Eve and the fall of mankind. Take a few moments to read the original version in Genesis 2:7–3:24.

The account of Adam and Eve paints a tragic "before-after" picture of creation. No less than seven times in Genesis 1, God looked at each element He had fashioned and affirmed the goodness of the world. Then the first humans risked the security and pleasure of paradise for the momentary satisfaction of thinking they didn't have to submit to another's authority. But shortly after nibbling a sweet piece of fruit, they realized just how sour life becomes when you disregard God. Among other catastrophic consequences of the fall, they experienced the death of four crucial relationships, and doomed all of their offspring—including you and me—to experience that nightmarish reality as well.

RELATIONSHIP #1: CUT OFF FROM GOD

Our relationship with God is broken, and we are spiritually disconnected from Him because of our sin. When I unplug a lamp from the power source, the light goes out. The same has happened to us. We are cut off from the One who made us, gives us life, provides for our needs, and gives us purpose. Now we enter the world with a subconscious awareness that God exists but we lack the ability or even the desire to locate Him. Consequently, we emerge from the womb with a hole in our souls that nothing else can fill. We might fill our lives with things to make us feel alive, feel meaningful, or feel hopeful, but nothing will ever replace what we're missing from the Life-giver. King David's son, Solomon, the wisest man who ever lived, said it best when in the depths of despair he wrote, "When I surveyed all that my hands had done and what I had toiled to achieve, everything was meaningless, a chasing after the wind" (Ecclesiastes 2:11).

RELATIONSHIP #2: CUT OFF FROM OURSELVES

As we grow up and strike out on our own in the world, we feel an eerie, inner loneliness. Most pastors and counselors acknowledge that few people really know themselves and these wise teachers spend hours helping others come to terms with their own identity. Until people understand their true identity is in Jesus Christ, their futile search for fulfillment will continue to spawn an endless variety of vices, addictions, psychological problems, and coping mechanisms. The fact is, we're born with a fundamental estrangement from our true selves. Everyone has the "me I experience and know" and the "me everyone else sees." And deep within, where no one can see, a battle rages between what we know is right and what we end up doing. The apostle Paul put it succinctly when he said, "I have the desire to do what is good, but I cannot carry it out" (Romans 7:18). None of us has it all together socially, emotionally, mentally, physically, or spiritually.

RELATIONSHIP #3: CUT OFF FROM OTHERS

Because of what Adam and Eve did, we find ourselves cut off from people around us as well. Our ancient ancestors attempted to hide their responsibility for sin by blaming someone else. God confronted Adam with a probing question intended to prompt his confession. "Have you eaten from the tree that I commanded you not to eat from?" But, instead of confessing, the man played the blame game. "The *woman* you put here with me—*she* gave me some fruit from the tree, and I ate it" (Genesis 3:11–12, italics added). When God confronted the woman, she said, "The serpent deceived me, and I ate" (Genesis 3:13).

The first people tried to cover their sin by blaming others and hiding their inner hearts from God. Countless generations later, we repeat the pattern they established: blame-shifting, denial, minimizing, or just plain lying. We avoid responsibility for our mistakes (sin) and hold others at arm's length. We keep secrets. We act independently. We refuse help. We hide our need for companionship in spite of our miserable private loneliness. "Each of us has turned to his own way" (Isaiah 53:6).

RELATIONSHIP #4: CUT OFF FROM GOD'S CREATION

We are cut off from God, ourselves, those around us, as well as the perfect world the Creator originally created for us. Ever since Adam and Eve's first rebellion, we became subject to the cause and effect laws of a flawed natural order, a world system that is prone to disorganization, disease, decay, and death. "Creation was subjected to frustration . . . the whole creation has been groaning as in the pains of childbirth right up to the present time" (Romans 8:20, 22). Ours is a world of environmental pollution and dirty politics, oil spills and slick televangelists, natural drought and manmade famine. Starvation and poverty plague poor countries. Abuse and addiction ravage the rich ones. Disasters ravage nature and the animal kingdom. AIDS and other strange new diseases threaten the kingdom of humankind. For years the human family held its breath for fear of a nuclear disaster due to a Cold War; now we tremble at the potential effects of environmental negligence. And in the midst of it all, innocent people sit in jail while the guilty escape through legal loopholes.

No wonder we're prone to cynicism and selfishness. It appears the defective planet we call home is doomed. What is worse, all the consequences of Adam and Eve's sin (spiritual, psychological, sociological, and ecological) continue to kill and destroy everything God once called "good."

JESUS IS THE SAVIOR OF THE WORLD

Fortunately, God has not left us to rot in the mess we made of His creation. He has heard our cry for help. We have reason for hope. While we cannot return to paradise, God has prepared something better. The good news found in God's Word declares that we may again enter the presence of God through a personal relationship with His Son, Jesus Christ. Paul describes how Jesus made this possible this way:

> If, by the trespass of the one man [Adam], death reigned through that one man, how much more will those who receive God's abundant provision of grace and of the gift of righteousness reign in life through the one man, Jesus Christ. Consequently, just as the result of one trespass was condemnation for all men, so also the result of one act of righteousness was justification that brings life for all men. (Romans 5:17–18)

When we begin a relationship with Jesus, we return to "Priority One" and experience relational healing. By getting to know God's Son, the chasm that separated us from our Creator becomes crossable. In fact, the restoration of that primary relationship helps us begin to heal other relationships. We can draw near to others from whom we have pulled away (or who have pulled

---

WHAT "ONE ACT OF RIGHTEOUSNESS" BROUGHT JUSTIFICATION FOR ALL MANKIND?

This single act was Jesus Christ sacrificing himself on a cross as atonement for the sins of mankind.

Old Testament religion was sacrificial from the beginning and continued until the destruction of the Temple in A.D. 70. Every Jew was familiar with the ritual attached to burnt offering, trespass offering, and their appropriate drink offerings, as well as with special occasions, daily, weekly, monthly and yearly when they had to be offered. No Jew could have failed to learn the fundamental lessons of this educative process that "the life of the flesh is in the blood" and that "without the shedding of blood there is no forgiveness of sins" (Leviticus 17:11, Hebrews 9:22). Jesus' sacrifice was foreshadowed in the Old Testament sacrifices, and by this one act he brought forgiveness for the sins of mankind.[8]

–John Stott, *Basic Christianity*

away from us). We also find the means in Christ to reconnect with ourselves. The apostle Paul describes that awesome truth in his letter to the Ephesians.

> But now you have been united with Christ Jesus. Once you were far away from God, but now you have been brought near to him through the blood of Christ.
>
> For Christ himself has brought peace to us. He united Jews and Gentiles into one people when, in his own body on the cross, he broke down the wall of hostility that separated us. He did this by ending the system of law with its commandments and regulations. He made peace between Jews and Gentiles by creating in himself one new people from the two groups. Together as one body, Christ reconciled both groups to God by means of his death on the cross, and our hostility toward each other was put to death.
>
> He brought this Good News of peace to you Gentiles who were far away from him, and peace to the Jews who were near. Now all of us can come to the Father through the same Holy Spirit because of what Christ has done for us. (Ephesians 2:13–18, NLT)

Isn't that incredible? If you've already entered into a personal relationship with Jesus, you now enjoy an unbreakable connection with God, Who promises complete restoration for those related to Him. *The Four Priorities* will help guide you in cultivating a deeper, more satisfying relationship with

---

IF YOU'RE AT THE PLACE RIGHT NOW WHERE YOU WOULD LIKE TO BOW YOUR KNEE AND ACCEPT THIS GIFT OF HEALING FROM THE DISEASE OF SIN AND THE PROMISE OF ETERNAL LIFE, YOU SIMPLY PRAY SOMETHING LIKE THE FOLLOWING. This is just an example prayer; there are no magic words. This is not about saying or doing the right thing. All you're doing is admitting you need God to save you, believing His promise to welcome you, and accepting His free gift of Himself in your life.

Dear Lord,
I admit that I am helpless to overcome my shortcomings to be the person You want me to be. I also admit that the things I have done and the disease of sin within me has disconnected me from You, and that I deserve eternal death as a penalty for my sin. Thank You for sending Your Son, Jesus, to die in my place. I trust in Him alone to pay the penalty of my sins and to grant me forgiveness. I accept His gift of eternal life, and I ask Jesus to be the Lord of my life. Fill me with your Holy Spirit and help me to become the man/woman You created me to be. Thank You.
In Jesus' name, Amen.

God, with others, and with the world around you.

If, however, you aren't certain about your salvation and where you stand with your Creator, we urge you to begin your relationship with Him today by praying the prayer on the previous page. At the end of this book, you will find a section titled "Establishing a Relationship with God." Stop here, turn to that section, and take care of this all-important business today. *The Four Priorities* will have little more than superficial meaning for those who do not have "peace with God" (Romans 5:1) through a relationship with Jesus Christ.

From this point forward, we will assume you now have peace with God through His Son, Jesus Christ. If so, tell someone you have made this life-changing decision! Your spiritual journey doesn't conclude the day you accept Him as your Savior. Far from it! On that day, you began to live—truly live—for the very first time. Salvation from the eternal consequences of sin is only the beginning of your new life. From that day forward, you began a process in which God replaces your old life with a new kind of living. Jesus has only begun to be your Savior. As you grow deeper in your relationship with Him, you increasingly allow Him to become the Lord and Master over *all* your life. He will save you from all sorts of things, including your own sinful way of thinking and behaving.

WHAT DOES THE "ETERNAL CONSEQUENCES OF SIN" MEAN?

The Bible tells of two locations where all mankind will spend eternity after death. For those who have trusted in Jesus Christ, their eternity is in Heaven with Him. For those who have not trusted in Jesus Christ, their eternity is forever apart from Him, in Hell.

Randy Alcorn explains it best:

What would keep us out of Heaven is universal: "All have sinned and fall short of the glory of God" (Romans 3:23). Sin separates us from a relationship with God (Isaiah 59:2). God is so holy that he cannot allow sin into his presence: "Your eyes are too pure to look on evil; you cannot tolerate wrong" (Habakkuk 1:13). Because we are sinners, we are not entitled to enter God's presence. We cannot enter Heaven as we are.

So Heaven is not our default destination. No one goes there automatically. Unless our sin problem is resolved, the only place we will go is our true default destination... Hell.[9]

–Randy Alcorn, *Heaven*

JESUS, THE LIFE CHANGER

Larry Snydal is an excellent example of Christ's transforming power. After succumbing to the numbing power of alcohol, this rugged construction worker lost his marriage and kissed his relationship with his three daughters good-bye. In exchange for a constant buzz, Larry lost everything. But not permanently. When Larry learned that Jesus loved him and was willing to give him a fresh run at life, the bearded boozer raced into the arms of the Savior. He found a new purpose for living, and through his growing relationship with Christ, he began to change (2 Corinthians 5:17).

Eventually, he met a fellow believer, a widow in her forties with five kids in need of a dad. Larry and Linda fell in love and married. As they grew together in their relationship with Jesus, they responded to a call from God to serve Him in foreign missions. Today they serve God fulltime with Wycliffe Bible Translators, first in Colombia and Brazil, and now as recruiters in the United States. The once hot-tempered, hammer-slinging sinner is known by his Christlike temperament. Just ask his daughters, who are no longer estranged. Larry Snydal is a living testimony of the power of Jesus Christ to transform a life. He is proof positive that Jesus Christ is nothing less than the living God.

TAKE ACTION

Read Genesis 2:7–3:24, which describes the Fall of humanity and its effect on the world.
How does this corruption of God's original design affect you personally? What has been the most damaging or painful consequence of "the Fall?"

What relationships have suffered the most from your own failures?

In what ways do you think they would change if, today, you were more like Jesus Christ?

Read Romans 5:1–21, which proclaims the restoration available to those who trust in Jesus Christ.

Those who have "peace with God" through faith in Jesus Christ can have peace in other strained relationships. What relationships would you like to see restored?

What did God do to offer restoration to humanity? Which of God's actions and attitudes can you emulate when trying to restore your broken relationships? (See also Philippians 2:5–8.) List those below.

Be intentional: What are you going to do about what you've learned?

Be specific: What action will you take in the near future to begin applying what you've learned? When will you do it?

Be accountable: Pray it through. Share your plan with a friend and seek his/her prayer and counsel for your next step.

CHAPTER 2: WHAT'S THE BIG PICTURE?

Scan here to watch the video!

New York City can be an overwhelming experience for first-time visitors. Few are prepared for the crush of people, the densely packed buildings, the constant sense of urgency, and the cacophony of voices, horns, engines, and jackhammers. If, however, they begin their visit with an elevator ride to the observation deck of the Empire State Building, they can make sense of the chaos. Eighty-six floors above street level, the whole city comes into perspective. You can see the network of sidewalks, streets, and highways that connect downtown neighborhoods and distant suburbs. You can appreciate the design that city planners put into place as buildings were laid out. You can see a traffic jam that commuters won't discover for ten more miles. You can observe a building on fire even before emergency services have been dispatched. Then, having seen the city from above, the clamor down below seems less confusing and unruly. The big picture has a way of providing a sense of peace and purpose.

God has this perspective when viewing our lives. He has an unobstructed view of our past, present, and future. He sees how all the thoroughfares and detours of our lives fit together. He is not caught off guard by news that sets us reeling emotionally. When a phone call in the middle of the night jangles our nerves and shatters our emotions with word of a loved one's death, God is not surprised. When a pink slip at work turns our finances upside down, God doesn't wring His hands, wondering how we'll make ends meet. When the consequences of our past indiscretions parade down Main Street, God isn't shocked. He sees it all and has a plan for it all to work out.

WHAT'S WRONG WITH THIS PICTURE?

All the same, it's easy to feel as though some things don't make sense. Even after you have begun a relationship with Christ by trusting in Him as Savior and Lord, certain events can fill your heart with doubt. For example, you still sin. You have embraced the Lord of truth, yet you still shade the truth when you fear total honesty will make you look inadequate. You still allow anger to guide your responses when insulted or cheated. You still struggle with lust. At times you use language you hope no one in church hears. These constant indicators of imperfection would cause any reasonable person to wonder, *Is this the normal Christian life?*

Maybe you're wondering if you were sincere enough when you trusted in Christ for salvation from sin. Maybe you're questioning if you've held up your end of the bargain, and if more depended on you to receive God's gift than what you were led to believe. Or maybe you wonder if the Lord, for some unknown reason, didn't accept you. Come to think of it, left to your own logic, you can think of a number of reasons why He shouldn't. If you're like a lot of Christians, you might ask yourself in quiet moments, "Did my prayer of repentance and faith have any effect, or was I just caught up in the moment?"

Don't despair. It's time for a metaphorical "elevator ride" to the top of the Empire State Building for some perspective. You need to see the big picture, what God sees as He observes your life of faith. If you asked Jesus to come into your life, He is there. And He isn't going anywhere. If you were able to see your own life from God's vantage point, you would see that you are in the process of transformation. If you could see what God sees, your anxieties would melt away and your heart would fill with hope. Furthermore, you would discover a greater capacity to endure the inevitable struggles and setbacks you continue to experience. Author John Maxwell says it so well, "Hope is the foundational principle for all change. People change because they have hope." So, let's take a look at your life from God's point of view. First, we'll examine Scripture. Then, we'll consider a helpful illustration.

GOD'S PLAN FOR YOU
When Paul wrote to the Christians living in Ephesus during the first century, they struggled with the same kinds of doubts we have today. They had accepted God's invitation to receive forgiveness for their sins through faith in His Son, Jesus Christ, yet they still wrestled with temptation and sometimes repeated past moral failures. The apostle reassured them with two monumental truths; one dealing with their past, the other pointing to their future.

He began by reminding the believers of their recent past. They did not begin their spiritual journey in Christ because of their good behavior; they were rescued from sin while still helpless to overcome it. "It is by grace you have been saved, through faith—and this not from yourselves, it is the gift of God—not by works, so that no one can boast" (Ephesians 2:8–9). They, of course, already knew this. And, if we're honest with ourselves, we know it too. We did nothing to become followers of Christ other than admit our need for a Savior and accept His gift of eternal life. Paul used this truth to reassure the Ephesians (and us) of God's *continuing* work of salvation in us. "For we are God's workmanship, created in Christ Jesus to do good works, which God prepared in advance for us to do" (Ephesians 2:10).

The "for" at the beginning of the verse could be translated "because." God saved us from sin—by grace, through faith—*because* we are His personal work-in-progress. Yes, you chose to trust in Christ as Savior and Lord, but the Bible also states that God knew *you* before you were born and He chose *you* to fulfill a destiny He had established before the beginning of time. The almighty, all-powerful Creator of the universe has dedicated Himself to transforming you into the kind of person who does "good works" as easily and as naturally as breathing.

In his letter to the Romans, Paul reassured believers in Christ with a divine promise that's so amazing, it's difficult to comprehend:

> We know that in all things God works for the good of those who love him, who have been called according to his purpose. For those God foreknew he also predestined to be conformed to the likeness of his Son, that he might be the firstborn among many brothers. And those he predestined, he also called; those he called, he also justified; those he justified, he also glorified.
>
> What, then, shall we say in response to this? If God is for us, who can be against us? He who did not spare his own Son, but gave him up for us all—how will he not also, along with him, graciously give us all things? Who will bring any charge against those whom God has chosen? It is God who justifies. Who is he that condemns? Christ Jesus, who died—more than that, who was raised to life—is at the right hand of God and is also interceding for us. Who shall separate us from the love of Christ? Shall trouble or hardship or persecution or famine or nakedness or danger or sword? As it is written:
>
> "For your sake we face death all day long;
> we are considered as sheep to be slaughtered."
>
> No, in all these things we are more than conquerors through him who loved us. For I am convinced that neither death nor life, neither angels nor demons, neither the present nor the future, nor any powers, neither height nor depth, nor anything else in all creation, will be able to separate us from the love of God that is in Christ Jesus our Lord. (Romans 8:28–39)

God has saved us from the eternal consequences of sin (Romans 6:23), and He is now saving us from the daily affliction of sin by making us new creatures. He made those who believe in Christ His own personal renovation projects. Because God has taken this responsibility upon Himself, we can be certain He will complete the work. Paul put it succinctly in his letter to the Philippians: "[I am] confident of this, that he who began a good work in you will carry it on to completion until the day of Christ Jesus" (Philippians 1:6).

So, if God has taken responsibility for transforming us into good people, what is our part? What responsibility do we have? Paul answered that question later in his letter to the Ephesians. He wrote, "Surely you heard of him and were taught in him in accordance with the truth that is in Jesus. You were taught, with regard to your former way of life, to put off your old self, which is being corrupted by its deceitful desires; to be made new in the attitude of your minds; and to put on the new self, created to be like God in true righteousness and holiness" (Ephesians 4:21–24).

While God will be faithful to complete the work of transformation, He nevertheless invites us to participate in the process. As we live our daily routine, we "put off the old self" by remaining sensitive to the work of God within. As He changes our patterns of thinking, and frees us from old habits and cravings, and heals old wounds, we walk away from our old lifestyle. We "put on the new self" by growing deeper in our relationship with Jesus Christ and begin imitating Him. As God completes the work within us, this process of "putting off the old self" and "putting on the new" becomes more natural. It's never easy, but it becomes increasingly natural.

Unfortunately, this transformation doesn't take place overnight. It is a progressive work of God. An illustration might help make this clearer.

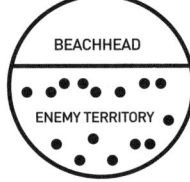
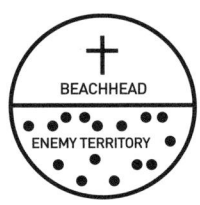

THE BEACHHEAD

Lane Adams, a Presbyterian minister, compared Christ's entrance into a new believer's life to the establishment of a beachhead on an enemy-controlled island. He recalls how the Allied Forces established beachheads to liberate occupied South Pacific islands during World War II, which was an arduous and lengthy process.

First, the Allied Forces took aerial photographs of the island to determine enemy positions. Then, based on this reconnaissance, they would shell the island with powerful bombs launched from battleships and dropped from planes. This would weaken the enemy's resistance. Not long afterward, a small group of Marines would slosh ashore, invade the island and secure a stretch of coastline, which they called a "beachhead." Although only a tiny portion of the island, it would soon be filled with more troops and supplies. The Allies had arrived, set up camp, and were determined to drive back the remaining enemy-held territory; eventually possessing the entire island beginning with this small, secure position.

THE GREAT INVASION

Got it? That's what happened to you. When you, by faith, trusted Jesus to be your Savior, He entered your life, established His position, and began equipping your offense to drive back the enemy. Jesus' position is established, but we're willing to bet you keep struggling with the enemy forces that were driven back. The enemy in your life comes to steal, kill and destroy (John 10:10). Sometimes you conquer the enemy; sometimes you are defeated. Do you find yourself asking, "What's the problem here? If Christ has set up His position, why does it take me so long to get better? Why do I still do stuff that I know isn't right?"

Everybody's got stuff they need to deal with. Everybody. This "stuff" is what is hidden behind your enemy lines; the issues of life that work against God's best for you (Romans 3:23).

The first thing you need to understand about Jesus Christ is that His beachhead position is *permanent*. Once Jesus comes in, He's here to stay. He says, "I'm here. This is my house now" (John 10:27-29). He comes in and forgives you of everything in the past, the present, and the future, and He gives you His Holy Spirit to reside within you to help become like Him.

Even though the *position* of Christ in your life is secured, your *condition* still stinks. The enemy is crouched at your battle lines. Why? Because when Jesus Christ enters your life, He doesn't do a total takeover; He only sets up a beachhead. There is still enemy-held territory. He's headquartered in your life, but under His command He gives you free will to operate. You can choose to battle the enemy-held territory in your life, or you can choose to live in bondage to the enemy. For your sake, we hope you choose to fight to take back what's rightfully yours.

The second thing you need to understand about the life of a Christ-follower: It's a *process*, and that process is a fight on your own personal battlefield to reclaim the enemy-held territory. In Romans 7 the apostle Paul talks about his battle. He says, "My own behavior baffles me. The very things I don't want to do, that's what I do. The things that I know I ought to do that the Lord would want me to do, I don't do that. I don't seem to have the power to pull that off" (J. B. Phillips Paraphrase). Settle in for the long haul – you will see victories and defeats in battles against the enemy – but remember, this is a process that will continually transform you throughout the rest of your life.

> *The Christian life is a process. The first step is to trust Jesus Christ as your Lord and Savior. The second step is to grow! 2 Peter 3:18*

God's bird's eye view allows Him to see what you were like before trusting Christ, where in the growth process you stand now, and—most important of all—what you will be like in the future. He sees the beginning, the middle, and the end of your transformation process all at once. By adopting God's point of view, you can set aside your doubts, stop worrying, and then join Him in the renovation of your heart (Romans 12:1–2). That's how an occupied island (and an occupied life) is liberated—a progressive pushing out of alien thoughts, idols, and actions. And the result is gradual growth or maturity. Then you can stand with God and boldly proclaim, "If anyone is in Christ, he is a new creation; the old has gone, the new has come!" (2 Corinthians 5:17).

WHAT'S THE BOTTOM LINE?

A beachhead signals the start of countless battles, seemingly endless wins and losses, before the Lord has accomplished His intended purpose for us. What is His *intended purpose*? Romans 8:28a says, "For those God foreknew he also predestined to be conformed to the likeness of his Son." Simply put, His purpose is for us to become like Jesus! The spiritual journey of a Christian is often three steps forward, two steps back. Gratefully, the Lord isn't put off by our setbacks and struggles. He sees the end from the beginning, and road closures and inevitable detours are no concern to Him. He knows how the traffic jams in our lives will resolve. When we focus on the long-term process of spiritual growth, we begin to see the big picture and trust God with the process. The following inspirational piece by an unknown author illustrates this fact.

> At first, I saw God as my observer, my judge keeping track of the things I did wrong, so as to know whether I merited heaven or hell when I die. He was out there sort of like a president. I recognized His picture when I saw it, but I really didn't know Him. But later on, when I met Christ, it seemed as though life were rather like a bike ride, but it was a tandem bike, and I noticed that Christ was in the back helping me pedal.
>
> I don't know just when it was that He suggested we change places, but life has not been the same since! When I had control, I knew the way. It was rather boring, but predictable . . . it was the shortest distance between two points. But when He took the lead, He knew delightful long-cuts, up mountains, and through rocky places at breakneck speeds. It was all I could do just to hang on! Even though it looked like madness, He said "Pedal!"
>
> I worried and was anxious and asked, "Where are You taking me?" He laughed and didn't answer, and I started to learn to trust. I forgot my boring life and entered into the adventure. And when I'd say, "I'm scared!" He'd lean back and touch my hand. He took me to people with gifts that I needed. Gifts of healing, acceptance, and joy. They gave us gifts to take on my journey, my Lord's and mine. And we were off again. He said, "Give the gifts away; they're extra baggage, too much weight." So I did, to the people we met; and I found that in giving I received, and still our burden was light.
>
> I did not trust Him, at first, in control of my life. I thought He'd wreck it; but He knows bike secrets, knows how to make it bend to take sharp corners, knows how to jump to clear high rocks, knows how to try to shorten scary passages. And I am learning to shut up and pedal in the strangest places, and I'm beginning to enjoy the view and the cool breeze on my face with my delightful companion, Jesus Christ. And when I'm sure I just can't do anymore, He just smiles and says, "Pedal!"

Simply put, God's purpose for us is not a random spur-of-the-moment idea. Long before we were born, He decided what He wanted our lives to amount to. And it's that purpose that adds meaning to the times we feel like we've blown it or feel buried without a shovel. As the story above illustrates, God never loses sight of the big picture—He is omniscient (knows everything infinitely) and He remains sovereign (in complete control of every circumstance)!

Even before He establishes a beachhead in our lives, God's strategy is at work in His mind. And that strategy is this: Once He takes hold of our heart (Ezekiel 11:19; 36:26), He is committed to transforming us into the likeness of His Son (Romans 8:29). It may take a lifetime, but He is determined to liberate us from ourselves.

What an awesome thought that is. Because of God's plan and perspective, we can better understand how God changes us, about the process of Christian maturity when we begin to wonder if the Holy Spirit is really at work in our lives. God observes (and celebrates) what isn't always evident to us. Because of His ability to weave our lives together into a beautiful tapestry, the knotty or dark threads need not steal our joy or cause us to give up on the process.

While some define the Christian life as the sum and substance of what happens to you when you first trust Jesus Christ as your Savior, that kind of definition sets a person up for disillusionment and despair. A much more Biblical definition of discipleship is not explained by virtue of the starting line, but by the finish line. Whereas we begin the race of faith when we invite Jesus to take possession of our hearts, the Christian life has more to do with a process that has only just begun.

TAKE ACTION

When did Jesus establish a beachhead in your life? What were the circumstances surrounding your receiving Jesus Christ into your life? Were other people involved in this important decision?

Do you know for certain you have trusted in Jesus Christ? Read John 1:12, John 3:16, John 5:24, and 1 John 5:11–13.

Read Romans 8:28–39, which proclaims the restoration of those who trust in Jesus Christ.
As long as the world remains in a fallen state, people will continue to suffer the effects of evil. How does a relationship with Jesus Christ help the Christian experience these difficulties differently?

What do you see as your greatest challenge to becoming more like Christ? What areas in your enemy-held territory continue to challenge you? How does this affect your ability to live well and to do what is right? Choose an area and, with the help of a trusted advisor or mentor, put together a game plan to grow in this part of your life.

ESPN frequently plays reruns of classic football games, usually involving a major upset or an amazing comeback victory. Use your imagination for a moment. When watching the rerun several years later, how does your perspective differ from those who watched the live event? As you watch the rerun, how does your knowledge of the outcome affect your view of the winning team when they are trailing by three touchdowns in the third quarter?

Based on Romans 8:28–39, how do you think God views your moral failures?

God has promised to finish the transforming work He began in you (Philippians 1:6). How can you take part in His renovation project?

Be intentional: What are you going to do about what you've learned?

Be specific: What action will you take in the near future to begin applying what you've learned? When will you do it?

Be accountable: Pray it through. Share your plan with a friend and seek his/her prayer and counsel for your next step.

CHAPTER 3: WHAT IS THE CHRISTIAN LIFE? PART 1

Scan here to watch the video!

Author and Bible teacher extraordinaire Steve Brown tells the story about a guy who played piano at a bar. Every night was the same. He'd play while men and women at various stages of intoxication leaned against the piano listening. Often the inebriated individuals would engage the piano man in conversation. To break the monotony of the nightly routine, the piano player started asking his listeners a provocative question. "What is the meaning of life?" It didn't matter who the people were, he asked the same question night after night. Although some people offered trite clichés, most just smiled and said nothing. One night a guy responded to the question by saying, "I don't know what the meaning of life is, but I know someone who does." The piano man listened with interest and asked for more information. "He's a guru who lives alone high up in the Himalayas."

Several weeks later, when the piano player realized how insignificant he felt pounding out meaningless songs he became very depressed. Although he was a gifted musician, those for whom he played were oblivious to his talent because they were self-medicated with booze. He determined he would find a way to discover for himself what life was all about. But where would he start? Then he remembered the comment about the guru.

Booking a flight, he traveled halfway around the world. At the base of the Himalayas, he hired a guide to take him to the guru who knew the meaning to life. Upon finding the sage, he asked, "What is the meaning of life?"

The guru never stirred from his lotus position. He didn't bother to stand up or even look the musician in the eye. He simply responded, "Life is a fountain."

Unwilling to accept that abstract definition as a final answer, he persisted. "Look, sir, no disrespect intended, but I'm extremely tired. I traveled thousands of miles to find you, to learn the answer to the question weighing heavily on my heart."

The guru, still sitting crossed-legged on a carpet, looked up at the desperate man and asked, "Life is a fountain . . . isn't it?"

THE MEANING OF LIFE

Sadly, millions of people seek answers to the mystery of life from those who aren't really sure of life's meaning themselves. If you Google the question, you'll find more than 400 million search results. But life can only be fully understood when a person enters into a relationship with the One who created life in the first place. When an inquisitive seeker by the name of Nicodemus came to Jesus by night, Jesus announced that He, Himself, was the source of eternal life. He declared, "God so loved the world that he gave his one and only Son, that whoever believes in him shall not perish but have eternal life" (John 3:16). You will spend eternity somewhere, either in God's presence or in eternal torment. If you have placed your trust in Jesus Christ (see "How to Begin a Relationship with Jesus Christ" in the appendix), you will live forever with Him.

Fortunately, we don't have to wait for physical death to begin experiencing "eternal life"; our new life starts when we begin a relationship with Him. Jesus later said, "I have come that [My people] might have life, and have it to the full" (John 10:10). Another translation renders the verse, " . . . and have it abundantly" (NASB). If you have begun a relationship with God's Son, your new life, "the Christian life," has already begun!

No, the meaning of life cannot be discovered on some snowcapped mountain. No eastern mystic holds the secret to the abundant life. Instead, we learn the answers to our deepest questions from Jesus, a rabbi (teacher), who gathered His most trusted companions in a second floor banquet room on the eve of His crucifixion and declared, "I am the way and the truth and the life. No one comes to the Father except through me" (John 14:6). The meaning of life starts with Jesus (Acts 4:12) and, in Him, you find ultimate, eternal satisfaction (Revelation 21:6–7).

The church will let you down. Finely tuned Christian programs will lose their appeal. People to whom you've looked as spiritual mentors will fail you. Given enough time, even your pastor will disappoint you. And merely taking in the pastor's sermons won't bring the abundant life Jesus promised. The life Jesus promised doesn't begin with believing the right facts and doctrines. Christianity is not a *statement* about a person called Jesus. It's neither a set of principles to endorse nor a creed to affirm or proclaim. It's not a philosophical system; the abundant life in Christ doesn't depend upon merely holding a Christian worldview. Too many people understand the Christian life to be a set of actions or a checklist of dos and don'ts or a set of propositions they must memorize or study. Such tragically shortsighted perspectives lead many to become overly concerned with right beliefs or right behavior, distracting them from the kind of life Jesus offers. Jesus consistently opposed the self-righteous teachers of His day who had become so preoccupied with manmade propositions, traditions, and rules that they forfeited the abundant life God offers. They exchanged a personal relationship with Him for a religious set of rules.

WHAT IS THE CHRISTIAN LIFE?

Howard Hendricks defines Christianity as "the life of Christ reproduced in the believer by the power of the Holy Spirit in obedient response to the Word of God."[10] Make sense? Let's break it down step by step.

God didn't design us to live independently of Him. Like a lamp must remain plugged into a wall socket, we must maintain intimate connection with the Source of life to experience the new kind of life Jesus promised (John 10:10). You can't simply take up a Bible and say, "I'm going to be a

Bible-believing Christian." The Christian life doesn't begin with a decision to become good enough to earn God's acceptance. On the contrary, the Bible is clear—and so is our experience of human nature—we cannot become good enough for God to accept us. His love is not based on our performance. Even on our best day we fall far short of qualifying for God's endorsement (Romans 3:23).

Amazingly God comes to us anyway. The life He promises is the life He produces. We tend to get it backwards. It's not about what we can do for God; it's all about what He wants to do in us and through us. It doesn't matter who we are, or how badly we've blown it in the past, because we are simply the beneficiaries of His sovereign grace. Paul encouraged the Christians living in Ephesus with these words:

> [God] chose us in [Christ] before the creation of the world to be holy and blameless in his sight. In love he predestined us to be adopted as his sons through Jesus Christ, in accordance with his pleasure and will—to the praise of his glorious grace, which he has freely given us in the One he loves. In him we have redemption through his blood, the forgiveness of sins, in accordance with the riches of God's grace that he lavished on us with all wisdom and understanding. And he made known to us the mystery of his will according to his good pleasure, which he purposed in Christ, to be put into effect when the times will have reached their fulfillment—to bring all things in heaven and on earth together under one head, even Christ. In him we were also chosen, having been predestined according to the plan of him who works out everything in conformity with the purpose of his will, in order that we, who were the first to hope in Christ, might be for the praise of his glory. And you also were included in Christ when you heard the word of truth, the gospel of your salvation. Having believed, you were marked in him with a seal, the promised Holy Spirit, who is a deposit guaranteeing our inheritance until the redemption of those who are God's possession—to the praise of his glory. (Ephesians 1:4–14)

Three great truths emerge from this passage that directly influence our understanding of the abundant life Jesus promised.

First, *God decided before creation that His people—those who place their trust in Jesus Christ for salvation from the eternal consequences of sin—would become "holy" and "blameless."* The Greek word for "holy" is often translated "sacred" or "sanctified." While these terms sound hyper-religious, the idea they describe is actually very down-to-earth. The word "holy" means simply "set apart for special use" in the same way a household might have "everyday dishes" for normal use and then a set of "good china" reserved for entertaining. You might not think of yourself as "holy," "sacred," or "sanctified" because you can't go a full day without doing something wrong or failing to do what you should. In truth, however, we have been set apart from the rest of the world by God for His own purposes.

God's purpose for you: to become "blameless." The word means "morally spotless." That sounds like He's set an impossible standard, doesn't it? Fortunately, He didn't place this expectation on us; He made Himself responsible for success. This leads to the second truth concerning the abundant life in Christ: *Because we are "in Christ," we have been declared "blameless" in advance of actually becoming blameless.* He has already determined that our moral success is a foregone conclusion. God has promised to make us morally blameless and, because He *never* fails, He has already transferred the rewards of success into our names!

God knows these two truths are hard to believe. He has declared us "holy" and has already credited the rewards of success into our accounts, but we don't *feel* holy and we don't *feel* like we deserve the blessings that accompany God's favor. So, Paul declares a third crucial truth concerning the abundant life in Christ: *To give us hope, God gave us His Holy Spirit.* The apostle describes the Holy Spirit as a "deposit guaranteeing our inheritance" (Ephesians 1:14). In real estate, they call this "earnest money." On Wall Street, they call this a "marker." This "deposit" is a down payment made in good faith, guaranteeing the full sum will be paid at an appointed time in the future.

In ancient times, a wealthy or powerful person wore a signet ring, a custom-made piece of jewelry designed to serve an important business function. Upon signing a contract or a written proclamation, the owner dripped hot wax onto the document and then pressed the face of the signet ring into the wax blotch to create a unique seal. Because no one else possessed that signet ring, the wax seal authenticated the document as binding upon the signer. Paul declares that God has pressed His Holy Spirit onto the souls of His people to authenticate the agreement He has made. He will make us "holy" and "blameless," and the presence of the Holy Spirit within guarantees the fulfillment of His pledge.

Eugene Peterson paraphrases God's promises this way:

> Long before he laid down earth's foundations, he had us in mind, had settled on us as the focus of his love, to be made whole and holy by his love. Long, long ago he decided to adopt us into his family through Jesus Christ. (What pleasure he took in planning this!) He wanted us to enter into the celebration of his lavish gift-giving by the hand of his beloved Son.
>
> Because of the sacrifice of the Messiah, his blood poured out on the altar of the Cross, we're a free people—

> **WHO IS THE HOLY SPIRIT?**
>
> After Jesus' resurrection, he spent time with some of his followers. When he prepared to leave them he said, "If you love me, you will obey what I command. And I will ask the Father, and he will give you another Counselor to be with you forever – the Spirit of Truth. The world cannot accept him, because it neither sees him nor knows him. But you know him, for he lives with you and will be in you."
>
> "The Counselor or Paraclete, from the Greek word parakletos (meaning one who gives support), is a helper, advisor, strengthener, encourager, ally, and advocate. [The word] 'another' [in John 14:16] points to the fact that Jesus was the first Paraclete and is promising a replacement who, after he is gone, will carry on the teaching and testimony that he started (John 16:6-7)."[11]
>
> – J.I. Packer, *Concise Theology*

free of penalties and punishments chalked up by all our misdeeds. And not just barely free, either. Abundantly free! He thought of everything, provided for everything we could possibly need, letting us in on the plans he took such delight in making. He set it all out before us in Christ, a long-range plan in which everything would be brought together and summed up in him, everything in deepest heaven, everything on planet earth.

It's in Christ that we find out who we are and what we are living for. Long before we first heard of Christ and got our hopes up, he had his eye on us, had designs on us for glorious living, part of the overall purpose he is working out in everything and everyone.

It's in Christ that you, once you heard the truth and believed it (this Message of your salvation), found yourselves home free—signed, sealed, and delivered by the Holy Spirit. This signet from God is the first installment on what's coming, a reminder that we'll get everything God has planned for us, a praising and glorious life. (Ephesians 1:4–14 MSG)

The Holy Spirit resides within God's people to live a morally spotless life in us and through us. To please God and reap the rewards of moral success, we no longer have to depend upon our own feeble will-power; we must learn to let the Holy Spirit do the work for us. Sadly, however, most of those to whom God extends grace fail to accept it. They receive the gift of salvation and then ignore the incredible gift of abundant living now. They discard it as irrelevant or too-good-to-be-true, or they settle for intellectual knowledge. The life that Jesus espoused in the pages of the New Testament is grounded in a personal relationship with Him. As with any other relationship, it calls for spending time together, conversing, pouring out your hearts to one another, and listening. That's why Christianity isn't really a religion as much as it is a *relationship*. It's a relationship by which you respond to the risen Christ *daily*, living out His life in you day by day, moment by moment.

"IN CHRIST"

The Bible describes the believer's association with God in terms unlike any other kind of relationship. We don't usually describe one person as being "in" or "within" another. We go "to" others and we can be "with" another, but the relationship is rarely "in" or "within" (unless we're talking about an expectant mother). Even so, God has promised to replace our fallen, sin-obsessed nature with a new spirit (cf. Jeremiah 31:31–34; John 16:13–15). This is what Paul means when, in his letter to the Colossians, he refers to "Christ in you, the hope of glory" (Colossians 1:27). The moment we believe in Christ as Savior, God places His Spirit within us. More often, however, Scripture views the Christian as "in Christ."

On the eve of His crucifixion, Jesus urged His followers, "Abide in Me" (John 15:4), promising that He would "abide in you." Paul declared to the Roman believers that we are "dead to sin but alive to God *in Christ*" (Romans 6:11, emphasis mine). Throughout his writings, Paul refers to Christians as those who are "in Christ." But what does this mean? How can we "abide in Christ" or be "in Christ"? Before we discuss this in practical terms, use your imagination to explore this illustration.

A good analogy of "abiding in Christ" might be a potted plant, such as a miniature rose bush. While the plant thrives on sunlight from above, it also draws nourishment and water through its roots. Plants require rich, moist soil. As any grade school child knows, bad soil grows sickly plants, and sickly plants don't bloom. Moreover, rose bushes wither and die in parched ground. For a Christian to thrive, he or she must be rooted in a relationship with God. While some people are rooted in themselves (trying to draw nourishment from self!) and others are rooted in what the crowd thinks (the shifting sands of popular opinion), to be "in Christ" means to pull the roots of one's life out of inferior, toxic soil and then transplant them into a relationship with Him. To be in Christ involves giving up whatever it is you're holding on to for life and then surrendering yourself to His plans and purposes. You stop trying to live the Christian life through your own strength, and you allow the Holy Spirit working in you to live the Christian life for you. Instead of trying to live for God, you draw life from Him. This is what distinguishes Christianity from all other world religions. Buddha pointed to his teachings, not his life. Islam is not defined by the life of its leader but the Quran. While other world religions require their followers to live according to a specific philosophy or adhere to a particular standard or follow a set list of guidelines, Christianity is a relationship with our Creator. Christianity—the Christian life—is defined by the One after Whom it is named. Without the life of Jesus Christ living in us and through us, we have no "Christianity." We do not have the capability in ourselves to be Christian. When you accepted Jesus Christ as your Savior, you placed your trust in Him to save you from the eternal punishment for sin and to give you eternal life as a free gift. But remember from Chapter 2, it doesn't end there. The apostle Paul reminds us, "[I am] confident of this, that he who began a good work in you will carry it on to completion until the day of Christ Jesus" (Philippians 1:6).

HOW DOES IT WORK?

Are you wondering how God will "carry it on to completion until the day of Christ Jesus" (Philippians 1:6)?

We will explore our responsibilities in the chapters to follow. For now, however, simply absorb this amazing spiritual truth: The life of Jesus Christ is reproduced in the believer by the *power* of the Holy Spirit, who makes your obedience to the Word of God possible.

We will discuss practical ways we can participate in God's transforming work, but for now—before rushing ahead—rest in God's promise. When you stop trying to impress God by trying hard to be good, the goodness of His Son takes over. He makes you a more responsible person than you have been before. You will find yourself setting priorities that reflect His values and not those of the culture around you (Romans 12:1–2). You will become a more dependable husband, wife, leader, parent, friend, employee, or associate than you previously had been. You will start engaging in the lives of people in effective ways. And it all starts by claiming the free gift of forgiveness that Jesus died to make available to you. Once you drop that heavy backpack of guilt, you will be free to respond in gratitude and love. As you submit to Christ as King—relinquishing control to the Holy Spirit—Jesus empowers you to make right choices and Christlike actions. Freed from the burden of striving to be good or trying to convince yourself that you're worthy of being loved, you relax and let the Holy Spirit take over. As you surrender your life to God's control, you will find rest in your "peace with God" (Romans 5:1).

TAKE ACTION

Read Ephesians 1:4–14 again.
God has promised to make you "holy" (set apart for His special use) and "blameless" (morally spotless). How does that influence your understanding of "the Christian life" and what it means to be a Christian?

Everybody looks to something for strength, security, or significance. Some turn to relationships. Others hope to find what they need in career or achievement. Still others mask their needs with habits. A lot of people even try to become good at religion.

In the past, what did you think might give you strength, offer you security, or make you feel significant? What was the result?

The abundant life "in Christ" requires you to turn away from the things you once expected to meet your deepest needs and then depend upon God to provide what you lack. This might sound strange, but take a few moments to write a goodbye letter to anything you once depended upon to help you feel strong, secure, or significant. For example, an overachiever might begin his or her letter, "Dear Career . . ."

Dear _____,

Be intentional: What are you going to do about what you've learned?

Be specific: What action will you take in the near future to begin applying what you've learned? When will you do it?

Be accountable: Pray it through. Share your plan with a friend and seek his/her prayer and counsel for your next step.

CHAPTER 4: WHAT IS THE CHRISTIAN LIFE? PART 2

Scan here to watch the video!

In the last chapter we discovered that the Christian life is the **life of Christ reproduced in the believer**. It's not our attempt to impress God with our best efforts. Rather, it's depending upon God to live the Christian life in us, and through us, in spite of us. We begin to live abundantly when we stop looking to other things to provide what God wants to give us personally. As we surrender control to the Holy Spirit, we are increasingly marked by Jesus' values and motives. It's an inside job! On our own, the Christian life isn't hard; *it's impossible!* Thank God He achieves the impossible in us supernaturally. The key to becoming "holy" (set apart for God's special use) and "blameless" (morally spotless) is being connected to the power source by which the current of Jesus' life flows through us (Ephesians 1:1–14).

The "Christian Life" can be defined as The life of Christ, reproduced in the believer, by the power of the holy spirit, in obedient response to the word of God

Suppose you just purchased a new home. You know, the one you've been dreaming about for years. It has all the latest gadgets and conveniences. The extra-large kitchen comes fully equipped with state-of-the-art appliances. The master bedroom suite includes a luxury bathroom with a Jacuzzi for two. You have an elaborate entertainment room, complete with big-screen high-definition TV and theatre-quality surround sound. In addition to the intercom and computerized security system, the backyard features a heated in-ground pool and hot tub. The house has everything you dreamed possible except . . .

Upon moving in, you discover the house isn't connected to the power grid. No electricity. The lights don't work. Appliances sit idle. The air conditioning system does nothing. So making the best of your real estate nightmare, you sit in the dark, dripping with sweat, admiring all the wonderful gadgets with all their time-saving potential.

Soon after sunrise the next day, your neighbor introduces himself. During the conversation you learn that he is an electrician with the city utility company. He explains that your home is wired for power but lacks a simple connection to the power grid. He adds that, as an employee with the power company, he can make the connection that will bring electricity to your lifeless home.

So what's your next move? Suppose you tell your spouse about your new neighbor and what he does for a living. You complain about the wasted potential of your house. You endure the darkness, you suffer heat and cold, and you learn to ignore your useless appliances, but you never ask the electrician to make the crucial connection you need.

That's what it's like for too many believers in Jesus Christ. They *say* they have a relationship with the Son of God and they thank the Father for forgiving their sins, but they never plug into the available power that is necessary to live the abundant life Jesus mentioned in John 10:10. They neglect an essential connection that will provide the kind of life Jesus promised; they fail to tap into the power of the Holy Spirit. To make that crucial connection, we must first understand something about the Holy Spirit.

GETTING PERSONAL

First of all, we need to understand that the Holy Spirit is not an "it." Just as God the Father is a person, and Jesus the Son is a person, so the Holy Spirit is a person as well. Note what Jesus said in John 16:13–14: "But when he, the Spirit of truth, comes, he will guide you into all truth. He will not speak on his own; he will speak only what he hears, and he will tell you what is yet to come. He will bring glory to me by taking from what is mine and making it known to you." Jesus spoke of the Holy Spirit in personal terms. He didn't refer to the Spirit as an impersonal power, or a supernatural force, or a directed energy emanating from heaven. The Holy Spirit is a person with thoughts (John 14:26), emotion (Ephesians 4:30), rationality (1 Corinthians 2:10–13), a will (Acts 8:29; 13:2), and the ability to relate (1 John 2:27).

Secondly, we need to understand how we encounter the person of the Holy Spirit. Jesus told His disciples, "You will receive power when the Holy Spirit comes on you; and you will be my witnesses in Jerusalem, and in all Judea and Samaria, and to the ends of the earth" (Acts 1:8). In other words, before we can *do* something, we have to *receive* something. Before we can point others to Christ verbally or through our lives, we have to receive the Holy Spirit. In order for Jesus' life to be reproduced in our lives, the power needs to be abiding and then flowing through us (cf. John 15; Romans 8).

Here's some good news from God's Word: believers already have a connection to divine power. If you have accepted Jesus into your life, you've already received the Holy Spirit (Ephesians 1:13–14, Romans 8:9-10). When you become a Christian, your life is wired so that you have access to His power. That's one of the ways the Holy Spirit functions in our lives. He enables us to know Christ.

In his famous encounter with Nicodemus (John 3), Jesus explained what being born again is all about. Jesus said, "I tell you the truth, no one can enter the kingdom of God unless he is born of water and the Spirit" (John 3:5). In other words, if the Holy Spirit does not bring you to the point where you see your need for Christ, you'll never invite Him in.

The Holy Spirit also is the One who inspired a human writer with the words, "Prophecy never had its origin in the will of man, but men spoke from God as they were carried along by the Holy Spirit" (2 Peter 1:21).

THE SPIRIT AND THE WORD

Still another way the Holy Spirit works in our lives is to open our minds to the Word of God, giving us the ability to understand and apply what we read in the Scriptures. Jesus explained that function of the Holy Spirit this way: "The Counselor, the Holy Spirit, whom the Father will send in my name, will teach you all things and will remind you of everything I have said to you" (John 14:26). It's as though we were given a third ear called the "ear of faith." This is the ability the Holy Spirit gives us to understand, comprehend, and then live out what we've read in the Bible. The Holy Spirit brings God's Word to life within us. What seems boring, irrelevant, or even nonsensical to those who do not have the Spirit of God suddenly becomes a source of inspiration and instruction to those "in Christ." Just before His crucifixion, Jesus promised His followers, "When he, the Spirit of truth, comes, he will guide you into all truth" (John 16:13).

The Holy Spirit also calls to our remembrance what we have read and studied. For example, when we find ourselves struggling with pride, the Spirit brings to mind the self-emptying example of Jesus becoming human, which Paul uses as an example of selflessness in his letter to the Philippians (2:5–8). The Spirit of God takes what we have read and then uses it to transform our minds. His application of Paul's illustration in Philippians then derails our tendency to focus on "what's in it for us." Through this crucial inward ministry, the Holy Spirit actually keeps us from failing more than we do. He takes principles we've encountered and brings them to the forefront of our thinking so that we find it more difficult to violate what we know God wants. Eventually, our conscience becomes attuned to God's mind.

The Spirit also prays for us (Romans 8:26–27) when we aren't sure what to pray about, or don't know exactly what to say, or when we know what is on our heart but find it difficult to come up with the right words. Even when we fail to pray, the Spirit of God prays on our behalf.

The Holy Spirit reproduces the character of Jesus in the lives of those who are spiritually alive. In Galatians 5:22–23, Paul notes that the qualities of "love, joy, peace, patience, kindness, goodness, faithfulness, gentleness and self-control" were characteristic of Jesus. When His life is reproduced in us, those qualities mark us too. If, on the other hand, some of those qualities are not evident in your life, He is the One who can make the change. For example, if you struggle with stress or worry, the Holy Spirit can transform your mind to become supernaturally confident in God's care. Peace will become your default state.

EMPOWERED

The Holy Spirit also empowers followers of Jesus to talk about their faith in a sane and sincere way. God doesn't want us to be weird or fanatical, but He does want us to offer valid testimony on His behalf, not unlike taking the stand in a courtroom. We simply talk about what we've experienced to be true in our lives. The Holy Spirit makes that kind of testifying possible. After all, that's what Jesus said would be the inevitable result of the Spirit living within us. He said, "You will receive power when the Holy Spirit comes on you; and you will be my witnesses" (Acts 1:8). Acts 4 reports that the very ones who heard Jesus speak those words before He ascended into heaven were in a prayer meeting. "After they prayed, the place where they were meeting was shaken. And they were all filled with the Holy Spirit and spoke the word of God boldly" (Acts 4:31).

The Holy Spirit's primary purpose in our lives, however, is to point to Christ. Jesus Himself said so. On that somber night before He was betrayed by Judas, Jesus hinted to His disciples in the upper room that He would be going away. He said, "I tell you the truth: It is for your good that I am going away. Unless I go away, the Counselor will not come to you; but if I go, I will send him to you . . . But when he, the Spirit of truth, comes, he will guide you into all truth. He will not speak on his own; he will speak only what he hears, and he will tell you what is yet to come. He will bring glory to me by taking from what is mine and making it known to you" (John 16:7, 13–14).

Take note of this important truth: Whatever begins with the Holy Spirit always ends with Christ. The Holy Spirit manifests Himself by reproducing Christ-like character in the believer, and He empowers God's people with gifts for the sake of ministry, but we must never forget this very important point: The overriding purpose of the Holy Spirit is to point to Jesus, not to become so conspicuous as to pull our attention away from Christ. He never wants us to become distracted from the end by becoming preoccupied with the means.

> *The Holy Spirit will never contradict the Word of God. The Holy Spirit always points to Christ.*

ONE STEP AT A TIME

Through the Holy Spirit, God has given us the power to be different in our homes, at our places of work, and in our neighborhoods. We have all we need to talk boldly about our faith with those in our spheres of influence. Through the Spirit we have the available resources to be courageously Christ-like in the way we act, decide, and think. But how do we begin to access the Spirit's resources?

According to the apostle Paul, the answer lies in learning how to walk in the awareness of the Holy Spirit. In his letter to the first-century Christians in Galatia, Paul wrote, "Since we live by the Spirit, let us keep in step with the Spirit" (Galatians 5:25). Keeping in step with the Holy Spirit means learning how to walk one step at a time. Just like a toddler has to start out by crawling and then taking a few steps and falling, so we have to start out with our arms outstretched to the Lord and head in His direction. In the process of learning to depend on His power, we'll fall flat on our faces. Falling down is inevitable when you're learning how to walk. Failure is an inevitable part of learning. The Lord knows we'll stumble and fall. Fortunately, "there is now no condemnation for those who are in Christ Jesus" (Romans 8:1). God has already declared us "blameless," morally spotless (Ephesians 1:4), and will not hold our failures against us. Instead, He provides a remedy for getting back up again.

Let's take a lesson in walking from an old disciple who learned from Christ how to crawl and then walk. John wrote,

> This is the message we have heard from him and declare to you: God is light; in him there is no darkness at all. If we claim to have fellowship with him yet walk in the darkness, we lie and do not live by the truth. But if we walk in the light, as he is in the light, we have fellowship with one another, and the blood of Jesus, his Son, purifies us from all sin.
>
> If we claim to be without sin, we deceive ourselves and the truth is not in us. If we confess our sins, he is faithful and just and will forgive us our sins and purify us from all unrighteousness. If we claim we have not sinned, we make him out to be a liar and his word has no place in our lives.
>
> My dear children, I write this to you so that you will not sin. But if anybody does sin, we have one who speaks to the Father in our defense—Jesus Christ, the Righteous One. He is the atoning sacrifice for our sins, and not only for ours but also for the sins of the whole world.
>
> We know that we have come to know him if we obey his commands. The man who says, "I know him," but does not do what he commands is a liar, and the truth is not in him. But if anyone obeys his word, God's love is truly made complete in him. This is how we know we are in him: Whoever claims to live in him must walk as Jesus did. (1 John 1:5–2:6)

John's lesson can be divided into three sections:

The Ideal Christian Life (1:5–7)
The Real Struggle with Sin (1:7–2:2)
The Ideal Christian Life (2:3–6)

The Ideal Christian Life (1:5–7)
John begins his lesson by describing the ideal Christian life in which a believer "walks in the light" of divine truth. He or she understands, accepts, embraces, and lives out the truths of Scripture. The ideal Christian isn't hypocritical, living righteously one minute and then committing sins the next. When we're living the ideal Christian life—utterly sinless and completely obedient—we enjoy unhindered fellowship with God and complete harmony with other believers. This is the goal. This is what we hope to achieve here and now on earth. This is the abundant life Jesus promises in John 10:10.

The Real Struggle with Sin (1:7–2:2)
While the apostle John hopes for the ideal Christian life—for himself and all believers—he also recognizes our ongoing struggle with evil. The Lord wants His people to conquer sin, He nevertheless understands that our

When Jesus spoke again to the people, he said, "I am the light of the world. Whoever follows me will never walk in darkness, but will have the light of life." John 8:12

journey toward "the light" will carry us through dark places. He knows we will experience failure. Therefore, He has made provision for restoring fallen Christians. His Holy Spirit not only empowers us to succeed, He restores us when we fail.

We experience the Holy Spirit's empowering presence in our lives when we are honest with God and admit we have impure thoughts, faulty motives, divided loyalties, and selfish attitudes. When we come to our loving Father as needy children, acknowledging that we've messed up, His Spirit picks us up and steadies us so we can start walking again. Consequently, failure—even the most serious moral tumbles—become a tool for instruction in the hand of God, never a weapon for abuse. The atoning death of Jesus Christ paid the penalty for past sin; His sacrifice also covers the sins we have not yet committed.

The Ideal Christian Life (2:3–6)

Most teachers would conclude their lesson with the reassurance that Christians can still have hope after moral failure. John, however, brings us full-circle to reinforce the ideal Christian life. He didn't want his readers to become complacent. The grace of God is not a license to sin. John challenges us with a sobering reality check: "The one who says, 'I have come to know him,' and does not keep his commandments, is a liar, and the truth is not in him" (v. 4). In other words, if a person who calls himself a Christian becomes complacent about sinful behavior and there is no spiritual growth in his life, then that person should reexamine his spiritual condition.

Later in this letter, John reassures his readers, "I write these things to you who believe in the name of the Son of God so that you may *know* that you have eternal life" (1 John 5:13 emphasis mine). He wants us to have assurance in the faithfulness of God to those who trust in Christ. Even so, John maintains an element of healthy self-doubt. Sin is serious business! A complacent attitude toward wrongdoing should cause one to ask the question, "Am I *really* a Christian?" If so, then go to 1 John 1:7–2:2 and ask the Holy Spirit for help! John affirms, "My dear children, I write this to you so that you will not sin" (2:1).

THE UNTAPPED RESERVOIR

Before he died, Dr. Bill Bright loved to tell about a man who lived during the depression. Ira Yates owned a sheep ranch in West Texas, but wasn't able to make enough on his ranching operation to pay the principal and interest on the mortgage. As time passed, he risked losing his ranch. Eventually, he had to live on a government subsidy. Day after day, as his sheep grazed on the rolling West Texas hills, he wondered how he would pay the bills. Then a seismographic crew from an oil company came into the area and told him there might be oil on his land. They asked permission to drill a well and he signed a contract.

A daily confession of sin is vital to the Christian's spiritual growth. The Bible tells us to daily examine our hearts. King David prayed, "Search me, O God, and know my heart; test me and know my anxious thoughts. See if there is any offensive way in me, and lead me in the way everlasting" (Psalm 139:23-24).

At 1,115 feet they struck oil—big-time! The first well came in at 80,000 barrels a day. Many subsequent wells produced twice as much. In fact, 30 years after the discovery, a government test on one of the wells showed that it still had the potential to yield 125,000 barrels of oil a day. And Yates owned it all! Actually, he owned it all on the day he purchased the land. Yet he had been living on government relief. A multimillionaire living in poverty! The problem? He didn't know about the riches lying beneath his feet and he lacked the ability to get to it.

In the Holy Spirit you have more energy for living the Christian life than you could possibly imagine. It's as if you are sitting on an undiscovered oil well. Sadly, too many followers of Christ are living below the poverty level when they have unbelievable resources available to them. Just imagine the impact we could have if only we would allow the Spirit of God to fill us and flow through us!

Now that you know about the abundant life available to you, don't overlook the huge reservoir of spiritual riches waiting to be tapped. God stands ready to help you reach the incredible wealth that is yours.

> "We are half-hearted creatures, fooling about with drink and sex and ambition when infinite joy is offered us, like an ignorant child who wants to go on making mud pies in a slum because he cannot imagine what is meant by the offer of a holiday at the sea. We are far too easily pleased."[1]
>
> —C.S. Lewis, *The Weight of Glory*

TAKE ACTION

Review 1 John 1:5–2:6, which helps us understand the "normal Christian life."
No one lives the ideal Christian life perfectly; we all have room for improvement. With that in mind, reflect on your own spiritual walk. Describe your progress. What are you doing to cultivate an ongoing relationship with God?

What unconfessed sin do you need to discuss with God? What habitual, compulsive, or repetitive sin interferes with your spiritual life? What steps are you taking to address your sin?

Write out a prayer expressing your desire for the Holy Spirit to heal your wounds and to transform your character:

Be intentional: What are you going to do about what you've learned?

Be specific: What action will you take in the near future to begin applying what you've learned? When will you do it?

Be accountable: Pray it through. Share your plan with a friend and seek his/her prayer and counsel for your next step.

CHAPTER 5: OUR RESPONSE TO THE GRACE OF GOD...OBEDIENCE

Scan here to watch the video!

Thus far we've discovered that a basic definition of the Christian life is the **life of Christ reproduced in the believer by the power of the Holy Spirit**. While God has promised to complete the spiritual renovation He began when we first trusted in Christ for salvation (Philippians 1:6), He calls us to take an active role in the work He's doing. Jesus urged His followers to "Abide in Me" (John 15:4), promising that He and His words would abide in us (v. 7). Paul urges us to "be filled with the Spirit" (Ephesians 5:18) and to "throw off everything that hinders and the sin that so easily entangles, and let us run with perseverance the race marked out for us" (Hebrews 12:1). The transformation of our character is the work of God; He gives us a genuine stake in the process. The means by which the Holy Spirit brings about Christ's life reproduced in us is a fourfold response to God's grace.

The "Christian Life" can be defined as The life of Christ, reproduced in the believer, by the power of the Holy Spirit, in obedient response to the word of God.

Our response to God's grace includes:

- Obedience to the Word of God
- Conversation with God in prayer
- Appreciation for God in worship
- Sacrifice to God in giving

Earlier, we considered the illustration of a house loaded with modern conveniences yet disconnected from the power grid. What happens when the electrician establishes that crucial connection? Everything in the house sparks to life! The power produces activity. The house didn't make the connection to the power grid by causing the appliances to operate. Quite the opposite. The activity within the house is a response to the energy supplied from an outside source. Similarly, when the grace of God connects with the lifeless believer, the Holy Spirit's power begins to flow and the energized Christian responds.

It is important to note that all four responses to God's grace are relational. That is, each response—every activity a Christian undertakes—is an effort to know God personally and experientially. Paul described the motivation for his spiritual activity this way:

> I consider everything a loss compared to the surpassing greatness of knowing Christ Jesus my Lord, for whose sake I have lost all things. I consider them rubbish, that I may gain Christ and be found in him, not having a righteousness of my own that comes from the law, but that which is

Every activity a Christian undertakes in response to God is an effort to know God personally and experientially.

through faith in Christ—the righteousness that comes from God and is by faith. *I want to know Christ and the power of his resurrection and the fellowship of sharing in his sufferings, becoming like him in his death,* and so, somehow, to attain to the resurrection from the dead. Not that I have already obtained all this, or have already been made perfect, but I press on to take hold of that for which Christ Jesus took hold of me. (Philippians 3:8–12 emphasis mine)

We don't engage in spiritual activities to please God; He's already pleased with us because we are "in Christ." We don't obey to earn God's favor; He has already transferred to our accounts every blessing heaven can bestow. We don't "walk in the light" to gain salvation or earn eternal life; by the grace of God we now have the light living within us. Therefore, every spiritual activity, every good deed, every act of obedience is a response motivated by a singular desire to know God.

In this chapter, we will consider the first three responses to God as we participate in the relationship He initiated.

OBEDIENCE TO THE WORD OF GOD

Obedience builds spiritual muscles. What we do with the Bible determines how much we grow in our faith. As an old country preacher once said, "This book will keep you from sin, or sin will keep you from this book." Someone else put it this way, "Dusty Bibles lead to dirty lives." How we incorporate God's Word into our lives determines the degree to which the character of Christ is reproduced in our lives. We either allow the Word to shape our thinking and behavior through the power of the Holy Spirit, or we allow the world to squeeze us into its mold.

WHAT'S THE BIG DEAL?

So what is so special about the Bible? For one thing, the Bible presents itself as God's unique revelation to humanity. Scattered throughout the sixty-six books of this ancient collection of God's revelation are numerous statements that the words and messages are from God Himself. In other words, God guided the writers as they wrote so that their words communicated truth about the human condition that could not be discovered any other way. The writers were not taking dictation. God used the culture, personality, and vocabulary of each contributor.

The Bible not only claims to be God's Word, the evidence points to the fact that it has a Divine origin. For one thing, all sixty-six books were written over a fifteen-hundred-year span with the earliest portions written more than three thousand years ago. Still the work displays an amazing unity. The writers included kings, statesmen, poets, fishermen, farmers, and physicians. They wrote independently of each other, yet their writings all tell the story of Jesus. Furthermore, the Bible has survived intact despite many attempts to destroy all existing copies. Even so, we have more physical evidence for the authenticity of the books in the Bible than for any other ancient literature.

Historical authenticity aside, the message of the Bible continues to be timeless as well as timely. It addresses the origin of life as well as the meaning and purpose of our existence. Scripture points to ethical issues of justice and mercy in this life as well as what to expect in life beyond the grave.

THE BENEFITS OF THE BOOK

The value of the Bible is not just seen in its Divine origin but in the practical way it benefits our lives. First, it is a light that provides illumination about the human condition as well as God's plan for the world (Psalm 119:105). The Bible is also a mirror. Not just any mirror, mind you, but the kind of looking glass that reflects our personalities and souls rather than our physical appearance. Through God's Word we have the opportunity to see ourselves from God's perspective and determine what in our lives is in need of change (James 1:23–24).

The Bible is also an essential source of food that sustains our souls (Matthew 4:4). Call it spiritual nourishment, if you like. The simple, direct instruction of Scripture, when acted upon, results in growth with essential benefits of fruitfulness, areas of wisdom, character, love, integrity, and courage. What is more, the Word of God provides appropriate weaponry to respond defensively as well as offensively to spiritual attack (Ephesians 6:10–18). It is a shield that protects us from assaults on our emotions, our self-esteem, and our faith—not to mention doubt, guilt, fear, insecurity, and feelings of inferiority (Psalm 119:114). But the Bible is also a sword that defends the man or woman of God from the lurking enemies of false truths or half-truths lying in wait ready to ambush us (Hebrews 4:12; 2 Corinthians 10:4-5). Furthermore, the Bible is the means by which we understand how to access the presence of the living God. A daily reading of God's Word provides us with the awareness that He is

"To be sovereign is to possess supreme power and authority so that one is in complete control and can accomplish whatever he pleases."

—Bob Deffinbaugh

WHAT IS A SPIRITUAL ATTACK?

It's a battle against your mind, will, and emotions motivated by Satan in an effort to defeat you in your walk with Jesus. Satan is the leader of the fallen angels, or otherwise known as the head of the demons. His name means "adversary" (opponent of God and his people). The New Testament gives him revealing titles, which are translated: devil, accuser, destroyer, tempter, evil one, and more. Jesus, in John 8:44, said that Satan was always a murderer and is the father of lies—meaning, he is both the original liar and the sponsor of all subsequent lies.[12] "Satan and his demons will try to use every type of destructive tactic to blind people 'from seeing the light of the gospel of the glory of Christ' (2 Corinthians

> 4:4). They will also use similar destructive tactics—such as temptation, doubt, lies, murder, guilt, fear, confusion, sickness, envy, pride, and slander—to hinder a Christian's witness and usefulness."[13]
>
> The picture (of Satan) is one of unimaginable meanness, malice, fury, and cruelty directed against God, against God's truth, and against those to whom God has extended his saving love. But do not be alarmed! Satan is a creature, superhuman but not divine; he has much knowledge and power, but he is neither omniscient (all-knowing) nor omnipotent (all-powerful); he can move around in ways that humans cannot, but he is not omnipresent (present everywhere at the same time); and he is an already defeated rebel, having no more power than God allows him and being destined for the lake of fire (Revelation 20:10).[14]
>
> But God has given us the most effective means of spiritual warfare, "the sword of the Spirit," which is the Word of God (Ephesians 6:17). Using the powerful Word of God is our #1 weaponry defense, enabling us to not only take a stand against the enemy—but to be victorious in defeating him.

good, powerful, and sovereign in directing our lives. Through the Bible we learn that He has expectations of us and resources for us.

It is possible, however, to know and understand the contents of Divine revelation without ever applying it. Unfortunately, knowledge is not enough. We must act upon what we discover for the Bible to impact our lives. The more we respond to the Word of God, the greater our capacity to understand its mysteries. Reading without an obedient response produces nothing.

THE BENEFITS OF BIBLE STUDY

Many Christians merely absorb information. But what does that accomplish? Here's an illustration that might explain the superficiality of mere Bible exposure. Ninety-three million miles away from earth there is a star called the sun. With a diameter 109.3 times that of the earth and a surface temperature of 27 million degrees Fahrenheit, tremendous energy bursts out into space. The earth receives this radiant energy at a rate of four million horsepower per square mile. Pretty amazing, huh? Fascinating study, but it may not impact the way you go about your day, right?

That's the way many deal with the truths they read in the Bible. A person reads an interesting passage. It's information that he had never heard before. After scratching his chin and opening his mouth to yawn, he closes the book. He can check off that he read that section of Scripture on his read-through-the-Bible-in-one-year chart, but that's about all.

If, on the other hand, a reader opens the science book with a desire to apply what he or she reads, everything changes. The sun's energy is ultraviolet

---

We must act upon what we discover for the Bible to impact our lives. The more we respond to the Word of God, the greater our capacity to understand its mysteries.

radiation. If it hits exposed skin, those UV rays penetrate the upper layers to produce a tan. Too much tanning could result in skin cancer. The wise reader will adjust his or her behavior based on the information gleaned from reading. With the purchase of SPF 30 lotion, knowledge has become application.

Do you understand the progression illustrated here? Once a correlation is made between the truth and how that truth impacts life, we pay better attention to the topic in question and then act upon the knowledge gained. That's the essence of Bible study. We ask questions of the text and then ask questions of ourselves.

Here's a simple way to visualize the process:

```
              TRUTH
              STATED


         IMPLICATIONS
         FROM THE TRUTH


     APPLICATIONS FOR MY LIFE
```

After reading a passage ask yourself, "What did I just read? What did the passage say?" Then go ahead and look to the text through the lens of understanding. This may require the use of a dictionary to make sure you understand the meaning of a word that you don't normally use. It also may require accessing a concordance in the back of your Bible to see how the word is used elsewhere in Scripture.

On this second level you are basically asking yourself, "What is the implication of this truth when taken at face value? What are the conditions, promises, or consequences of this verse? To whom does it apply? How are those people like me?"

Finally, ask yourself, "If I were going to put this truth into practice, what would I have to do or say or choose? What impact would this reality have on my marriage, my job, my character, my relationships, or the goals that I'm currently pursuing?" That's where obedience to God's Word shows up. First you have to know what is expected. Then you have to know what it means. Finally you are in a position to act on what you understand to be true, to obey the instructions God has communicated through His written Word.

OBEDIENCE DEFINED

Dietrich Bonhoeffer was a brilliant young Lutheran pastor in Germany who lived during the first half of the twentieth century. When Hitler attempted to hypnotize pastors and church leaders into thinking his regime was consistent with the teachings of Christianity, this stocky, blond, bespectacled theologian could not ignore what he saw as a gross violation against people created in God's image. Bonhoeffer led a courageous resistance movement that resulted in an underground church. In the process, he gained first-hand knowledge of what it means to take God's values seriously. He identified the price tag associated with obeying the law of love. He referred to it as "the cost of discipleship." This thirty-something cleric was arrested and sent to a concentration camp where he was executed just two weeks before the allied forces liberated his cell. Before his death, Bonhoeffer wrote, "Only the believer is obedient, and only he who obeys believes."[15] Even though obedience, or submission, is difficult for many Christians, it lies at the heart of being a joyful Christ-follower.

"Only the believer is obedient, and only he who obeys believes."

—Dietrich Bonhoeffer

WHY OBEY?

Obedience is a way to prove one's love for another. When your child purposely chooses to do what you have asked him to do (even though his little heart would rather do the opposite), what is going on? Compliance probably goes beyond simply valuing what you think. It's more than obeying in order to avoid discipline. More likely, your child's obedience flows from his love for you.

The same goes for you and your mate. The laws of Christian marriage prohibit infidelity. While standing before a preacher and a packed church you had agreed to God's demands. But after every wedding comes a marriage. That's when the "I dos" simply fall to the floor and shatter or they are faithfully lived out and eventually become "I dids." Chances are you have found (or will find) yourself tempted to disregard the promises pledged at the altar. When you choose to keep your word and do what your mate expects (and longs for) you prove that you really do love that person.

The night before Jesus was betrayed, arrested, and crucified, He provided a litmus test of love for His followers. He said, "If you love me, you will obey what I command . . . Whoever has my commands and obeys them, he is the one who loves me. He who loves me will be loved by my Father, and I too will love him and show myself to him . . . If anyone loves me, he will obey my teaching. My Father will love him, and we will come to him and make our home with him. He who does not love me will not obey my teaching. These words you hear are not my own; they belong to the Father who sent me" (John 14:15, 21, 23–24). According to Jesus, actions speak louder than words. Anyone can profess love for another; actions reveal the heart.

Earlier, we explored the concept of being "in Christ." In that same conversation with His friends, Jesus said, "As the Father has loved me, so have I loved you. Now remain in my love. If you obey my commands, you will remain in my love, just as I have obeyed my Father's commands and remain in his love" (John 15:9–10). We learn from this that to "abide in Christ" is to obey His commands. Furthermore, He stated that a person's willingness to obey was the primary indicator of whether that person was truly committed to Him. Why else do you think Jesus would say, "You are my friends if you do what I command" (John 15:14)? Obedience is one way that we participate in the relationship God initiated. Obedience is how we respond to God's grace and then grow closer to Him personally and experientially.

Obedience is one way that we participate in the relationship God initiated. Obedience is how we respond to God's grace and then grow closer to Him personally and experientially.

What is more, as we obey God's commandments, His activity in our lives changes us. Obedience is a fertilizer that promotes healthy growth. It enables us to fully benefit from God's process of growing us into the likeness of His Son. The apostle Paul thought deeply on that when he wrote, "Therefore, I urge you, brothers, in view of God's mercy, to offer your bodies as living sacrifices, holy and pleasing to God—this is your spiritual act of worship. Do not conform any longer to the pattern of this world, but be transformed by the renewing of your mind. Then you will be able to test and approve what God's will is—his good, pleasing and perfect will" (Romans 12:1–2). Becoming a living sacrifice means sacrificing our own desires in order to obey what God wants. As that daily decision becomes more habitual, we begin to think more and more like Jesus and we gain an even clearer understanding of what brings God pleasure (Hebrews 13:20–21). In fact, joy increases as we have an increased desire to do it.

We aren't the only ones who benefit from our obedience. Others who might not yet be Christians do as well. As you might guess, if we consistently follow the moral map God has laid out for us in the Bible, those who observe our lives will take notice. Uncompromising devotion and loving commitment to others is uncommon in our culture; therefore, we will stand out. Jesus hinted at the fact that when we obey His command to make His glory and the love of others the overriding aim of our lives, people will know that we are different.

WHAT GOOD IS OBEDIENCE?

Can't you hear the reaction of some? "Obey, obey, obey. Just what's the big deal with obedience? I thought Christianity was all about grace. Obedience smacks of legalistic performance. I don't get it." Those who think that way are looking at obedience the wrong way. God isn't out to make our lives miserable by insisting on meaningless demands. His requirements dealing with sexual purity, fidelity, integrity, generosity, forgiveness, justice, and worship are not onerous have-to's meant to make life difficult. Far from it! These are keys that unlock the secrets to happiness and fulfillment. The owner's manual that you get with your new car doesn't complicate your life; those instructions (like changing the oil every 3,000 miles) are given to extend the life and performance of your car. The same is true with God. Everything He asks us to do is grounded in His love for us.

HOW DO WE OBEY?

Obedience may be the very best way to show that we believe. It is also one of the most difficult choices to make. A life of obedience isn't something we wake up one morning and decide to live out. It's a process of going three steps forward and two steps backward. Remember, as the beachhead metaphor illustrates in Chapter 2, each person still has an enemy-held territory that is in the process of being liberated. The takeover takes longer than we had hoped. Though we belong to the Father and have been cleansed of our sin, we still have a sinful nature that resists doing what we know we should (1 Corinthians 9:27). Barreling down the freeway of faith toward a destination of God's choosing, we find ourselves choosing the nearest exit in order to do what seems more freeing for the moment.

If you are serious about learning obedience, you have to be honest with yourself and God. That means admitting that you have left the freeway. It means coming to the bottom of the exit ramp and asking yourself, "What am I doing here? I really don't want to be here. I blew it by ignoring God's desires in order to serve my own momentary needs." Once you have recognized your mistake by getting off the freeway, the next step is simple. Find the nearest on-ramp, gather speed, and get back on-course (1 John 1:8–9).

THE CONSEQUENCES OF DISOBEDIENCE

When we choose to disregard the owner's manual that comes with our car, stuff happens. Not good stuff—bad stuff. Not as a result of divine punishment but as a predicted consequence of wrongdoing. We live in a cause and effect world. Even scientists who claim that God doesn't exist nevertheless accept certain laws. Newton's Third Law indicates every action has an equal and opposite reaction. The apostle Paul spoke of a similar law. He called this the law of the harvest: We reap what we sow (cf. Galatians 6:7–8). Ultimate salvation from judgment does not eliminate the consequences of disregarding God's dictates. Those consequences are sadly called "wasted opportunities," "blown chances," "wounded family members," "compromised health," "disqualification for public ministry," and sometimes result in a shortened life.

Just as the apostle Peter illustrates one who stayed with the process of learning how to obey God, Israel's first king illustrates the opposite. According to what we read in 1 Samuel 9:2, Saul stood head and shoulders above his peers in more ways than one. He was tall, handsome, and gifted. He began with a sincere desire to obey the Lord. He had a brilliant advisor in Samuel the prophet, so Saul knew what he was supposed to do. He knew what God desired and he knew he had the means to honor the Lord's wishes. Saul seemed to have it all. Still, the promising young king struggled with pride and jealousy (1 Samuel 18:8). When Samuel instructed Saul to wait for him before

---

Everything He asks us to do is grounded in His love for us.

beginning a ceremony, the impetuous king began slaughtering animals for the sacrificial offering (1 Samuel 13:9ff). Saul, who stood tall in physical stature, became a Pygmy in terms of humility. His ability to rationalize disobedience to God's orders proved to be his downfall. When Samuel finally arrived and realized that Saul had gone ahead without him, he rebuked the king with a sharp tongue and a word from God. "To obey is better than sacrifice" (1 Samuel 15:22). Sadly for Saul, his failure to embrace obedience as a core value cost him the crown. After this willful transgression, the Lord prompted Samuel to anoint David as Saul's replacement.

Yes, disobedience has consequences. It might not be the loss of your job, but it could be. One thing is certain—failing to take God's Word seriously will rob you of the joyful sense of God's presence He desires for you. On the other hand, the more you respond to the Word of God with appropriate action, the greater capacity you will have to understand the truth contained in His Book (Matthew 25:15ff; Luke 12:48). In other words, when you act on what you know, the Lord opens your eyes and your heart to experience even more of His presence. That's what Jesus was getting at with His friends in the upper room (John 13:13-17). The love relationship that exists between the Father and the Son, and the Son and His followers, is maximized when those involved respond with faith and action.

When you act on what you've learned from God's Word, the Lord opens your eyes and your heart to experience even more of His presence.

TAKE ACTION

Read Philippians 3:8–12.
When you begin a new relationship with someone, how do you get to know him or her? What kinds of things do you do to learn more about this person?

God has initiated a relationship with you, so there's nothing you must do to gain His favor or earn His love. Instead, He invites you to learn more about Him. Based on our study in this chapter, what will you do to discover God's character, His desires, His values, His priorities, and His plans for the future?

Like many activities, Bible study gets easier, more enjoyable, and more rewarding over time. Check out the resource "How to Study the Bible" in the back of this book to help you get started in your personal bible study. These resources will be helpful whether you begin studying on your own, or as part of a study group.

Be intentional: What are you going to do about what you've learned?

Be specific: What action will you take in the near future to begin applying what you've learned? When will you do it?

Be accountable: Pray it through. Share your plan with a friend and seek his/her prayer and counsel for your next step.

CHAPTER 6: RELATING WITH THE ALMIGHTY

Scan here to watch the video!

As any good marriage counselor will affirm, a growing intimacy between two people requires communication. The same can be said of any healthy relationship. Friendships grow stronger as two people express themselves and listen to one another. The interpersonal bond develops over time as each person learns what makes the other tick—how they respond under pressure, what they hope to accomplish in life, what values they hold in high regard, what priorities they serve. Friendships even grow stronger when the people involved learn to talk through conflict.

Our relationship with God, like any genuine relationship, requires communication. Two means of interpersonal sharing with the Almighty include prayer and worship.

PRAYER

An unforgettable scene in Mel Gibson's epic movie, *The Passion of the Christ*, depicts Jesus stooped in the shadows of an olive garden, the branches casting Him in an eerie darkness. His haunting moans make it clear that all is not well. Overwhelmed with sorrow, He painfully expresses His grief in Aramaic, pouring out His heavy heart to the Father. His agonizing monologue reveals His desire to be kept from the cross, to forego His dreadful destiny. The anticipation of bearing the punishment of all the world's sins had pressed the Son of God to His limits.

As His conversation with His Father concluded, a snake slithers from a nearby bush. With a confident resignation to imminent suffering and death, Jesus does not draw back in fear. With a calculated stomp, He guides His leather-sandaled foot down upon the serpent's head, crushing the personification of evil as He walks through the trees toward the cross. The image is a powerful reminder of the first promise of God's redemption recorded in Genesis 3:15. After the fall of humanity, God cursed the tempting serpent, saying, "I will put enmity between you and the woman, and between your offspring and hers; he will crush your head, and you will strike his heel."

Through prayer Jesus triumphed over temptation and responded obediently to His Father's plan. In the atmosphere of prayer, we also learn to breathe the air of obedience. Prayer is a critical component for all those who want the life of Christ reproduced in them. As Oswald Chambers powerfully stated, "We look upon prayer as a means of getting things for ourselves; the Bible's idea of prayer is that we may get to know God Himself."[16] He continues, "Prayer is not simply getting things from God, that is an initial form of prayer; prayer is getting into perfect communion with God."[17]

PRACTICING THE PRESENCE OF JESUS

Typically, we think of prayer as talking to God—either alone or in a group—with bowed head, closed eyes, folded hands, and perhaps bended knee. But that's only one form of prayer. We learn from the example of Brother Lawrence that prayer involves much more than a particular posture and need not be limited to specific times, such as meals or bedtime. Brother Lawrence lived in a monastery outside Paris more than three hundred years ago, and as a member of the Carmelite community, served his Lord and his brothers in the kitchen as a cook. Aware that Jesus was with him at all times, Lawrence viewed everything he did in that little room as an act of prayer. He called his unorthodox definition of prayer "practicing the presence of Christ." In his own words, "God is everywhere, in all places, and there is no spot where we cannot draw near to Him, and hear Him speaking in our heart; with a little love, just a very little, we shall not find it hard."[18]

For this remarkable man, prayer was his opportunity to share every moment with the Lord and to bring every detail of his life into His available presence. With a view of prayer like that, the intimidating ideas of what it takes to communicate with God no longer are an excuse. If prayer is nothing more than practicing the presence of Christ, it is as simple (and natural) as breathing.

HOW DO WE PRAY?

For the follower of Jesus, prayer is not some religious ritual. It is candid conversation with Someone we care about Who cares for us. As a result, we don't need to be overly concerned about parroting someone else's words or attempting to sound religious. We aren't praying for the benefit of anyone other than the One who can already read our thoughts before we verbalize them. So we can relax and be creative.

A popular model for praying is A.C.T.S., which stands for Adoration (worship, proclaiming who God is and the attributes of His character), Confession (personal repentance of sins), Thanksgiving (gratitude, praising Him and remembering the works of the Lord), and Supplication (asking for your needs and the needs of others).[19] If kneeling helps you feel close to God, take a knee (or two). A case can be made that bowing or kneeling helps us assume a posture of reverence and humility. But Jesus taught us to talk to God as if He were our father (Matthew 6:9). If closing your eyes helps you concentrate on what you are saying and to Whom you are speaking, then go for it. If you can close out distractions while keeping your eyes open, then by all means watch and pray. After all, that's Biblical (Colossians 4:2). It's also a safety precaution if you are attempting to pray while commuting to work. Remember—no occasion is inappropriate for talking to the Lord.

Dr. Leighton Ford, evangelist and respected Christian author, is right on

Prayer is your opportunity to share every moment with the Lord and to bring every detail of your life into His available presence.

the mark when he suggests, "Don't limit your prayers to a formal act once a day. Get in the habit of sending flash prayers to God many times a day. Pray when you wake up; pray before meals; pray as you walk or ride or wait; pray when you can't sleep. Even doing your work or your recreation to the glory of God can be a prayer." The only restrictions Jesus placed on prayer had to do with words spoken without thinking or with wrong motives. He really got on the religious leaders of His day for mindlessly babbling religious sounding words that had become a ritualistic exercise (Matthew 6:7). Jesus warned against equating prayer with vainly repeating canned phrases or chanting our requests like an incantation. The words may be valid, but if they are offered with corrupted motives, they have no value. And praying as a means to impress others is just as worthless.

Praying A.C.T.S.

Adoration
(Matthew 6:9)
Confession
(Matthew 6:12)
Thanksgiving
(Psalm 118:1)
Supplication
(Philippians 4:6-7)

If prayer is really the interaction between friends, however, it should not be seen as motivated solely by need. Praying that is always looking for a handout is nothing more than verbal coins inserted in a cosmic vending machine. The kind of communication Jesus calls us to is primarily relationship building. That means talking to the Lord about issues that have a tendency to come between Him and us. It also has to do with asking forgiveness when we know wrong choices or willful actions have created a distance between us.

Relationship building prayer involves protracted periods of time conversing about little things—admiring the beauty of a sunset, commenting on undeserved blessings, or letting the Lord know how special He is to you. You know, the glue of commitment is the stickiness of what we used to call "sweet nothings." In other words, it is important that we talk to the Lord about crises in our lives. It's important that we petition Him about issues that are beyond our control. And it's important that we relate to Him as a cherished friend.

WHAT SHOULD WE PRAY FOR?

For starters, ask God to provide you with growth options and opportunities that will enhance your relationship with Him. Ask the Lord to give you a willingness to obey what you know He desires. Ask Him for the faith to trust Him when you're tempted to worry or doubt (Matthew 6:31–33). Jesus said that when we pray according to God's will, we can be sure that He will answer (Matthew 7:7–8). And you can be sure that God wills for you to mature in your relationship with Him.

Remember—no occasion is inappropriate for talking to the Lord. The only restrictions Jesus placed on prayer had to do with words spoken without thinking or with wrong motives.

Praying for your own personal growth is also appropriate. How are things at your job? Most likely you have issues there that concern you. Bring those to the Father. Are there those with whom you have difficulty working? Don't pretend with God that all is well. Talk to Him about those relationships. Are you apprehensive about your job security? Tell the Father.

Ask God for insight into situations that overwhelm you. In his epistle, the apostle James states, "If any of you lack wisdom he should ask God" (James 1:5). Also acknowledge your desire for physical health to the Lord. When you are sick, ask for His healing touch. Confess your need for rational thinking. If you are prone to depression, ask the Lord to bring into your life people and treatment options that will stop the emotional spiral.

In addition, pray for family members and close friends. If they do not yet know the Lord, ask Him to surround them with Christians who will share their faith (Colossians 1:6) and stir them with questions of eternity to whet their appetite for spiritual matters. If they are believers, ask the Father to open their eyes to evidence of His faithfulness in their lives and their dependence upon Him.

Don't stop with family and friends—pray for your church family. Ask God to encourage your pastor as he guides the congregation. Name those who teach your kids and request that the Lord would reward their commitment with creativity and patience.

> **DO I PRAY FOR EVERYONE EVERY DAY?**
>
> When we begin praying for others, sometimes we can feel guilty if we don't pray for everyone everyday. Our prayer time becomes a laundry list of burdens, overwhelming us until we stop praying altogether.
>
> For help on organizing your prayer life, see the resources "How to Set Up a Prayer Notebook" in the back of this book. You'll find tips to avoid being overwhelmed with your prayer requests, and as a result see God's goodness in how He answers your requests.

If we take our cues from Jesus' model on how to pray (Matthew 6:9–13), we should talk to God about everything that matters to us (or Him). We should feel free to ask Him for daily sustenance. More than food, that's whatever it takes to survive day to day. We should ask the Father for forgiveness because acknowledging our spiritual indebtedness to God and cashing in on His forgiveness prompts us to be more patient and forgiving toward others. We are to call on the Lord for strength when tempted and for deliverance when we find ourselves kidnapped by calamity.

HOW DOES GOD ANSWER PRAYER?

Someone once said, God answers every prayer. Sometimes He says "yes." Sometimes He says "no." And sometimes He says "wait." Experience has shown this to be very true. God doesn't have a spam folder. Every message reaches Him and He responds to every contact. We must, however, remember that God is not a blessing dispenser. He's the sovereign King of the universe who knows what's best. He may choose to deny our earnest request because

> **WHAT IS JESUS' MODEL ON HOW TO PRAY?**
>
> - Pray like this: "Our Father in heaven, may your name be kept holy. May your Kingdom come soon. May your will be done on earth, as it is in heaven. Give us today the food we need, and forgive us our sins, as we have forgiven those who sin against us. And don't let us yield to temptation, but rescue us from the evil one" (Matthew 6:9-13 NLT).

we don't necessarily ask for what will serve our long-term best interests. As one friend said, "I have lived long enough now to thank God for the requests He denied!"

Sometimes, God denies our request because a "yes" would compromise our spiritual health. The apostle Paul was plagued with an undisclosed ailment he described as a "thorn in the flesh." By his own admission he pleaded with God to have it removed, but the Lord did not answer in the way Paul had hoped. Instead, the Lord responded, "My grace is sufficient for you . . ." (2 Corinthians 12:9). In that case, the answer to Paul's prayer was "no." Paul later admitted that the denied request made him spiritually powerful. He came to see the affliction as his greatest asset, saying, "Therefore I will boast all the more gladly about my weaknesses, so that Christ's power may rest on me. That is why, for Christ's sake, I delight in weaknesses, in insults, in hardships, in persecutions, in difficulties. For when I am weak, then I am strong" (2 Corinthians 12:9–10).

The Bible also reports those occasions when people who were praying for God's deliverance learned how to wait. Isaiah wrote to such folks. He knew that freedom from Babylonian bondage would come. The Lord had given him a preview of coming attractions. But he also knew that the motion picture of God's redemption would not be released in the near future. No wonder he wrote, "Those who wait for the Lord will gain new strength" (Isaiah 40:31 NASB).

FASTING

After Jesus was baptized, He immediately went into the wilderness in response to the leading of the Holy Spirit. While there, He fasted forty days and forty nights (Matthew 4). Choosing to forego eating for a period of time is a discipline worthy of great study—entire books have been written on the subject—but for the purposes of this book, we will highlight three authors who have extensively studied the topic, and have expressed themselves well. For further study, see the "Recommended Reading" resource in the appendix.

"Throughout Scripture fasting refers to abstaining from food for spiritual purposes. Like prayer, fasting doesn't coerce God, or earn His favor, or prove our spiritual worth. Biblical fasting isn't a hunger strike, the purpose of which is to gain political power or attract attention to a good cause. It is also distinct from health dieting which stresses abstinence from food for physical rather than spiritual purposes. Because of the secularization of modern society, people are often motivated by vanity or perhaps a desire for spiritual power. As a political or social tool, fasting can be effective, but biblical fasting has a very different purpose."[20]

Biblical "fasting is not an end in itself; it is a means by which we can worship the Lord and submit ourselves in humility to Him. One of the greatest spiritual benefits of fasting is becoming more attentive to God—becoming more aware of our own inadequacies and His adequacy, our own contingencies and His self-sufficiency—and listening to what He wants us to be and do. Christian fasting focuses on God. The results are spiritual results that glorify God, both in the person who fasts and others for whom we fast and pray."[21]

"Fasting confirms our utter dependence on God by finding in Him our source of sustenance beyond food. Through it, we learn by experience that God's Word to us is a life substance, that it is not food ("bread") alone that gives life, but also the words that proceed from the mouth of God (Matthew 4:4). We learn that we too have meat to eat that the world does not know about (John 4:32, 34). Fasting unto our Lord is therefore feasting—feasting on Him and on doing His will."[22]

WORSHIP

We worship to bring the Lord pleasure by revering Him, thanking Him, and celebrating His goodness and power. The words to an old gospel song say it well: "Turn your eyes upon Jesus. Look full in His wonderful face. And the things of earth will grow strangely dim in the light of His glory and grace."[23] Rick Warren says it well in his book, *The 40 Days of Purpose*. On page one he bottom-lines it for us: "It's not about you." Worship is first understanding Who God is and then praising Him for who He is, all that He has done, and all that in faith you know He will do in your life.

Dr. Larry Crabb teaches, "Efforts to worship God without first getting to know Him tend to reduce worship to mere appreciation when God cooperates with our agendas. And thanking God without true worship, without first being stunned that the holy God who has every right to abandon us instead draws us closer, leaves us still thinking that at least a few things ought to go our way. But when true worship is the spring from which gratitude flows, we take nothing for granted. The fact that anything is right in our lives becomes a cause for celebration, and we feel humble gratitude for undeserved blessings—which, of course, all of them are."[24] Those who focus on Jesus in a worshipful lifestyle and participate in singing, praying, contemplating in silence, or listening to a sermon experience a tangible payoff. Consider the following benefits.

When you gather with other believers on a regular basis you have the

It's in worship that your doubting, anxious heart finds confidence and hope to face the uncertainties that await you during the week.

opportunity to release your cares and concerns. The founder of the Vineyard movement[25] wrote a praise song that contained these words: "O let him have the things that hold you and His Spirit like a dove will descend upon your heart." Doesn't that sound inviting? When you enter into the Lord's presence in a place or a time set apart for the express purpose of considering His attributes, something significant occurs. Even though you've come to worship with unresolved issues and intimidating challenges in your life, those problems are dwarfed when contrasted to the answer of Whose presence you're keenly aware.

Your concept of God will be shaped by your worship of God.

When you exercise your faith in the context of worship, you discover long-term results. Just as with physical muscles, working your faith muscles makes them stronger. No wonder the person who wrote Hebrews felt so strongly about maintaining a core value of regular worship. The inner strength that is derived from consistently being in corporate worship is not an exercise in vanity. Those well-chiseled faith muscles aren't intended for showing off or gaining a sense of fulfillment while looking at yourself in the mirror. They have a practical benefit. They allow you to lift the responsibilities that come with maturing in your understanding of the Christian life. When you make worship a priority, you discover you are not a solitary pilgrim on the path of faith. Rather, as you are surrounded by others confessing the same creeds, singing the same lyrics, and facing the same cross on the back of the platform, you are relieved to realize there is an entire congregation headed in the same direction you are. Chances are, you need to be reminded of that sense of community (and unity) at least once a week.

Finally, it's in worship that your doubting, anxious heart finds confidence and hope to face the uncertainties that await you during the week. It's as though faith (like a focused ray of sunshine through a magnifying glass) ignites into contagious trust and courage in light of what lies ahead. There's a moving scene near the end of that great Civil War epic movie *Glory*. The Union's first black regiment has enthusiastically volunteered to lead an assault on a Confederate fort. Given the circumstances, many of the regiment are highly likely to be killed. The night before the invasion, the soldiers gather around a fire worshiping Jesus. As they sing and pray aloud, their obvious fears give way to an inexplicable confidence that God is in control.

HOW WE WORSHIP

Our culture knows all about worship. Unfortunately, we rarely worship an object worthy of our devotion. We worship sports teams and sports personalities. We worship movie stars. We worship golden ladders whose rungs promise promotion and big paychecks. In fact, the god of a personal career is the deity before whom more people bow than their favorite football team. Gordon Dahl wrote, "Most middle-class Americans tend to worship their work, to work at their play, and play at their worship."[26] Work is good. So is play. Worship is essential. But how we embrace these three activities is critical.

For those who are committed to having Jesus live out His life in them, being intentional in worship is a must. It's a non-negotiable. Here's why: Your concept of God will be shaped by your worship of God. Private worship (on your own) is good and necessary; however, if you only worship on your own, your God will be limited to your understanding of Him. Chances are, that's not very big. In J. B. Phillips' book, *Your God Is Too Small*, he denounced our tendency to force God into a conceptual box of our own making. As one skeptic quipped, "In the beginning God created us in His image, and ever since we've attempted to return the favor."

When we join others for public worship the context of our contemplation about the Creator is multiplied exponentially. As with a crowded sporting event, the atmosphere is charged with expectation of how we will experience the Lord of the universe. But whereas the presence of others raises our experience of God to a new level, worship ultimately does not have to do with other people, or even the externals we often associate with worship. It really doesn't matter whether we hold a hymnal in our hands and sing lyrics written two hundred years ago or we sing songs that were composed two months ago. It doesn't matter if the church has a worship team holding microphones or a choir wearing robes. Meaningful public worship doesn't depend upon stained glass windows; worship can take place in a high school gymnasium. The reason is this: Worship has everything to do with spending time in the presence of the Lord acknowledging His greatness and expressing gratitude. While the setting can facilitate worship, God is the focus.

POINTERS FOR PUBLIC WORSHIP

Imagine you were preparing for a major presentation next week. You and your coworkers are to present to your CEO a 360° status review of the company and your role within it. Let's consider the preparation you would undergo to prepare – everything from what suit you would wear to making sure you arrived a few minutes early – you would take every advantage to maximize this experience with your boss.

The avid worshiper of God is no different. He takes advantage of every opportunity to worship with other believers. He has a checklist of things to keep in mind on the way to a worship service.

- *Positive attitude:* This isn't denial that hardships exist in your life. This means you come with an expectant attitude that something significant will happen. Obviously, this will involve spending time in private worship between Sundays so you will be in the habit of hearing from the Lord, with that frequency dialed in. Come with the intention of interacting mentally (James 1:23–25).
- *Come with the right gear:* If you were headed to a football game, you might take binoculars as well as purchase the program to read up

on the players and statistics. For the serious worshiper, this means bringing a Bible, a notebook, and a pen. You're not a passive bystander; you're an active participant.

- *Arrive rested:* To offer God the praise, imagination, and worth that He deserves demands that we are capable of creative thought and energetic participation. That isn't likely to happen if we have been out past midnight on Saturday. We also are apt to be out-of-tune or blurred in our focus if we have filled our minds with entertainment that undermines the kind of life we are attempting to live out. Filtering our thoughts during the week and going to bed at a decent hour the night before Sunday (or whatever day you worship) is critical to giving God our best and full attention.
- *Be prompt:* Those who lead worship at your church have taken great pains to plan a seamless experience in which one element builds on another. If you show up ten minutes late, you will have missed a foundational aspect to the service that will prevent you from experiencing the desired impact. In addition, tardiness distracts those you have to step over to find your seat. It's also discourteous to those who are speaking or leading when you barge in.
- *Be alert:* This means being intentional in your worship. Don't simply be reactionary. Be proactive. Meditate on the words you are singing and how true they are (or aren't) in your life. Read any programs or orders of service before the service begins so that you aren't distracted (or become a distraction) to others during the service.
- *Prioritize the pattern of weekly worship:* If you recognize the importance of public worship celebrations, factor them into your week. Make it habit-forming. You tend to value what you accommodate. Jesus put it this way, "Where your treasure is, there your heart will be also" (Matthew 6:21). The person who wrote the first-century epistle to persecuted Jewish Christians put it this way, "Let us not give up meeting together, as some are in the habit of doing, but let us encourage one another—and all the more as you see the Day approaching" (Hebrews 10:25).

Sören Kierkegaard, a Danish philosopher, suggested that in terms of a drama our view of worship often spotlights the preacher as the star performer and ourselves as the audience. He contended, however, that worshipers are the performers, with the pastor, choir, and other participants the prompters with God as the audience.

Finally, be a learner. Don't come to church as though you know it all, even if you've previously heard a sermon on a certain topic or scripture. A big reason for gathering with other believers is to place ourselves in a setting where we stretch our understanding. If the living Christ is present whenever His people are gathered in His name, we had better believe that Jesus can bring us to a place of understanding that is deeper than we've known before.

PUTTING IT ALL TOGETHER

If anyone knew how to commune with God, it was the composers of biblical psalms. These poems, originally set to music, bring prayer and worship together to show us how God's people should communicate with our Heavenly Father. One of the best examples can be found in Psalm 73, in which the composer, Asaph, laments a problem we still see today. He could barely contain his frustration at seeing evil people prosper while honest, decent people suffer injustice. In fact, his disillusionment became so overwhelming, he began to doubt the goodness of God. He admitted, "My feet had almost slipped; I had nearly lost my foothold. For I envied the arrogant when I saw the prosperity of the wicked" (Psalm 73:2–3).

That's the kind of honesty God longs to hear in our prayers!

Fortunately, the psalmist found the solution to his spiritual crisis. After struggling with his frustration and doubt to the point of exhaustion, he writes, "When I tried to understand all this, it was oppressive to me till I entered the sanctuary of God; then I understood their final destiny" (vv. 16–17). Worship became the remedy for his disillusioned, doubting heart. In the process of worship, he took his eyes off temporal circumstances to gaze into the eternal greatness of God. In giving worth-ship to God, he received healing and hope. In the end, prayer—honest communication with God—and worship—recognition of God's sovereignty and goodness—became the means of greater intimacy between the Creator and His beloved creature.

In the end, prayer and worship became the means of greater intimacy between the Creator and His beloved creature.

TAKE ACTION

Read Psalm 73 in its entirety, taking time to identify with the composer's emotions.
When you pray, how honest do you get with God? How do you think God would respond if you became completely transparent and spoke your mind?

Just like many Old Testament characters set up "places of remembrance" to honor what the Lord had done for them, so we should remember what the Lord has done for us. Many do this through a prayer notebook—keeping track of who they pray for, the needs they submit to the Lord, and the way He answers them.

Do you keep a prayer notebook or journal to record God's answers to your requests? See "How to Set Up a Prayer Notebook" at the end of this book for help.

God is a person, not an impersonal power. How well do you know this almighty Person? How often do you worship God, either by yourself or with others?

What will you do, beginning this week, to use prayer and worship to become more familiar with God as a friend, Father, and mentor?

Be intentional: What are you going to do about what you've learned?

Be specific: What action will you take in the near future to begin applying what you've learned? When will you do it?

Be accountable: Pray it through. Share your plan with a friend and seek his/her prayer and counsel for your next step.

CHAPTER 7: WHY DO I NEED TO GIVE?

Scan here to watch the video!

Giving is never about money, time, or possessions; it's always a matter of the heart. As we have received grace for our sins, we also forgive those who have offended us. As the Lord freely provides for our needs, we respond in generosity to help others. As God has freely given us talents and abilities, we use His gifts in service to one another to further and to build His kingdom. Like all good works, giving is supposed to be a product of faith and an act of worship. Generosity is at least one measure of spiritual maturity (Matthew 6:21).

"He is no fool who gives what he cannot keep to gain what he cannot lose."
—Jim Elliot

Charles Swindoll tells the story of a man named Davis. During his ninety-two years of life near Lincoln, Nebraska, this reclusive farmer amassed a considerable fortune. He worked his way up from a hired hand to a successful rancher. In the process, however, he alienated himself from neighbors and extended family. Davis became so embittered when his wife's family suggested she had married beneath her, he vowed he would never leave them or their other children any of his estate.

When his wife died, the old man spent an incredible amount of money on monuments in her memory. He hired a sculptor to create a stone loveseat on which were perched the likeness of both his wife and himself. Then he commissioned another monument of himself kneeling at the grave of his wife, laying a wreath. After that he commissioned a statue of his wife with angelic wings depositing a wreath at his future grave. As more and more ideas came to his mind, he commissioned more and more works of art until he at last had spent more than a quarter of a million dollars on monuments to his wife and himself.

For where your treasure is, there your heart will be also.
Matthew 6:21

When civic leaders approached him for a major contribution for a hospital, park, or community project, however, Mr. Davis slammed the door in their faces, complaining that the community had never done anything for him. He continued to live detached and depressed, grieving his deceased wife. By the time his miserly heart quit beating, he had exhausted his fortune. He died penniless and alone in the poorhouse. According to a published report, only one person even bothered to attend his funeral: the tombstone salesman.

Sadly, he ended up a bitter man who never learned the joy of sharing with others, having lost scope on an eternal key to legacy investing (Matthew 16:26). In fact, those cherished monuments on which he wasted his money fell into disrepair and gradually sank into the black Nebraska soil. Mr. Davis failed to realize that the secret to an abundant life is giving generously from what you have received.

A SIGN OF LIFE

Christian tourists in Israel often note the stark contrast between the Sea of

Galilee and the Dead Sea. The Sea of Galilee is fed by fresh water from the melting snows of Mount Hermon and deep underground springs. The deep blue lake is only thirteen miles long and seven miles across, but it teems with fish. As was the case in Jesus' day, fishing boats continue to harvest a bounty that helps to fuel Israel's economy.

At the southern end of the Sea of Galilee, the famous Jordan River flows freely as it winds its way southward, separating Israel from its neighbors to the east. Eventually the Jordan empties into the Dead Sea—more than 1,300 feet below sea level. It doesn't take a Rhodes scholar to understand how this sea got its name. The sea is truly "dead" because the concentration of salt and minerals—six times that of the ocean—destroys all life. While the Sea of Galilee receives fresh water and gives off fresh water, the Dead Sea receives fresh water but passes nothing on. The Sea of Galilee sustains life; the Dead Sea remains toxic to living organisms. Curious, don't you think? It's a great metaphor for life. People who have learned how to pass on their God-given resources to others are fresh and vital. Those who don't turn stagnant and "dead."

You may have experienced the principle of "receiving and giving" firsthand in the context of a local church. Those who attend on a regular basis soak in what the pastor dishes out Sunday after Sunday. Bibles get marked up, and notebooks fill up. If you are blessed to have a gifted communicator of God's truth, each sermon is an anticipated feast. You eat it up and long for more. But you may be oblivious to the weekly notices in the bulletin crying out for the need for volunteers in the nursery, teachers in Sunday School, or attendants in the parking lot. After all, you go to church to get your tank filled, right? Continually on the receiving end, we can grow indifferent toward the needs of others. In time this apathy joins with a critical spirit toward others. What seemed to satisfy our appetite no longer does. A sweet spirit that once flowed through us like the Jordan River becomes bitter and disgusting like the Dead Sea.

This syndrome can happen with our finances as well. When we soak up the teachings of the local church without sharing in the ministry, we are apt to become sour and mildew-filled sponges that no one enjoys being around. The blessings that should flow through us to others become like stagnant water.

JOYFUL LIFE OF A FAITHFUL STEWARD

Pastors are often criticized for preaching about money. Some might, indeed, place too much emphasis on the topic, but Jesus talked about money more than He did about heaven or hell. Much of the Lord's teaching dealt with stewardship: one sixth of the Gospels and one third of the parables deal with what people do with their money—and what that says about them and their priorities. As James Moffat stated, "A man's treatment of money is the most decisive test of his character—how he makes it and how he spends it."

What good will it be for a man if he gains the whole world, yet forfeits his soul? Or what can a man give in exchange for his soul?
Matthew 16:26

Each man should give what he has decided in his heart to give, not reluctantly or under compulsion, for God loves a cheerful giver.
2 Corinthians 9:7

God desires that we give of our wealth. In the Old Testament, Abraham gave one tenth of a windfall as an offering of thanksgiving (Genesis 14:20). God commanded His people to dedicate ten percent of their income and return it to Him (Leviticus 27:30; Numbers 18:21–32; Deuteronomy 14:22). This contribution was called a tithe (which means a tenth). God's insistence that His people contribute a portion of what they produced was God's creative way to remind the Hebrews that they were tenants on His earth and they could not live independent of their Creator. In his book, *The Blessed Life*, Pastor Robert Morris explains, "God gives us stewardship responsibility over our lives. We demonstrate faithful stewardship–we show God that we realize we are stewards, not owners–when we give Him the tithe."[27] Giving a tenth of their livestock and produce helped the people learn to revere God's holiness and recognize His ability to provide for them (Deuteronomy 24:22-23).

God not only desires to provide for His people, He wants to bless us with an overflow! But He knows that "The tithe represents the ultimate 'heart test' for the believer."[28] To walk in this blessing, our hearts must release the grip our possessions and wealth have on them. God offers us a chance to test Him and His goodness through the tithe. Did you know this is the *only time* in the Bible that God says it's ok to test Him? He says, "'Bring the whole tithe into the storehouse, that there may be food in my house. Test me in this,' says the Lord Almighty, 'and see if I will not throw open the floodgates of heaven and pour out so much blessing that you will not have room enough for it'" (Malachi 3:10). If you haven't begun giving to the Lord, I would urge you to take God at His Word and test him! But don't stop there. "The tithe is God's historical method to get us on the path of giving," says Randy Alcorn in his book, *The Treasure Principle*.[29] "In that sense, it can serve as a gateway to the joy of grace giving. It's unhealthy to view tithing as a place to stop, but it can still be a good place to start."[30]

For God's people today, "tithing is life, not law."[31] The principle of the tithe is not an obligation. "Jesus validated the mandatory tithe, even on the small things (Matthew 23:23). But there's no mention of tithing after the Gospels. It's neither commanded nor rescinded... [but] every New Testament example of giving goes far beyond the tithe. However, none falls short of it."[32] The New Testament actually raises the stakes, teaching that all of our possessions and wealth belong to God, not just ten percent! Randy Alcorn continues, "There's a timeless truth behind the concept of giving God our first fruits. Whether or not the tithe is still the minimal measure of those firstfruits, I ask myself, *Does God expect His New Covenant* children to give less or more? Jesus raised the spiritual bar; He never lowered it (Matthew 5:27-28)."[33]

In truth, we are merely stewards of what God has entrusted to us. It is all at His disposal and we must hold loosely that which we claim as hard-earned income. When we admit that what we possess doesn't really belong to us, we can let it go a little more easily and then function as a manager, or steward, of God's property and begin to walk in the joy of giving.

Honor the Lord with your wealth, with the firstfruits of all your crops.
Proverbs 3:9

The earth is the Lord's, and everything in it, the world, and all who live in it.
Psalm 24:1

The Savior knows greed shrivels a person's heart and soul. Looking for more and more ways to get more and more money prevents a person from seeing the truth of life. (Think about it. Have you ever met someone who admitted they were too wealthy?) A preoccupation with income has a predictable outcome. It blinds you from seeing God's best for your life. But when you freely give generously to God, you exercise faith, acknowledging Him as your ultimate provider. This act of worship releases greed's grip on you, realigning your heart with God's, allowing you to trust Him to care for your basic needs. That's what Jesus meant when He said, "Do not worry, saying, 'What shall we eat?' or 'What shall we drink?' or 'What shall we wear?' For the pagans run after all these things, and your heavenly Father knows that you need them. But seek first his kingdom and his righteousness, and all these things will be given to you as well" (Matthew 6:31–33).

A GOOD INVESTMENT

Jesus also understood that sharing one's shekels liberates the heart from the prison of self-interest. The freedom that comes with being a conduit of blessings (whereby what God allows to flow into our lives is passed along to others) is only superseded by increased blessings. In other words, any attempts at generosity will be rewarded in kind. Jesus said, "Give, and it will be given to you. A good measure, pressed down, shaken together and running over, will be poured into your lap. For with the measure you use, it will be measured to you" (Luke 6:38). Would you call that incentive giving? You might just call it the way God wired His world.

If you grew up in a farming community, you know the truth of that principle. If you plant corn, you don't harvest pumpkins. You harvest what you sow. When you prepare the soil and then plant wheat, you harvest wheat, not soybeans. A person doesn't have to grow up on a farm to understand the Law of the Harvest. The Bible puts it this way: "Do not be deceived: God cannot be mocked. A man reaps what he sows" (Galatians 6:7).

In terms of the Sea of Galilee, it's "fresh water in—fresh water out." In terms of friendship, it's "A man who has friends must himself be friendly" (Proverbs 18:24 NKJV). In terms of prayer, when you spend time talking to God, you are more capable of discerning God's will. With money, the Law of the Harvest means that a believer will always gain a return on what he or she gives away. Give to a person in need and you will not likely go needy yourself. A life marked by a habit of being generous will be richly rewarded, either in this life or the life to come. "Richly rewarded" could mean cash returns, but more often it refers to contentment and joy and with an amazingly clear perspective of just how abundant life really is. When you develop a pattern of giving you make an investment in tomorrow.

GIVING WHAT IS NOT OWNED

One golfer in the Seattle area refuses to play with new golf balls. For one

---

Jesus has a treasure mentality. He wants us to store up treasures. He's just telling us to stop storing them in the wrong place and start storing them in the right place! (Matthew 6:20)

—Randy Alcorn, *The Treasure Principle*

Give, and it will be given to you. A good measure, pressed down, shaken together and running over, will be poured into your lap. For with the measure you use, it will be measured to you. Luke 6:38

reason, his modest salary causes him to grimace at the rising cost of green fees let alone the additional dollars for extras. Gregg just can't bring himself to pay $10 for a sleeve of three balls. While his thrifty approach to the game originated in Scotland—strangely appropriate!—the cost of new golf balls is not the only reason he balks at doing what most golfers consider normal. For Gregg, if you pay full price you are more apt to psyche yourself out hitting over a water hazard. After all, you are aware of how much you spent on that silly ball and you sure hope it doesn't end up in the bottom of the lake because that would be a waste of money. This distraction could keep a thrifty golfer from feeling free to swing away. Time and time again, that expensive ball takes a swim. The same is true of losing a ball in the rough or out of bounds. If you've just plopped down good money, you feel obligated to look for the lost ball. Not only does such a search break the rhythm of your game, it frustrates the foursome behind you.

So what does Gregg do? Following a round of golf (or on another day off), he'll wander through the woods bordering the golf course in search of lost balls. With a stockpile of almost-new balls, this golfing cleric has discovered a new freedom in swinging away. Since he didn't buy the ball to begin with, he doesn't get upset when forced to part with it. When we view what we have as something we've inherited from someone else, the power of possession loses its grip on us. As a result, we loosen our grip on it.

When we view what we have as something we've inherited from someone else, the power of possession loses its grip on us.

But it's not just the promise of reward or our place as stewards that should motivate our generosity. Perspective should make a difference. That is, in light of how little life we have left to live, why not give away more than our stingy, selfish hearts want to? We need a realistic view of what really matters in life and in death. You can't take any of your earthly possessions with you when you go to the grave. As Oswald Chambers has said, "You can't take it with you, but you can send it on ahead!"

Don't be like old Mr. Davis, who spent a fortune on monuments and gravestones. Instead, determine today to be a generous person who gives freely of the good things God has enabled you to acquire. Invest in the Kingdom of God. After all, the issue of money and sacrifice is far more crucial than we think. Not because God desires our money. He owns the whole universe! Rather, He wants our complete devotion and our attitude toward material possessions is a barometer of our love for Him.

Jesus made this clear during His encounter with a rich young man.

> Now a man came up to Jesus and asked, "Teacher, what good thing must I do to get eternal life?"
>
> "Why do you ask me about what is good?" Jesus replied. "There is only One who is good. If you want to enter life, obey the commandments."
>
> "Which ones?" the man inquired.
>
> Jesus replied, " 'Do not murder, do not commit adultery,

do not steal, do not give false testimony, honor your father and mother,' and 'love your neighbor as yourself.'"

"All these I have kept," the young man said. "What do I still lack?"

Jesus answered, "If you want to be perfect, go, sell your possessions and give to the poor, and you will have treasure in heaven. Then come, follow me."

When the young man heard this, he went away sad, because he had great wealth.

Then Jesus said to his disciples, "I tell you the truth, it is hard for a rich man to enter the kingdom of heaven. Again I tell you, it is easier for a camel to go through the eye of a needle than for a rich man to enter the kingdom of God."

When the disciples heard this, they were greatly astonished and asked, "Who then can be saved?"

Jesus looked at them and said, "With man this is impossible, but with God all things are possible." (Matthew 19:16–26)

During this encounter, the wealthy man wanted to know about salvation. Jesus probed his intentions with a challenge. He said, in effect, "To be saved, all you have to do is become morally perfect!"

The man surprised everyone with his pride, stating he had perfectly observed all five of the ten commandments regarding his relationship with people. Of course, this was a lie, but Jesus let it pass to focus on what the man lacked: a sincere devotion to God. To prove His point, Jesus challenged the rich young ruler to donate all of his material wealth to the poor, promising he would "have treasure in heaven." Unfortunately, the exchange of wealth for a relationship with God proved too costly, revealing the man's true master. His money ruled his heart; not his God.

The Lord's comments concerning the difficulty of wealthy people entering heaven reveals an important truth concerning the relationship between salvation and money. One cannot gain heaven's riches by sacrificing earthly wealth; however, a genuine believer should not consider giving away material wealth a burdensome sacrifice anyway.

Note also that Jesus didn't say "give the money to God" as though the almighty Ruler of the universe needed spare cash. Jesus told the man to use the money for the benefit of others. Use money for the sake of ministry and you have, indeed, given it to God!

With the rich young ruler in mind, let's look at a modern day man who has found the joy of giving. "Ray Berryman, CEO for a national municipal services firm, says he and his wife give at least half of their income to God's work each year. 'My joy in giving comes from serving God in a way that I know He's called me to and realizing that what I give is impacting people for

Christ,' Ray says. 'It's exciting to know we're part of evangelizing, discipling, helping, and feeding the needy. It just feels wonderful and fulfilling.' The more we give, the more we delight in our giving-and the more God delights in us. Our giving pleases us. But more importantly, it pleases God."[34] There is a deep and profound joy that comes when we freely and cheerfully give back to God with the purpose of advancing His kingdom on earth!

GIVING GUIDELINES

While God wants us to keep a loose grip on our material wealth and to give it freely to those in need, He nevertheless wants us to steward our money with wisdom. Therefore, by way of suggestion, you might want to order your giving to Christian causes as follows:

1. Give first to your local church, and then to the ministries that have benefited you and your family (either through Biblical instruction, service, ministry to your children, etc).[35] Here is a way to evaluate the value of a good spiritual investment—look for places where they are attempting to make Christ known in a variety of ways, looking in the areas of (1) Scope of Outreach, (2) Growth of Missions, (3) Multiplication, (4) Urgency, and (5) Impact. That is investing in good soil!
2. Prayerfully ask God what missionaries to support with a regularly, monthly check. This would include those who serve overseas as well as local and national ministries or organizations.
3. Be responsive to causes in your community that benefit those who have physical needs or are otherwise disadvantaged.
4. Why not get into the habit of carrying a certain amount of cash in your pocket each day. Designate that as God's money. When you encounter someone in dire need or someone you feel impressed to give that money to, offer it as a gift from God (not from you).

TAKE ACTION

Read Matthew 19:16–26.
God doesn't call everyone to give up all material wealth for the sake of ministry and He doesn't have anything against material possessions. He cares most about the heart. Set aside some extra time to contemplate the answers to these questions. Answer honestly. This is just between you and God.

Of all your material wealth and possessions, what sacrifice would cause you the most anxiety? What does this suggest about your relationship with that tangible asset?

Frankly, everyone could stand to give away more, but do you think God considers you a generous person? Examine your discretionary spending (entertainment, dining out, hobbies, etc.) and compare that amount to your giving. How much of your net income goes to each?

What sacrifice can you make right now for the sake of helping others? Let this become an opportunity to allow God to stretch your faith and expand your vision. Share your plans with a trusted spiritual confidant and ask him or her to hold you accountable.

Be intentional: What are you going to do about what you've learned?

Be specific: What action will you take in the near future to begin applying what you've learned? When will you do it?

Be accountable: Pray it through. Share your plan with a friend and seek his/her prayer and counsel for your next step.

PRIORITY TWO

2

"LOVE YOUR NEIGHBOR AS YOURSELF."

MATTHEW 22:39

"You are only able to love your neighbor to the degree you are able to love yourself; you are only able to love yourself to the degree you understand God's love for you."

—Dr. John Tolson

A PERSONAL, PROGRESSIVE COMMITMENT TO YOURSELF

OVERVIEW

Let's face it; we live in a selfish, self-centered world. Many of our societal ills stem from the fact that people care too much about their own wellbeing and comfort. Conversely, we learn in church to regard others as more important. After all, doesn't Jesus present the ideal follower as one who lives out the teaching of the Beatitudes (Matthew 5:1–12)? Those who are part of His kingdom are blessed when they are poor in spirit, mourning, meek, merciful, peacemakers, and willing to suffer as one of His disciples. Sounds like the opposite of being committed to self, doesn't it? Are you surprised to learn God wants us to maintain a personal, progressive commitment to ourselves?

Priority Two is not about being self-centered or selfish. It is about seeing yourself as God sees you.

This priority is not about being self-centered or selfish. It is about seeing yourself as God sees you, near the apex of His creation. "What is man that you are mindful of him?" (Hebrews 2:6). "God created man in his own image, in the image of God he created him; male and female he created them" (Genesis 1:27). David was overwhelmed when he realized how special he was in the eyes of God (Psalm 139) and though he knew how easy it was to be offensive in His sight, it never changed the fact that God loved him and adored him as one of His children.

It takes a long time to really believe what David proclaimed. Our lives are a composition of both happiness and sorrow, accomplishments and defeat, obedience and horrid behavior. It also takes an understanding of how to grow spiritually, physically, mentally, emotionally, and socially. All of us, at some point in our lives, have been (or will be) profoundly impacted by another human being who pulled us out of a pit or shined a light in the darkness. Those who pulled others up were able to do so because they had something to offer. They had a reservoir of strength, assets they could draw on. At some point in their lives, they made a personal commitment to grow and in so doing, learned how life works with the abilities God gave us.

We are complex people with bodies, minds, emotions, and the need for social interaction. We aren't all full of strength in each of these areas by accident. In fact, many Christians find that their love for Christ hasn't made them a positive person or one who never battles depression or who has the ability to automatically forgive someone who has hurt them deeply. That only happens when we transform our thinking into a new way of being, through God's Word and the power of the Holy Spirit. We must intentionally and regularly add deposits of knowledge (God's Word) and experience (surrendering to the Holy Spirit) which will create in us a desire to serve and minister to others out of the joy of our own transformation.

That's what **Priority Two** is about. We never fully arrive, but that's why we say it is a personal, progressive commitment. Join us on this journey to personal growth and watch what happens.

> **HOW DOES GOD SEE YOU?**
>
> - You are His creation. God made you. (Genesis 1:27)
> - You are His child. God loves you. (Romans 8:17; Galatians 3:29; Titus 3:7; John 3:16)
> - You are worthy of being saved. Christ died for you. (Ephesians 1:4; Romans 5, 6)
> - You are blessed. God has gifted you (Ephesians 1:3; 1 Corinthians 12)
> - You have purpose. God has a plan for your life. (Jeremiah 29:11-13)

CHAPTER 8: PHYSICAL ASSETS – CARING FOR THE TEMPLE

Scan here to watch the video!

How long do you want to be productive? Be truthful, now. Many people think they want to be active and engaged in meaningful work into their eighties, which sounds good, but few realize what it takes to reach such a goal. Fewer still are willing to pay the price. Some anticipate what it will take to survive financially in their later years, and they prepare by saving and investing wisely over decades, but then pay little or no attention to the effects of time on their bodies. If we don't take adequate care of our bodies, all that hard-earned money will go to doctors, hospitals, pharmacies, and finally the undertaker.

If we hope to enjoy health and productivity in our later years, we must begin preparing today. Pardon the cliché, but we aren't getting any younger. And today *really* is the first day of the rest of your life. So, let's give adequate attention to our bodies, what the apostle Paul called "a temple of the Holy Spirit" (1 Corinthians 6:19–20; cf. 3:16; 2 Corinthians 6:16). Perhaps it would be helpful to first understand the process of aging, how this process affects the body, and what we can do about it.

AN AGES-OLD PROBLEM

The body begins the aging process at about ten or eleven years of age, or just before puberty.[1] After age twenty-five, the body has a decreased ability to keep up with the deterioration process. Physical deterioration continues at a rate of one percent per year and then accelerates dramatically near the end of life. While the average lifespan increased with each generation in the twentieth century—from forty-eight years to more than seventy-five in the United States—the rate of aging has remained the same. Our ability to combat infectious disease, increase the quality of our environment, and improve the quality of food has helped tremendously, but we still cannot slow the rate at which our bodies deteriorate.

The most significant change occurs in what physicians call "lean body mass." This includes bone, muscle, and connective tissue. Lean mass can be viewed as what is left of the body after all water volume has been removed. Over the years, we experience lean body mass reduction, primarily in skeletal muscle loss. This loss in muscle mass accounts for age-associated decreases in the body's metabolic rate, muscle strength, and activity levels. The loss of lean body mass leads to lower caloric needs. In other words, we need less fuel to run the engine. Unfortunately, we don't necessarily reduce our caloric intake. If the body can't utilize the extra fuel, it has to go somewhere, so the body converts this extra energy into fat.

How can we stop the effects of aging on our bodies? The answer is that

"What lays a young man up may lay his senior out."

—Peter Medawar, Nobel Prize-winning immunologist

we cannot. Any text or video program that says otherwise is wrong. However, we can slow the effects of aging, increase our quality of life, and even add years to our lifespan. To learn how, we need only examine the origin of humanity as described in the book of Genesis.

In the beginning, when God placed Adam and Eve in the garden, He gave them the task of caring for the world. He gave them work to accomplish.

> God created man in his own image, in the image of God he created him; male and female he created them. God blessed them and said to them, "Be fruitful and increase in number; fill the earth and subdue it. Rule over the fish of the sea and the birds of the air and over every living creature that moves on the ground."
>
> The Lord God took the man and put him in the Garden of Eden to work it and take care of it (Genesis 1:27–28; 2:15).

Ironically, technology surrounds us with time-saving conveniences, yet we can't find time for the single most important factor in combating the effects of age: moderate physical activity.

The first humans didn't lie around the Garden of Eden nibbling on produce all day long; they devoted themselves to activity that required strength and endurance. Today, however, most occupations are sedentary in nature, so most people struggle to maintain even modest physical activity. Consequently, we neglect the very best long-term remedy to a short life.

Physical activity has a greater impact on health and longevity than any other factor. A number of studies have examined laboratory mice, comparing the lifespan of sedentary versus active specimens, and have demonstrated that running in a cage wheel increased longevity by fifteen to twenty percent.[2] One can speculate about the results of the same type of study involving humans. We can safely assume that humans would have similar results.

When physical therapists are asked if those suffering from arthritis can safely participate in an exercise program, they quickly answer that regular, moderate-level exercise brings little risk of damage to joints. In fact, safe, low-impact physical activity actually protects against the development of chronic disease and disability, including arthritis. We are clearly blessed, therefore, with the ability to improve our physical status at any age and set the stage for an improved aging experience.

A veteran tennis coach, Jack Sanford, once stated, "There is no such thing as a self-motivated athlete." Every athlete has a source of inspiration or goal ahead of him that keeps him moving forward, pushing through the barriers that would halt his progress. The same truth applies to the everyday man as well. What is your motivation to engage in regular physical exercise? This might explain why there is such a lack of activity around us. The question then is, what better motivator can we have than our Lord, and how would He want us to take care of ourselves?

THE "REST" OF THE STORY

We also find in Genesis that God built R & R into His plan for creation.

> By the seventh day God had finished the work he had been doing; so on the seventh day he rested from all his work. And God blessed the seventh day and made it holy, because on it he rested from all the work of creating that he had done (Genesis 2:1–3).

Originally, God set aside the seventh day to commemorate His creation of the world and to celebrate His provision. In six days, He created the universe, crafted earth, gave it order and purpose, and then filled it with everything humanity needs to thrive. On the seventh day, He ceased all activity. The Hebrew name for this day, "Sabbath," derives from the verb "to cease." God paused to declare His work complete and good. The Sabbath day honors God for giving us everything we need.

When God brought the nation of Israel into the land promised to Abraham (Genesis 12:1–3), He commanded the Hebrew people to "cease" all work on the seventh day. This commandment (Exodus 20:8) commemorated the covenant He had established with Abraham and his descendants and reminded His people that God is their provider. He intended this day of rest to be a day for feasting and singing, a time in which families delighted in their God and bonded with one another. Their break from the grind of daily duties gave the people of God an occasion to celebrate His provision and protection.

Do you not know that your body is a temple of the Holy Spirit, who is in you, whom you have received from God? You are not your own; you were bought at a price. Therefore honor God with your body.
1 Corinthians 6:19-20

Unfortunately, we have a remarkable ability to twist God's design tragically out of shape. Somehow, we have managed to turn workaholism into a spiritual virtue and neglect God's provision of rest as though it were a burden! A missionary once boasted, "I'd rather burn out than rust out." But are those our only options? People who embrace this all-or-nothing approach to life usually attach their spiritual significance to their self-importance, taking pride in whizzing through life without taking a breath. On the other hand, those who "rust out" are no less self-important. They simply express their pride through laziness. They may live a long time, but so what? "Burn-out" people don't live long enough to accomplish all that they could and "rust-out" people lead meaningless lives.

The biblical perspective offers a healthy balance. God gave humanity work to keep us active, but He knows we need breathing room somewhere between vitality and exhaustion. He ordained one day in seven to be a "day of rest." Jewish rabbis refer to this as a day to let our souls catch up with our bodies. During His earthly ministry, Jesus affirmed this time of rest, saying, "The Sabbath was made for man, not man for the Sabbath" (Mark 2:27). Moreover, He maintained a balanced perspective of ministry and personal rejuvenation. Even though He was in constant demand, we never read, "Jesus *ran* over to Samaria," or "Jesus *rushed* to Bethany." He had a mission, and He knew where He was going, but He also set aside time to get away (Matthew 14:13, 23; Luke 22:39). Like any human, Jesus could become physically, emotionally, and spiritually drained. He took care of Himself so He could minister effectively to others.

DIET

While we exercise too little and rest too seldom, we eat too much. Strangely, Americans maintain a dual obsession with both food and weight control. The cable television lineup includes an entire network devoted to 24-7 programming on food. Nothing else. Just food. One program after another shows master chefs creating mouth-watering dishes so enticing you can almost smell the aroma coming through your screen. Those who have succumbed to these culinary temptations soon find themselves researching the latest diet fads. South Beach, Mediterranean, Atkins, Paleo, HCG . . . the list is truly endless, and each year adds another dozen diet fad failures. Add to those the more sensible programs—Weight-Watchers, Jenny Craig, Nutrisystem, Body for Life—and the issue becomes even more confusing. Everyone claims to hold the "secret" to weight control and fitness.

In truth, there is no "secret." Fads aside, legitimate programs simply market what should be obvious. People who eat a balanced diet of healthful food in reasonable portions avoid excessive weight gain. As Dr. Bina Patel says, "It's simple. If it doesn't go in, it doesn't stay on." Bottom line, weight management is a lifestyle, not a "quick fix." Our long term relationship with food can be measured in inches and pounds.

Age does not help. During adolescence, just thinking of doing a sit-up could melt away the unwelcome "handles." As an adult, losing flab takes three weeks with caloric restriction, careful food selection, and increased exercise. At the pivotal age of forty, it takes four weeks. The reason goes back to the issue of "lean body tissue," specifically muscle mass. Until approximately age twenty-five, our bodies automatically develop new muscle tissue as part of the growing process. Sadly, the process reverses around age twenty-five, after which we lose 1 percent of muscle mass each year. If a person weighs 150 pounds at age twenty-five, does little or no exercise for twenty years while maintaining the same weight, aging will convert thirty pounds of muscle into thirty pounds of fat. This proves that fitness involves more than weight. Just because you wear smaller sized clothes doesn't mean you're fit.

We can, however, do something about the loss of muscle. If we eat sufficient protein and regularly work our muscles, we can actually add muscle. This not only helps us look good in a swimsuit, and feel better in general, adding muscle mass helps with metabolism and weight control. Put simply, muscles burn fat. If you add muscle through good nutrition and regular exercise, your body will consume fat rather than store it around your waist and on your rear end. People with more muscle mass have an easier time keeping excess weight off. With a higher metabolism, they can enjoy more food with less risk of obesity.

A PERSONAL PLAN

Everyone is unique. Not every dietary lifestyle fits everyone. Some need more protein than others. Others fair better with high carbohydrate meals. In his book, *The Healthy Kitchen*, Dr. Andrew Weil does a nice job summarizing the present state of knowledge:

> You can lose weight on any kind of a diet; the trick is to keep it off by finding a healthful way of eating you can live with and a regimen of physical activity you can stick to. For initiating weight loss, more people find a low-carbohydrate regimen easier and more satisfying than a low-fat one, and medical research strongly supports the idea that many people are carbohydrate-sensitive as a result of their genetic makeup. Carbohydrate-sensitive individuals are particularly susceptible to weight gain if they eat refined carbs—that includes products made with flour or sugar, for example. But that does not mean they should follow the Atkins diet, which is overloaded with meat and deficient in fruits and vegetables. I do not recommend it for more than short-term dieting—six weeks or less. As a long-term strategy, this way of eating puts too much of a workload on the kidneys and undermines body defenses against cancer and other chronic diseases that tend to show up later in life.[3]

Clearly, the key to eating is to give the body what it needs in reasonable quantities. It's a mistake to think we can quickly reverse weight gain *and keep off the fat* by eating a certain combination of foods. The fact is, ninety percent of long-term weight maintainers consume a diet with twenty to thirty percent of energy from fat, they restrict total caloric intake, and they participate in regular physical activity. Only nine percent of the National Weight Registry sample maintains weight loss by diet alone, and only one percent achieves weight maintenance by physical activity alone. In other words, there are no shortcuts to maintaining good physical fitness. Good health results from a combination of three long-term habits: balanced diet, portion control, and regular physical activity.

Increasing evidence suggests that obesity is not a simple problem of willpower or self-control, but frequently involves the complex interactions of psychology and physiology. Some individuals may become overweight or obese partly because they have a genetic or biologic predisposition to weight gain. They have to work harder to balance their diet and exercise more than others. A great number of people—more than anyone realizes—maintain an unhealthy emotional relationship with food. Similar to people drinking too

Good health results from a combination of three long-term habits: balanced diet, portion control, and regular physical activity.

much or using drugs to alter their emotional state, many turn to food.

In most cases, however, the increasing prevalence of obesity reflects changes in society and behaviors over the past twenty to thiry years. In the early 1970s the average daily caloric intake by adults was 1,996. That figure increased to 2,234 by 2005 and continues to be on the rise.[4] We have become a society of gluttons who need to wake up to the dangers of obesity. Approximately two-thirds of adults and one-third of children in the United States are overweight or obese.[5] Obesity has become a chronic disease which causes serious medical complications, an impaired quality of life, and premature mortality.

An expert panel convened by the National Institutes of Health and the North American Society for the Study of Obesity has developed treatment guidelines for obesity:

Estimated annual cost of obesity-related illness in the USA = $190.2 billion

USA businesses experience annual losses of $4.3 billion because of obesity-related job absenteeism[6]

1. Begin with a physician's evaluation to identify which patients need obesity management and to determine what form of therapy is most appropriate for each individual.
2. Consider healthy meal replacements to enhance weight loss by helping control portion size and energy intake. Obese persons tend to underestimate their energy intake because they underestimate serving sizes or they fail to identify "hidden" calories from fat and sugar in the food.
3. Carefully consider a balanced meal plan. Many different dietary programs are available, but the patient should find the approach practical, sustainable, enjoyable, and healthful.
4. Exercise! The exercise chosen should be enjoyable, made a priority in the schedule, and most importantly, performed consistently over time.

Keys to success include creating an individualized approach based on each patient's specific health risks and habits, using various resources (for example, support groups, registered dieticians, and naturopathic doctors), and encouraging and empowering patients to become active participants in their weight-loss program.

CONCLUSIONS

Clearly, the satellite image shows obesity in the United States is at a crisis level. The U.S. Surgeon General declared we have an epidemic of childhood obesity and noted that one out of every eight deaths in America is caused by an illness directly related to being overweight and obese. Yet this crisis is completely preventable.[7] Where does all of this bring us?

As individuals, what is the clear answer? Can we predict the future of healthy eating to prepare our children? We can safely assume in five to ten years from now, we will know even better how to pursue weight management

> **OBESITY CAN CAUSE OTHER PROBLEMS SUCH AS:**
>
> Cardiovascular disease
> High blood pressure
> Sleep apnea
> Depression
>
> Type 2 diabetes
>   **37%** of adults are pre-diabetic
>   **3%** of adults who have type 2 diabetes are undiagnosed
>   **8%** of adults have type 2 diabetes[8]

in a healthy manner. We can probably predict that caloric restriction will remain a fundamental cornerstone to optimizing the temples we know as our bodies. The next generation of dieticians will probably steer us away from processed foods and encourage a diet filled with vegetables and fruit for long-term healthy weight control. Fish will remain a good idea, likely followed by poultry, pork and beef. Other predictions? Exercise will largely retain a dose-dependent relationship to good health.

Regardless of what the future holds, remember the age-old maxim "everything in moderation." As a general observation, similar to addictions, a person with weight-control concerns needs to decide that he or she is serious about addressing the issue and then become committed to a lifestyle change. At that point, pursuit of the guidelines above has a significant chance for long-term success.

Only 19% of Americans get the recommended amount of physical activity[9]

What is your specific situation? Talk to your physician (for example, are you prone to diabetes or do you have a history of cardiovascular disease?). If standard measures are not getting you to your goal, consider a monitored, reputable weight loss clinic with medical oversight. This has to be a lifestyle change. Just reading about physical fitness will clearly not achieve it.

The old adage is true. "You only live life once. But if you live right, once is enough." Isn't it time to adopt this approach with our own bodies? Remember, good health results from a combination of three long-term habits: balanced diet, portion control, and regular physical activity. As the wise Solomon said in Ecclesiastes 9:10, "Whatever your hand finds to do, do it with all your might."

TAKE ACTION

Read Genesis 1:27–28 and 2:15, which describe the creation and commissioning of humanity.
In the beginning, God gave humanity certain responsibilities that required physical activity. After all, He designed the human body to improve with use. In this way, the first people experienced personal fulfillment as they lived in harmony with their design.

How do you give your body the physical activity it requires to remain healthy?

What physical activity do you most enjoy? When can you take part in this activity next?

Read Genesis 2:1–3, which describes the origin of the Sabbath rest.
God also designed the human body for rest. One day out of seven was the right amount according to our Creator. How much time do you set aside for R & R each week?

For much of human history, "work" necessarily required physical activity. For sedentary occupations today, "rest" might include some form of activity, such as hiking, golf, or team sports. What helps you feel rejuvenated after working at your vocation?

Traditionally, the Sabbath included time with family and loved ones. In what ways do you regularly spend quality relationship time with important people in your life?

If you will be completely honest with yourself, how would you rate your current diet and weight? Have you seen your general physician within the last 12 months? If you haven't recently completed a thorough medical review, make it a goal this week to schedule an appointment to review your physical well-being.

Be intentional: What are you going to do about what you've learned?

Be specific: What action will you take in the near future to begin applying what you've learned? When will you do it?

Be accountable: Pray it through. Share your plan with a friend and seek his/her prayer and counsel for your next step.

CHAPTER 9: PHYSICAL ASSETS – SEXUAL CONTROL

Scan here to watch the video!

Dave's vulnerability to an extra-marital affair was obvious to those who knew him. As the head of his corporate empire, he had reached the pinnacle of success by his mid-thirties. His employees admired his leadership savvy, which gave his company unprecedented dominance over its competition. All the same, they were jealous of his youthful appearance and athletic physique, which drew stares from beautiful women wherever he went.

His senior management team knew something wasn't quite right when Dave announced he'd be spending time alone at his lake cottage instead of accompanying the newest recruits on their field trip of Wall Street. "What's up with Dave?" they asked. "He never misses the opportunity to lead the troops to the frontlines of corporate warfare. He must be battling burnout."

His team was right. Twenty years of climbing the ladder of success had taken their toll. Dave sent his wife and kids home while he stayed at their vacation place. He told them he just needed time alone. In spite of the fact that he had achieved success in every imaginable definition of the word, Dave didn't feel satisfied. His wife's aging body no longer provided him the sexual turn-on he once enjoyed. To make matters worse, she complained of a headache more often than she used to when he wanted to be physically intimate. She blamed feeling tired for her lack of desire.

With the family gone, Dave surfed the cable channels on the cottage plasma TV. He sipped a glass of wine after landing on an adult channel with minimal dialog and maximum skin. Feeling aroused and guilty, the half-drunk, burned-out executive decided to take a walk along the lake. Within a hundred yards he saw his neighbor's wife, Beth, in their beachfront Jacuzzi. He called out a greeting; she smiled and gestured for him to join her.

As enjoyable as a midnight walk along the beach would have been on this balmy autumn night, sitting in a hot tub with a beautiful woman seemed an even more attractive option. When Beth offered him a glass of wine, he didn't indicate he'd had too much already. "My husband is back in the city, hard at work," she explained.

Dave knew Beth's husband well. Uri had been a top executive in his firm since the beginning. The two families had owned vacation homes next to each other for years. Although Dave and his wife and Beth and her husband had shared many a festive evening in one another's spas, this was the first time Dave and Beth had been alone. Before too long too much booze and too little clothing led to adultery. Dave's adult channel fantasy became an ugly reality when he took Beth into his bedroom.

While this story could have played out recently, it's actually quite old. "Dave" is King David of Israel. "Beth" is none other than Bathsheba, the wife of David's close friend, Uriah, the Hittite warrior. You can read the actual account in 2 Samuel 11:1–5. Sadly, this ancient story has been repeated in countless lives over the last 2,500 years. In fact, it continues today among Christians and nonbelievers alike. God gave humanity the beautiful and precious gift of sexual intimacy, yet we abuse it and pervert it like no other blessing.

THE BEAST WITHIN

In the words of author Frederick Buechner: "Lust is the ape that gibbers in our loins. Tame him as we will day-by-day, he rages all the wilder in our dreams by night. Just when we think we're safe from him, he raises up his ugly head and smirks, and there's no river in the world flows cold and strong enough to strike him down. Almighty God, why dost thou deck men out with such a loathsome toy?"[10]

Men aren't the only ones who struggle with the issue of sexual control. Consider the experience of Darla (not her real name). Her dad left her mother and abandoned her before she finished preschool. After the divorce, Darla longed for her daddy's affection, but he rarely picked her up on weekends when he was entitled to visitations. Darla projected her need for affection on her stepfather, but he never fully accepted her and didn't go out of his way to lavish love or attention on her.

As Darla entered adolescence, the reflection she saw in the mirror began to surprise her. Her flat chest transformed almost overnight into a full figure like her mother's. The boys at school began to notice as well. Soon Darla recognized that when she wore tight-fitting sweaters she received a lot of attention. Starved for affection, Darla soon played into the hands of boys who seemed sincere in their expressions of love. She found the attention and affection she craved in the back seats of Firebirds and Hondas. Or so she thought. In reality, she began a futile pursuit of true love in a life of sexual promiscuity along a rural road outside of town. She knew what to wear (or not wear) to gain what she most desired: the affection of a man.

Although Darla became a Christian through a campus ministry in college, she would be the first to say that her appetite for sex was stronger than most women. She would readily acknowledge that casual sex did not provide the security of commitment and unconditional love that she had been denied as a child, but she couldn't deny the pleasurable satisfaction to which she had become accustomed. Darla's "easy" reputation won her many dates, but her attempts to win the battle with promiscuity didn't succeed until she got married.

After ten years of marriage and three kids, Darla has maintained a physical appearance that turns heads. When men take a second look at her in the grocery store or at the gym, she feels a certain sense of excitement. Bedroom scenes on television easily trigger her imagination and, on more than one occasion, she has found herself fantasizing about romantic getaways with men she has seen across the sanctuary at church. Amazingly, Darla's dysfunctional

Men aren't the only ones who struggle with the issue of sexual control.

past and her overactive libido have not resulted in her having an affair. But if she fails to gain freedom from the stranglehold lust has on her thoughts, a moral tumble is only a matter of time.

David and Darla struggle with an issue that affects everyone. The Christian, however, bears additional responsibility. In the previous chapter, we learned that the body of the Christian is a temple of the Holy Spirit (1 Corinthians 6:19; cf. 3:16; 2 Corinthians 6:16) and that we have a responsibility to keep our temples in good repair. Paul's greater concern when writing to the Christians in Corinth, however, focused on their maintaining sexual purity. He said, in effect, "keep the sanctuary of your body pure." When a believer engages in sexual sin, he or she turns the dwelling place of God into a brothel.

When a believer engages in sexual sin, he or she turns the dwelling place of God into a brothel.

THE GIFT OF SEX

Lust may be "gibbering ape," but sex is a gift from God. The Creator Himself gave us this marvelous blessing of mutual pleasure, not only for the sake of reproduction, but as a wonderful secret to be shared between a man and a woman committed to one another for life. Sex invites us to explore and experience unconditional acceptance. The result of such delightful entanglement is becoming one in flesh and spirit without regret or fear or shame or dread.

Soon after God fashioned the first human, Adam, from the soil of the earth, He made an unprecedented declaration. Throughout the creative process, the Lord declared each stage "good." He created light and called it *good* (1:4). He separated dry land from the seas and "saw that it was *good*" (v. 10). He covered the earth with vegetation and "saw that it was *good*" (v. 12). He sprinkled the heavens with stars and planets and "saw that it was *good*" (v. 18). He filled the sea with creatures and the air with birds and "saw that it was *good*" (v. 21). He fashioned a marvelous array of animals and "saw that it was *good*" (v. 25). But of the solitary human, "God said, 'It is not *good* for the man to be alone'" (2:18).

> The Lord God said, "It is not good for the man to be alone. I will make a helper suitable for him."
>
> Now the Lord God had formed out of the ground all the beasts of the field and all the birds of the air. He brought them to the man to see what he would name them; and whatever the man called each living creature, that was its name. So the man gave names to all the livestock, the birds of the air and all the beasts of the field. But for Adam no suitable helper was found. So the Lord God caused the man to fall into a deep sleep; and while he was sleeping, he took one of the man's ribs and closed up the place with flesh. Then the Lord God made a woman from the rib he had taken out of the man, and he brought her to the man. The

man said,

> "This is now bone of my bones
> and flesh of my flesh;
> she shall be called 'woman,'
> for she was taken out of man."

For this reason a man will leave his father and mother and be united to his wife, and they will become one flesh. The man and his wife were both naked, and they felt no shame. (Genesis 2:18–25)

The longing for sexual pleasure and unrestrained intimacy is wired into the psyche of the human soul. The obvious reason that God factored the sex drive into our DNA was to propagate the human race. God's instructions to replenish and multiply were aided by the inner urge to let our hormones play. But the gift of sex was given for more than just procreation. God could have accomplished this through any conceivable means, but He made it an intensely pleasurable experience physically and emotionally. When shared by a man and woman unconditionally committed to one another for life, sex increases their sense of intimacy and intensifies their feeling of safety and acceptance.

God affirms the joy of sexual intimacy in the Song of Solomon, which celebrates the pleasure of sex.

> I have taken off my robe—must I put it on again? I have washed my feet—must I soil them again? My lover thrust his hand through the latch-opening; my heart began to pound for him. I arose to open for my lover, and my hands dripped with myrrh, my fingers with flowing myrrh, on the handles of the lock. (Song of Solomon 5:3–5)
>
> How beautiful you are and how pleasing, O love, with your delights! Your stature is like that of the palm, and your breasts like clusters of fruit. I said, "I will climb the palm tree; I will take hold of its fruit." May your breasts be like the clusters of the vine, the fragrance of your breath like apples, and your mouth like the best wine. May the wine go straight to my lover, flowing gently over lips and teeth. (Song of Solomon 7:6–9)

For this reason a man will leave his father and mother and be united to his wife, and they will become one flesh. The man and his wife were both naked, and they felt no shame.
Genesis 2:24–25

Solomon's amazingly candid exposé of the love of a husband and a wife is nothing short of steamy, R-rated, erotic poetry seductively veiled in figurative images. In the lines of this epic poem, Solomon celebrates sex as a shared spiritual experience, which reflects the act of marriage described in Genesis.

According to God, marriage occurs when a man and a woman leave their families of origin, unite to form a new family, and seal their commitment with sexual intercourse. Through this "one-flesh" union, the two spirits experience unity (Genesis 2:24).

After the fall of humanity, sin corrupted God's original design for sex. Consequently, sexual passion is a powerful force that pulsates within men and women regardless of their marital state. It doesn't just show up on the wedding night. It is a primal instinct that begs for attention and demands to be satisfied. Because sex is such a dominant desire, it has been known to nullify the logic center of the brain. As a result, responsible individuals have been branded as mindless fools after yielding to sexual temptation. Having gratified their selfish desires, men and women have lost jobs, reputations and marriages for the sake of a fleeting sexual high.

CAGING THE APE WHILE ENJOYING THE GIFT

Countless individuals have shipwrecked their potential on the reef of indiscretions. You could probably name a few. Some may have been people you once considered mentors. Perhaps you witnessed the pain they suffered themselves and the anguish they caused others by their selfish choices. The moral failure of these admirable people should be a warning that no one is immune from temptation and anyone can succumb. As Paul wrote to the Christians in Corinth, "If you think you are standing firm, be careful that you don't fall" (1 Corinthians 10:12).

To avoid your own moral fall, consider the following.

Be aware of your vulnerability. If you think you're incapable of sexual sin, think again. Take a personal inventory. Take note of what is going on in your life when you are most liable to sexual temptation. You know what tends to cause your sexual engine to increase its rpm—perhaps certain magazines or movies or the influence of certain people. Identify your personal escape route. Determine to put it down, turn it off, or leave the room.

Peter advised those immersed in a promiscuous culture to "abstain from sinful desires, which war against your soul" (1 Peter 2:11). Even though our culture may downplay the occasional one-night stand or excuse sexual indiscretions, you know what God thinks. If you are not married, ask God to give you the ability to remain sexually pure. If you have blown it, confess your sin and ask His forgiveness. Nonetheless, when it comes to temptation, you're not out of the woods. You need to be proactive. Paul's concern for his young unmarried friend Timothy is good advice. "Run from anything that stimulates youthful lust. Follow anything that makes you want to do right. Pursue faith and love and peace, and enjoy the companionship of those who call on the Lord with pure hearts" (2 Timothy 2:22 NLT).

If you are married, guard the marriage bed. If you and your spouse enjoy an active sex life, you can't assume you're impervious to sexual temptation. The enemy of our souls will never cease to entice us with bodies that are curvier,

---

Run from anything that stimulates youthful lust. Follow anything that makes you want to do right. Pursue faith and love and peace, and enjoy the companionship of those who call on the Lord with pure hearts.
2 Timothy 2:22 NLT

more muscular, or younger. But don't believe the lie. The Bible says, "Marriage should be honored by all, and the marriage bed kept pure, for God will judge the adulterer and all the sexually immoral" (Hebrews 13:4).

A wise Hebrew writer suggested a way that those who are married can maintain the integrity of their bedroom. It has to do with avoiding envy and practicing gratitude. Be content with what God has given you to enjoy. He wrote,

> Drink water from your own cistern, running water from your own well. Should your springs overflow in the streets, your streams of water in the public squares? Let them be yours alone, never to be shared with strangers. May your fountain be blessed, and may you rejoice in the wife of your youth. A loving doe, a graceful deer—may her breasts satisfy you always, may you ever be captivated by her love. Why be captivated, my son, by an adulteress? Why embrace the bosom of another man's wife? For a man's ways are in full view of the Lord, and he examines all his paths. (Proverbs 5:15–21)

Another way to derail the train of sexual temptation is to continue to court your mate. Express your love regularly. Take time for walks and hugs. Make time for sexual intercourse even when the "need" for sex is not as obvious as it once was.

Guard your thoughts. The power of suggestion can be mind-boggling—and mind controlling. We become what we think about. We do what we ponder. With that in mind, don't allow sexual fantasies to fill your thoughts. Obviously, you can't prevent lustful images or urges from gaining entrance into your brain. But you can limit the focus you give them. As Martin Luther stated, "You cannot prevent the birds from flying over your head. But let them only fly and so not let them build a nest in the hair of your head."[11]

When Paul wrote to the Christians in Philippi, he gave them a formula for living above reproach.

> Do not be anxious about anything, but in everything, by prayer and petition, with thanksgiving, present your requests to God. And the peace of God, which transcends all understanding, will guard your hearts and your minds in Christ Jesus.
>
> Finally, brothers, whatever is true, whatever is noble, whatever is right, whatever is pure, whatever is lovely, whatever is admirable—if anything is excellent or praiseworthy—think about such things. Whatever you have learned or received or heard from me, or seen in me—put

it into practice. And the God of peace will be with you.
(Philippians 4:6–9)

Establish accountability checkpoints. Don't underestimate the power of confession when it comes to keeping your nose (or other body parts) clean. Admitting your failure and your tendency to stumble is a strong deterrent to sinning. Ask one or two people to be part of an accountability small group with you. Meet regularly. Allow each person to express areas of temptation for which they would like to be held accountable. Chances are, if you have someone asking you on a periodic basis how you are doing with your struggle with lust, you will be less apt to give in to sexual promiscuity. Just knowing that someone (to whom you've confessed your struggle with lust) will ask you how you are doing should cause you to think twice.

If you are a businessperson who spends as many nights in a hotel room as you do in your bedroom at home, you know the availability of adult entertainment on in-room televisions. If you are tempted to watch such programming, ask someone from your church to pray for you to have strength. Invite this person to ask you upon your return if you avoided the trap. When Chuck Swindoll was pastor of First Evangelical Free Church of Fullerton, California, he had a list of questions he frequently asked his staff. While his questions probed issues beyond sexual temptation, his checklist certainly touched on that area.

1. Have you been with a woman (or man) anywhere this past week that might be seen as compromising?
2. Have any of your financial dealings lacked integrity?
3. Have you exposed yourself to any sexually explicit material?
4. Have you spent adequate time in Bible study and prayer?
5. Have you given priority time to your family?
6. Have you fulfilled the mandates of your calling?
7. Have you just lied to me?

TAKE ACTION

Read Genesis 2:18–25, which describes the first marriage relationship.
The first married couple "were both naked, and they felt no shame." What does this tell us about their emotional intimacy? What does this tell us about their physical intimacy?

What might cause "shame" in a marriage relationship today? How can a married couple remove shame as a barrier to their intimacy?

God has offered a specific remedy for the problem of sin and shame (1 John 1:8–9). Before you do anything else, address any source of shame with God and then, if you are married, with your spouse.

Read Proverbs 5:15-21, which encourages sexual integrity in marriage.
What steps are you taking to remain faithful to your spouse?

Be intentional: What are you going to do about what you've learned?

Be specific: What action will you take in the near future to begin applying what you've learned? When will you do it?

Be accountable: Pray it through. Share your plan with a friend and seek his/her prayer and counsel for your next step.

CHAPTER 10: MENTAL ASSETS – THE IMPORTANCE OF INFLUENCES

Scan here to watch the video!

The human mind is one of God's most amazing creations. Unfortunately, it is also one of the most neglected, abused, and underutilized assets given to humanity. Our creator gave us a unique mental capacity that, in part, reflects His image and gives us the exclusive ability to relate with Him. Unfortunately, the hectic lives of modern families and the access to unlimited amusement opportunities threaten to reduce all of us—Christians and non-Christians alike—to culturally perceptive yet spiritually clueless slaves to whomever has the jazziest jargon and the slickest presentation. We have become victims to pop-up internet ads, witty propaganda (whether political or commercial), and cunning entertainment, all guided by a secular mindset. Whether overtly marketed through media outlets or subtly permeating the kingdom of God by deceit, the effect on our spiritual development is not good.

Obviously, a single chapter will not solve the problem of secular infiltration, but we have to start somewhere. So let's kick-start a dialogue with two questions.

One of the best ways to keep a healthy mind is to meditate on Scripture. Deep thinking is essential for brain health, especially as we age.

QUESTION 1: WHAT ROLE DOES THE MIND PLAY IN OUR SPIRITUAL DEVELOPMENT?

Our mind forms ideas—good, inane, or unsound—and ideas can be powerful things. In 1849, Lord Palmerston addressed the British House of Commons, saying, "Opinions are stronger than armies. Opinions, if they are founded in truth and justice, will, in the end, prevail against the bayonets of infantry, against the fire of artillery."[12] Note his qualification, "if they are founded in truth and justice." We must use our minds to examine and sift ideas, measuring them against the Scriptures to determine whether or not they conform to

---

WHAT DOES IT MEAN TO HAVE A SECULAR MINDSET?

Secular, according to dictionary.com, is defined as "of or pertaining to worldly things or to things that are not regarded as religious, spiritual, or sacred; temporal."

To have a secular mindset then, is to perceive our world without regard to biblical principles – to make decisions, act on those decisions, and speak those thoughts which are contrary to the character of God.

God's way of thinking. The Bible challenges us, "'Come now, let us reason together,' says the Lord" (Isaiah 1:18). God knows that our minds develop and grow through the process of reasoning. According to educators, we are prompted to reason, examine problems, discover solutions, and then adjust behavior when challenged by a phenomenon called *cognitive dissonance.*

According to this theory, we live with a set of assumptions about life until something causes a serious disruption and shakes up our world, forcing us to think or reason differently. A horribly negative example of this occurred when terrorists attacked the United States on September 11, 2001. Until that day, most Americans felt confident that we were protected from foreign attack by two large oceans. By the end of the day, our sense of invincibility crumbled and fell into a heap of twisted metal and shattered glass. That was cognitive dissonance (knowledge disruption) for all Americans. 9-11 precipitated a dramatic reshaping of our minds.

From a positive standpoint, the apostle Paul was convinced that cognitive dissonance could occur voluntarily. He wrote a letter to the Romans explaining how each believer could progressively think more like Christ.

> Therefore, I urge you, brothers, in view of God's mercy, to offer your bodies as living sacrifices, holy and pleasing to God—this is your spiritual act of worship. Do not conform any longer to the pattern of this world, but be transformed by the renewing of your mind. Then you will be able to test and approve what God's will is—his good, pleasing and perfect will. (Romans 12:1–2)

Paul challenges us to examine the "pattern of this world," reject its flaws, and then seek a better way from God. Like all of the Bible writers, he begins with the assumption that sin has corrupted or darkened the thinking process, but that thinking God's thoughts can transcend every aberrant view. God invites us to "reason together" with Him as we read and obey His Word, which allows us to see truth more clearly and to think more rationally over time.

QUESTION 2: HOW DOES A TRANSFORMED MIND THINK DIFFERENTLY FROM "THIS WORLD?"

Harry Blamires, in his book *The Christian Mind*, highlights the following marks of the Christian mind or evidence that a person is thinking like Christ.

The first mark is to think supernaturally. This means having an eternal perspective. When a person who thinks supernaturally looks at nature, that person sees the complex yet beautiful design of a Creator. When this individual looks at the events of life, he or she sees the sovereign hand of providence. When looking at insurmountable problems like illness or financial setback, this person sees prayer as a life-changing resource. A supernatural perspective sees aging and death as the inevitable journey of mortal flesh but without succumbing to despair because of the promise of eternal life in Christ.

Those who think supernaturally also see the resources of talent or wealth as a means to help others or as an investment in eternal matters, such as the work of evangelism and the mission of the church. The supernatural mindset says, God "is able to do immeasurably more than all we ask or imagine, according to his power that is at work within us" (Ephesians 3:20). "This world," by contrast, clutches to things that will disappear. The supernatural mind clings to Christ and holds all other things lightly.

The second mark is to be aware of evil. Humans can be remarkably cruel to other humans, the animal world, or the environment. Lurking in the shadows of every seemingly upright person is the capacity to do very ugly things. Wars have a way of making this point. Where does the capacity to exterminate a whole ethnic group of people come from? Where does the selfish behavior in all of us arise? What is the source of the vanity and pride often displayed in the religious profession? Rather than learned behavior, these are constantly reverberating echoes of a fallen world and the prompting of Satan and all his schemes.

The third mark is to focus on truth. Every culture and generation has its own interpretation of values, prejudices for certain appetites, philosophical assumptions, and interpretation of reality. Thus, people can be lured by mass-preference and ideas without questioning whether those preferences and ideas are true. New York Times bestselling author Andy Andrews notes, "We occasionally read history or watch history presented on film. But in terms of why we do what we do, how we govern each other, what our society allows and why – very few of us intentionally connect the truth of the past with the realities of where we have ended up today."[13] Most people have become quite comfortable with today's societal values, premises, and assumptions without questioning their validity or considering their impact on future generations. "Mass-preference" societies allow for individual preferences as long as no one claims to have absolute truth.

Christianity, on the other hand, values acts and facts. These acts and facts are the foundation for our faith and they transcend all time, all cultures, and all personal preferences. Christianity is founded upon events that actually happened and follows a God who lived among us and revealed truth through His life. Truth is the way things are, not the way we want them to be. Truth stands the test of time and will always be supported, either directly or indirectly, by Scripture. Not all truth comes from Scripture, but all that Scripture teaches and validates is true.

The fourth mark is to accept authority. Any monarch has the option of becoming a benevolent ruler or a tyrant. The Christian mind asserts that God is benevolent; that is, He wants to be followed and worshiped voluntarily rather than forcibly. The Christian not only bows his knees before a sovereign Lord but also does so eagerly and willfully. Therefore, the believer doesn't take a pick-and-choose approach to obedience. The old cliché, "God said it, I

"Come now, let us reason together," says the Lord.
Isaiah 1:18

believe it, that settles it!" applies. That is not the statement of an idiot leaping blindly into the dark but of a grateful child acknowledging the authority and security of a loving parent.

This mark of the Christian mind can be difficult to accept at times. The Scriptures contain commandments that can seem impossible to follow. "Love your enemies" (Matthew 5:43). "Overcome evil with good" (Romans 12:21). "Give, and it will be given to you" (Luke 6:38). "Don't commit adultery" (Romans 13:9). "If someone wants to sue you and take your tunic, let him have your cloak as well" (Matthew 5:20). Yet the Christian with a Christian mindset will not question whether he or she must respond to every admonition of Scripture. Like the apostle Paul, this person will not always obey perfectly (Romans 7:14–20), but the intent is to obey out of our love and desire to honor our Creator.

The fifth mark is to have concern for the individual. Tension will always exist between goals, agendas, systems, and productivity and a concern for the human beings who make all those things happen. Our society has been extremely successful in creating crowded cities with roaring traffic, accompanied by modern technical innovations that speed up communications through the internet, mobile phones, and other forms of social media. At times, however, an eerie loneliness pervades this progress because we lack real connectedness with other humans. We participate in various cultural systems, and we're surrounded by people, yet we fail to form close, mutually dependent bonds.

In many respects, Christians and non-Christians behave similarly, both "conforming to this world" and its values. When Jesus ministered on earth, He gave little attention to organizational systems, preferring to deal with people. He cared about relationships, who they were as family members, their eternal values, how they worshiped God, and how they treated one another. Christians, like their non-believing peers, can be consumed with hierarchy and the political machinery of the church. They obsess over bureaucracy while ignoring the Beatitudes.[14] Consequently, the church begins to resemble a corporation with a steeple and a cross as its logo. They focus on bottom-line issues, such as attendance numbers and income, while people, with their joys and sorrows, their struggles and their victories, get lost in the quarterly financial report.

A person with a Christian mind-set—one who is "transformed by the renewing of his or her mind"—knows how to step back from the functions that consume him or her and how to think about others with the mind of Christ. When these people begin to lead the church, ministry becomes the focus. Rather than looking inward with a survival mentality, the church turns outward to change the world . . . one individual at a time.

POSITIVE AND NEGATIVE INFLUENCES

Clearly, we are to be "transformed by the renewing of our minds" as we expose ourselves to the truth of Scripture and submit ourselves to the leading

---

We do not dare to classify or compare ourselves with some who commend themselves. When they measure themselves by themselves and compare themselves with themselves, they are not wise.
2 Corinthians 10:12

of the Holy Spirit. That would be easier if we could remove ourselves from the daily influence of the world, but we can't, short of shaving our heads and joining monasteries. Somehow, we must learn to cope with daily interaction with non-Christians without "being conformed to this world." Fortunately, the Bible offers lots of wise counsel to help us with this challenge.

The Bible says more about emotional well-being than cleanliness, hygiene, or diet. Clearly, a person with a positive, kingdom-oriented outlook is better equipped to meet and overcome the challenges of life than someone who's enslaved to the world's mindset and living without hope. Even medical research agrees. For example, depressed heart attack patients are five times more likely to die than heart attack patients who cultivate and maintain a positive attitude.[15]

When Jesus ministered on earth, He gave little attention to organizational systems, preferring to deal with people.

- Emotions, not events, cause stress-related illnesses.
- Emotions affect our immune system and the ability to resist disease.
- Thoughts can cause physical problems like ulcers, indigestion, and high blood pressure.
- In some cases, depression is a better detector of heart problems than physical measurements.

Cognitive distortions are warped, self-defeating patterns of mental function. Like a fun-house mirror, they reflect a distorted image that is often assumed to be real but isn't. As a result, they lead to anger, fear, guilt, and other emotions that accelerate the negative image rather than help it. Here are the "Seven Cognitive Distortions" as summarized by Brenda Polk of Lifeway Christian Resources.

1. *All-or-Nothing Thinking:* If your performance falls short of perfect, you see yourself as a total failure.
2. *Overgeneralization:* You see a single negative event as a never-ending pattern of defeat. The extreme form of overgeneralization is called Labeling or Mislabeling. When a single event or error leads to a negative label of yourself: "I'm a loser."
3. *Jumping to Conclusions:* You form a negative interpretation even though there are no definite facts that convincingly support your conclusion.
4. *Magnification (catastrophizing) or Minimization:* You exaggerate the importance of things (such as a minor goof-up) or you inappropriately shrink things until they appear tiny (your own desirable qualities).
5. *Emotional Reasoning:* You assume that your negative emotions reflect the way things really are: "I feel it, therefore

it must be true."
6. *"Should" Statements:* You try to motivate yourself with "shoulds" and "should nots," as though you had to be punished before you could be expected to do anything. "Must" and "ought to" statements are common offenders. The emotional consequence is guilt. When we direct these statements toward others, the emotional consequence is anger, resentment, and frustration.
7. *Personalization:* You see yourself as the cause of some negative, external event for which you were not primarily responsible.

Clearly, the best and only response to negative thinking is to cultivate a habit of positive thinking. According to the Bible, positive thinking even affects our physical health.

> "A cheerful heart is good medicine, but a crushed spirit dries up the bones." (Proverbs 17:22)

> "A heart at peace gives life to the body, but envy rots the bones." (Proverbs 14:30)

> "Pleasant words are . . . sweet to the soul and healing to the bones." (Proverbs 16:24)

Boldness, confidence, diligence, zeal are all great approaches to life. They are also great for your health. If you want these characteristics to be in your life, start with five strategies offered by the Bible for a mental (extreme) makeover.[16]

Strategy One: Take every thought captive. "We demolish arguments and every high-minded thing that is raised up against the knowledge of God, taking every thought captive to obey Christ" (2 Corinthians 10:4–5 HCSB). To overcome the continuous pattern of negative thinking, listen to your thoughts and realize when they do not match up to the truth of God's Word. Write down the negative thoughts, and ask the Holy Spirit to show you His truth that counters it. Use the Bible Study Tools in the Appendix for help with searching God's Word. List the truth beside the negative thought. When that negative thought returns and attempts to drag you down, replace it with the Scripture or truth you have discovered. Pray it through. You might pray something like this, "Lord, I'm feeling like _____. But I know Your Word says that I'm _____ and that's the truth. Help me believe and walk out what I know to be true in You." Don't worry about trying to conquer every thought at once. Focus on the thoughts that are most pervasive to you right now, and when you have experienced freedom by replacing them with the truth (and walking it out in faith), then ask the Holy Spirit to reveal more negative thoughts that need truth spoken over them.

Strategy Two: Release condemning thoughts. "Therefore, no condemnation now exists for those in Christ Jesus" (Romans 8:1 HCSB). Thoughts that belittle are destructive and compound the negative conclusions we draw. Mistakes and errors are common in life; remember, only Jesus was perfect. Ask for forgiveness when necessary from God, others, and yourself and move on without continuing to belittle or berate yourself.

Strategy Three: Realize you are powerless to change on your own, but you can change through Christ's power working in you. "I am able to do all things through Him who strengthens me" (Philippians 4:13 HCSB). Ask for God's help in making these mental changes. Seek help from another qualified person who can also help you work through the negative thoughts. A Christian counselor or your pastor may be helpful in making changes in your mind, attitude, and habits. A trusted accountability partner who understands your struggles can help to keep you on track.

Strategy Four: Renew your mind. "Do not be conformed to this age, but be transformed by the renewing of your mind" (Romans 12:2 HCSB). Negative thoughts are developed over many years and often a lifetime. Many times these thoughts began from someone else's comments that stuck and made an impression. Other outside influences to our thoughts are television, books, magazines, pictures, advertisements, and music. Transform your mind by learning and meditating on God's truth. Commit to turning off the outside influences that most strongly impact your thinking.

Strategy Five: Think on these things. "Finally brothers, whatever is true, whatever is honorable, whatever is just, whatever is pure, whatever is lovely, whatever is commendable—if there is any moral excellence and if there is any praise—dwell on these things" (Philippians 4:8 HCSB). Test your thoughts against this checklist. If your thoughts do not match up to the criteria God has provided, release the thought as unworthy of your mental energy.

Renewing your mind will not happen overnight.

As you gradually realize and change the way you think about yourself, you will change your attitude and then your actions. Even with a mental makeover, you will continue to need "attitude adjustment" work. Trust God for the consistent renewal of your mind and reap the benefits from making daily, sometimes small, but significant steps from a negative to a positive frame of life.

Computer programmers used to quote an old acronym GIGO, which stands for "Garbage In, Garbage Out." Like a computer, a brain receives input, processes what it's fed, and then guides the individual's response. The formula is fairly simple. Feed the brain negativity, what response should we expect? How might we respond if our minds receive a steady stream of positive (Biblical) input?

Trust God for the consistent renewal of your mind and reap the benefits from making daily, sometimes small, but significant steps from a negative to a positive frame of life.

TAKE ACTION

Read Romans 12:1-3, which challenges believers to examine their mental influences.
What influences associated with "this world" have the greatest impact on your thinking and behavior?

How can you replace, or at least balance, each of these influences with something more spiritually constructive?

When you read the "Seven Cognitive Distortions" as summarized by Brenda Polk, which causes you the most difficulty and why?

Read the apostle Paul's challenge to choose positive influences in Philippians 4:8-9 and identify two that come least naturally to you. Write them on a small card. Keep it handy over the next several days, remind yourself often to think on these things and put them into practice, and see for yourself if the apostle's promise is true: "The God of peace will be with you."

Be intentional: What are you going to do about what you've learned?

Be specific: What action will you take in the near future to begin applying what you've learned? When will you do it?

Be accountable: Pray it through. Share your plan with a friend and seek his/her prayer and counsel for your next step.

CHAPTER 11: EMOTIONAL ASSETS – GRIPING OR GRATITUDE

Scan here to watch the video!

Take a few moments to reflect on the answer to this question: "What is it like to live with me every day?"

Seriously. Don't blow this off. This little exercise could literally change your life. When you come home from work, does your family scurry off to their respective rooms or do they welcome you as a breath of fresh air? What kind of energy do you bring home? Stress or Joy? What are you like at work? Do people want to drop by your office for comfort or encouragement, or do they avoid chance encounters in the hall or around the coffee pot?

Take some time now to think. We'll wait.

Ask yourself: "What is it like to live with me every day?"

All of us would like to forget the cranky way we have responded both inside and outside the home. Who doesn't want to defeat crankiness before it hijacks our personality and then pushes others away? John Maxwell's *Maximum Impact Simulcast* gathered the nation's top gurus of industry and leadership to share their top three or four ideas about success in life. All of them agree that one of the most important characteristics is a positive attitude.

Herb Kelleher, former CEO of Southwest Airlines, explained his hiring process this way: "What we are looking for, first and foremost, is a sense of humor. . . . We don't care much about education and expertise because we can train people. . . . We hire attitudes."[17] For years, Southwest Airlines actively

> **"ATTITUDE"** by Charles Swindoll
>
> "The longer I live, the more I realize the impact of attitude on life. Attitude, to me, is more important than facts. It is more important than the past, than education, than money, than circumstances, than failures, than successes, than what other people think or say or do. It is more important than appearance, giftedness, or skill. It will make or break a company … a church … a home. The remarkable thing is we have a choice every day regarding the attitude we will embrace for that day. We cannot change the inevitable. The only thing we can do is play on the one string we have, and that is our attitude … I am convinced that life is 10% what happens to me, and 90% how I react to it. And so it is with you … we are in charge of our Attitudes."

sought and trained people who listen to others, who smile, and know how to say thank you.

So how can we cultivate the kind of attitude that lifts our own spirits and pulls others out of the dumps? Clearly, not by gritting our teeth and promising to be a better person tomorrow. Willpower alone won't have any lasting effect. We need a model to follow, an example worthy of emulating. Moreover, we need supernatural help, divine power to accomplish what internal motivation cannot.

The ultimate model is Jesus. He wants to rule and reign over every aspect of our lives. For a while the wrist bracelet WWJD became fashionable because certain Christian, professional golfers wore it. Anything that is overexposed can become trivialized, but the core message of that wristband offered a worthwhile reminder. It challenged believers to approach every circumstance in life with the question, "What Would Jesus Do?"

What would Jesus do when someone takes advantage of you at work? What would Jesus do when someone cuts into your traffic lane? What would Jesus do when your five-year-old throws a temper tantrum? We may not know what He would do in every situation, but we know He would think less about Himself and seek the greatest good of others. He wanted nothing more than to transform the lives and attitudes of others, and He's still in the business of changing people.

Several years ago, Randy Pope and several church leaders of Perimeter Church in Atlanta decided to purchase a special piece of property in order to create another congregation as a part of their master plan. The lady who owned the property had a reputation for being hard to deal with, and they anticipated that their request would be met with negativity. But, when they laid out their plans, she said, "I think you are just the right group to buy it." They were shocked. They told her they had expected her to resist. She agreed that her response would have been negative before she trusted Christ, but He had made her into a different person. She didn't use the phrase, but she was asking and answering, "What would Jesus do?"

Learning what Jesus would do takes some time but the first step is to make Him first in your life. Jesus said, "Seek first his kingdom and his righteousness, and all these things will be given to you as well" (Matthew 6:33). "These things" refers to all your basic needs. His constant and faithful provision gives us the opportunity to reject grumbling in favor of gratitude. He also wants us to examine and then change our motivations, our reasons for doing what we do. This emotion renovation begins with a hard look at why we have become so negative.

POSSIBLE REASONS FOR GRIPING

A primary cause for griping is spoilage; that is, like a child, the person may become spoiled. This is characterized by a general spirit of entitlement, the unconscious expectation that life owes us certain rights or privileges. People

---

WWJD?
We may not know what Jesus would do in every situation, but we know He would think less about Himself and seek the greatest good of others.

who grow up getting what they want find it difficult to handle circumstances that are less than perfect. They have come to believe that life is all about their own wellbeing and happiness, a notion that runs contrary to everything Jesus taught about priorities. He consistently taught that contentment is the result of selflessness, not self-indulgence. In fact, we learn from Jesus that the more we hoard wealth and possessions, the less grateful we become. Let us join the Old Testament sage, who prayed, "Keep falsehood and lies far from me; give me neither poverty nor riches, but give me only my daily bread. Otherwise, I may have too much and disown you and say, 'Who is the Lord?' Or I may become poor and steal, and so dishonor the name of my God" (Proverbs 30:8–9).

Another cause for griping is negative friends. The writer of Proverbs 13:20 observes, "He who walks with the wise grows wise, but a companion of fools suffers harm." Complainers tend to flock together and feed off the cynicism of one another. They exaggerate, contaminate, ridicule, and sour life's experiences for everyone. They can't wait to share bad news. Negativity becomes such an ingrained personality disorder that good news threatens their stability and undermines their identity. They aren't happy unless they're complaining, and their complaining makes them mad! If the company you keep poisons your attitude, it's time to run. Far better to suffer the displeasure of your friends than waste your future.

A negative, griping attitude can also be caused by comparing one's self to others. Paul wrote, "We do not dare to classify or compare ourselves with some who commend themselves. When they measure themselves by themselves and compare themselves with themselves, they are not wise" (2 Corinthians 10:12). The habit of measuring oneself for the sake of comparison is a by-product of ingratitude. We can look at the talents or possessions that others have and become either jealous or intimidated. Some enjoy good health while others endure sickness. Some look like Greek sculptures while others struggle with disabilities. Some are born into wealth; others struggle to make ends meet. Some are born with natural good looks, and others are not. Some have a boatload of charisma, while others struggle to attract friends.

Measuring one's self against others is a losing proposition. We can always find someone richer, healthier, better looking, and more successful. Therefore it is both spiritually defeating and an act in futility to gripe about what is or what is not.

GRUMBLING AND GOD

God doesn't like grumbling. When the Israelites fled the iron grip of Pharaoh in Egypt and wandered the desert, they eventually joined the grumblers, chorus and whined, "Why have you brought us up out of Egypt to die in the desert? There is no bread! There is no water! And we detest this miserable food!" (Numbers 21:5). God's response sent a clear message that grumbling is unacceptable behavior (Numbers 21:6–9). Many centuries later, James, the

Jesus consistently taught that contentment is the result of selflessness, not self-indulgence.

brother of Jesus, warned the New Testament people of God, "Don't grumble against each other, brothers, or you will be judged. The Judge is standing at the door!" (James 5:9).

The Bible regularly condemns grumblers as thankless people, brimming with ingratitude toward God (2 Timothy 3:2), ingratitude toward others (2 Timothy 3:1–4), and ingratitude toward their Savior (Luke 17:12–18). They have fallen into a grumblers' rut and have become what Gordon MacDonald calls VDP (very draining people). Because ingratitude is a communicable disease, we must treat ingrates like people with the flu. Give them plenty of compassion . . . from a safe distance! Instead, seek out people like the apostle Paul, who learned how to see the potential good in all circumstances. We learn from him that contentment is a choice.

While imprisoned in Rome, Paul wrote to the believers in Philippi, in part to express his thanks for the provisions they sent. First, however, he reassured his friends that he didn't resent his unjust incarceration. Far from it! He wrote,

Contentment is a choice.

> I want you to know, brothers, that what has happened to me has really served to advance the gospel. As a result, it has become clear throughout the whole palace guard and to everyone else that I am in chains for Christ. Because of my chains, most of the brothers in the Lord have been encouraged to speak the word of God more courageously and fearlessly. (Philippians 1:12–14)

Most people would have resented the injustice Paul endured, but he accepted his circumstances as the will of God and looked for unforeseen opportunities. Later in this letter, he explained how he could remain so positive in the midst of such negative circumstances.

> I rejoice greatly in the Lord that at last you have renewed your concern for me. Indeed, you have been concerned, but you had no opportunity to show it. I am not saying this because I am in need, for I have learned to be content whatever the circumstances. I know what it is to be in need, and I know what it is to have plenty. I have learned the secret of being content in any and every situation, whether well fed or hungry, whether living in plenty or in want. I can do everything through him who gives me strength.
>
> I have received full payment and even more; I am amply supplied, now that I have received from Epaphroditus the gifts you sent. They are a fragrant offering, an acceptable sacrifice, pleasing to God. And my God will meet all your needs according to his glorious riches in Christ Jesus. (Philippians 4:10–13; 18–19)

Paul found several reasons to be grateful in his circumstances. He was delighted to see the gospel preached among people who would not otherwise have heard the good news. He was gratified to know the Philippians cared about him. He was thankful for the comfort of his provisions. He had already chosen to be content, but the physical support was appreciated. He was thankful that his friends would feel God's pleasure because of their generosity. The apostle chose to be content, which came easily after he intentionally looked for reasons to give thanks.

The Thanksgiving holiday gives us this same opportunity each year. It's a great time to pause and reflect on why we are grateful. Most people thank God for family, health, good fortune, material blessings, and so forth. There's nothing wrong with that, but perhaps we shouldn't limit ourselves. Don't limit gratitude to one day out of 365; take the holiday as a special reminder to thank God regularly. Moreover, we would do well to think creatively when counting our blessings. Genuine gratitude often starts with the lips and then engages the heart. When that happens, thanksgiving goes much deeper than material blessings. Here are three examples of gratitude for non-material blessings.

Gratitude for the Capacity to Understand. Not everyone can look at his or her personal situation or the awful mess the world is in and understand what is happening. A Christian is not surprised when either good or bad things happen. The Christian who has read Scripture with understanding knows the sinfulness of humankind creates unimaginable evil, but that God is ultimately in control. While vicious ways of humanity seem to have no limit and evil appears to run unchecked, we find peace in the capacity to understand these things from a heavenly perspective. Unlike those who do not have a relationship with Christ, we groan with great expectation (Romans 8:18–21) and we grieve the dead in Christ with hope (1 Thessalonians 4:13).

Gratitude for the Capacity to Care. Not everyone is touched by the needs of others. Some have experienced a sort of "compassion fatigue" by viewing too many villages devastated by earthquakes or wars, too many abused children, too many victims of crime, or too many starving people. So if you can look at any form of human need and still find a place in your heart to care about the suffering of others, you are a fortunate person. You are not emotionally dead. You still have the capacity to respond. God can still put you to work in His cause. That is worth celebrating, and you can thank God that you haven't become completely calloused by the overload of negative communication coming from the media.

Gratitude for the Compassion to Get Involved. It's one thing to see what needs to be done and another thing to respond. We usually have to overcome the inertia created by the overwhelming number of needs and the thought that one human being makes little difference. Ask those who have gone on a short-term mission trip how they felt about the experience. They usually are deeply grateful that they took the time and effort to make the trip. In fact, they usually respond that it meant more to them and their personal growth than to the people they were helping.

TAKE ACTION

Read Philippians 4:10–13; 18–19, in which Paul describes his contentment and expresses his thanks.
Describe a circumstance you experienced that some might characterize as negative. How did you respond to the situation?

Looking back, can you identify things for which you could be grateful? Name some of them.

Take some time now to list reasons to be thankful.

How do you think cultivating an attitude of gratitude will influence your effect on others in your family, among your friends, and at your job?

Be intentional: What are you going to do about what you've learned?

Be specific: What action will you take in the near future to begin applying what you've learned? When will you do it?

Be accountable: Pray it through. Share your plan with a friend and seek his/her prayer and counsel for your next step.

CHAPTER 12: EMOTIONAL ASSETS – BITTERNESS OR FORGIVENESS

Scan here to watch the video!

More lethal than a car bomb and more toxic than Sarin gas, yet cruelly slow to act, bitterness has the power to kill the human spirit. It is the corrosive bile that denies our peace; it is the seething wrath that craves vengeance; it is the vitriol that poisons relationships. The author of Hebrews warned of this corrupting influence and its aftermath: "See to it that no one misses the grace of God and that no bitter root grows up to cause trouble and defile many" (Hebrews 12:15).

Bitterness shows itself in three ways:

First, bitterness can be directed against God. A child loses a parent to an untimely death so the child becomes angry with God. A wife feels trapped in a loveless marriage, so she walks away from her faith. A man is fired from his job or is overlooked for the third time for a promotion, so he cries out against God in the night. In so many words they all say, "If you answer prayers, God, why didn't you answer mine?"

Second, bitterness can be directed against other people. A person may not blame God for his circumstances, but thinks he knows whom to blame so he looks for ways to make them pay for the pain they have inflicted. One event, forever seared on our minds, depicts what bitterness can do to others—the photos of airplanes flying into the World Trade Center towers on 9-11-2001.

Third, bitterness can be directed against oneself. A person finds it difficult to forgive himself for being so stupid and doing something so dumb. In doing this, he throws away the key that allows someone to unlock his heart and help him process his confusion and pain. This person may even feel deserving of life's harsh treatment and go through life with a cloud of bitterness over his head that he cannot remove. Until this bitterness is dealt with, this person will make everyone around him miserable.

The analogy referred to in Hebrews for bitterness is a root. It's the part of the plant you can't see because it runs beneath the soil. It feeds the plant and keeps it firmly in place. The roots of a plant can be so tough they can burrow under an asphalt road and crack the surface. If ignored, they can cause cracks and holes large enough to damage cars. Likewise in life, the roots of bitterness can detour all normal patterns of human interaction or bring them to a screeching halt.

The roots of bitterness cause all kinds of trouble. Let's consider the four most common problems people experience because of unresolved anger.

PHYSICAL PROBLEMS

Dr. S. I. McMillan's classic work, *None of These Diseases*, details the potential health benefits of following biblical advice and the possible hazards of ignoring God's instructions concerning cleanliness, diet, and the mind. He reported that anger, if not handled properly, could contribute to no less than fifty diseases.

Dr. Norman Wright, professor of psychology at Biola University, states that God has constructed us with a tube about thirty feet long that begins at our throat and runs to our rectum. Unresolved anger, which leads to bitterness, can cause any number of complications to this tube, including colitis, gastroesophageal reflux disease, diarrhea, and ulcers. Other physicians highlight the long term contribution of anger on hypertension, obesity, heart disease, and diabetes.

MENTAL PROBLEMS

One thing is certain: an angry, bitter person has no room for joy, creativity, imagination, or any other positive influence. Eventually, bitterness can lead to a borderline personality disorder (BPD)—a serious emotional disturbance characterized by unstable personal relationships and fears of abandonment leading to a constant state of emotional turmoil.[18] What triggers BPD is not the same for everyone; however, most causes can be linked to perceived or real neglect and abuse during childhood. Such abuse was never adequately dealt with, and the bitterness took an enormous toll.

RELATIONAL PROBLEMS

A person can camouflage bitterness for only so long before it begins to "defile" his or her relationships with others (Hebrews 12:15). The Greek word for "defile" means, literally, "to stain." Think of a permanent red blemish on a white shirt. Unresolved anger has the power to ruin something beautiful.

Steve had always felt neglected by his wife during the years the children were at home. He tried in vain to express his disappointment at receiving the emotional leftovers from the love and attention she showered on their three kids. Even though this barren relationship was painful, he endured for the sake of the children—that is, until the youngest left for college. Then Steve left. The lingering bitterness that had stained his marriage became an ugly parting gift for those who were closest to him.

SPIRITUAL PROBLEMS

A bitter attitude is so serious that Jesus said you should stop whatever religious "thing" you are doing and go settle the matter with the one with whom you have a problem. In fact, He strongly urged His followers to settle all disputes, knowing that bitterness always points to a deeper spiritual issue. Here are some of His most sobering warnings.

> If you are offering your gift at the altar and there remember that your brother has something against you, leave your gift

> there in front of the altar. First go and be reconciled to your brother; then come and offer your gift. (Matthew 5:23–24)
>
> If you forgive men when they sin against you, your heavenly Father will also forgive you. But if you do not forgive men their sins, your Father will not forgive your sins. (Matthew 6:14–15)
>
> If your brother sins against you, go and show him his fault, just between the two of you. If he listens to you, you have won your brother over. But if he will not listen, take one or two others along, so that "every matter may be established by the testimony of two or three witnesses." If he refuses to listen to them, tell it to the church; and if he refuses to listen even to the church, treat him as you would a pagan or a tax collector. (Matthew 18:15–17)
>
> When you stand praying, if you hold anything against anyone, forgive him, so that your Father in heaven may forgive you your sins. (Mark 11:25)
>
> If your brother sins, rebuke him, and if he repents, forgive him. If he sins against you seven times in a day, and seven times comes back to you and says, "I repent," forgive him. (Luke 17:3–4)

Both your relationship with Christ and your influence for Him are at stake. Pastor and author Charles Stanley understood this when he reflected on his relationship with his children:

> Not long ago, I sat down with my two children, Andy and Becky, and asked if they had resentful feelings toward me for any wrong I had perpetrated. At the time, they were both in their twenties, and so they felt freer to talk openly and honestly.
>
> Andy was the first to respond. He recalled a time when he was thirteen or fourteen and was practicing one part of a song. Over and over, the same melody. I asked him if that was all he knew. Andy recalled that to his adolescent ears, my words sounded like I was saying "I don't like you or your music." That damaging impression caused him to decide not to play any music for me again, even though he was a talented musician.
>
> Becky had her memory, too. "When I was five years old,

we lived in Miami. One day you put me in my room and you wouldn't let me out. I cried and cried, but you wouldn't let me out."[19]

He asked for their forgiveness, which they readily gave, and their reconciliation helped the three of them find emotional and spiritual healing. In Ephesians 4:31–32, the apostle Paul wrote that we need to eliminate a six-headed monster:

1. Bitterness. The internalized, smoldering resentment that keeps a person in perpetual animosity. If bitterness is not resolved by forgiveness, then monsters 2 through 6 kick in.
2. Rage. The explosion that leads to revenge.
3. Anger. Never-ending internal deterioration.
4. Brawling. Public outburst that reveals loss of control.
5. Slander. Defamation of character.
6. Malice. The determination to get even.

FORGIVENESS MAKES A DIFFERENCE

At the heart of the matter, forgiveness means setting someone free. When one person has hurt another, a debt needs to be paid. The forgiving person cancels that debt. The person who refuses to forgive maintains his or her right to seek justice or vengeance. We call it holding a grudge. Some people enjoy the feeling. It gives them a certain sense of power. But holding a grudge is like holding a rattlesnake by the tail. Sooner or later, you'll get bitten, and the venom of that serpent will snuff out your spiritual life.

Before entering the process of forgiveness, we need to understand three mistaken ideas about forgiveness. First, some assume that understanding an individual's behavior (the reasons for that person's actions) or explaining it away is the same thing as forgiveness. It is not. Knowing that a person lashed out at you in public because he is dealing with frustrations at home does not mean that you have forgiven him.

Another mistaken idea is that time heals all wounds. Many men have grown up without the affection or the affirmation of their fathers. During their twenties and thirties, they may talk about it and think that, in time, it will no longer bother them. Often, however, these men in their late forties or early fifties will face an emotional crisis where they realize that they can't go on without dealing with the rejection. At that point, these men usually need professional help. Time didn't heal the wound—it just temporarily masked it.

The third mistaken idea is that we should confess our bitterness and express forgiveness to someone who had neither solicited it nor wanted it. Actually this will do more harm. Expressing forgiveness with the other person being oblivious to his or her offense will come off as "holier than thou," and the other person may interpret this as one more control issue. It can come off as a feigned forgiveness. And, if the other party is not emotionally ready to deal with it, this can make him feel humiliated for not wanting to respond with his own forgiveness.

Fortunately, it only takes one person to forgive. It takes two to reconcile, but one person can clear the deck of his own bitterness and move on. For those who want to do so, there is a five-step process of forgiveness.

It only takes one person to forgive. It takes two to reconcile, but one person can clear the deck of his own bitterness and move on.

Step One: Forgive the Debt

One story about Robert E. Lee after the Civil War has him visiting a lady in Kentucky, who pointed to a battered tree outside her home. She said it used to be a beautiful magnolia, but no longer a thing of beauty without its limbs. The Union Army had blasted it with their artillery and she asked, "What do you think about that?"

Lee looked at her and responded simply, "Cut it down and forget about it."

That is the best advice. Forgive and move on. Refusing to dwell on an unhappy experience pays wonderful dividends. The discarded resentment no longer siphons your emotional and spiritual energy, and that freedom sets you free to use that energy where God has called.

Bob Hamp, a Licensed Professional Counselor and popular Christian author and pastor teaches when you forgive someone, "You must make a CHOICE. The choice is this: You choose to live with the consequences of the other's sin, and not charge it to their account. [This] is not easy. In some cases it may be the most difficult choice a human can make. Jesus made this choice in the Garden of Gethsemane the night before His crucifixion. This choice required such intense will-work, that the Son of God sweat drops of blood as He chose to take our sins upon Himself and not charge them to our account."[20]

Step Two: Release the Offender

When a debt is cancelled, the debtor is free to go. Sometimes he hangs around until he is invited to leave. That's what happened to John Tolson's father. He left home when John was two years old, never to return again. Like any boy who longs for a father, this left a hole in John's heart. For years, he wondered what it would be like to see his father again, to have him show up for one of his basketball games. John longed for words of affirmation that he would never hear. He would dream about a hug or an "attaboy," but the dream was never fulfilled.

It was difficult to forgive a father he never saw, until a special day at the beach where John had one last conversation with his father. John sat in a chair facing an empty chair just inches away. With carefully selected words, John spoke as though his father were sitting in the chair. John forgave his father and then released him and also years of bitterness and pain. It was a one-sided conversation, but it was enough to bring closure and healing to a middle-aged man.

When you forgive the offender and release their debt, three things are accomplished on your behalf:

> **A. It gives you back your Mind:** When you are angry with another, you give them real estate in your mind. Forgiving restores back to you possession of what you have given away. If you have ever wondered why it is difficult to control your thoughts, consider this; it is impossible to submit to God what you have already given to someone else.
>
> **B. It gives the offender Back to God:** When you release them, you give them over to God for Him to work justice in their lives. Justice is not an eye for an eye or a tooth for a tooth. (This approach simply results in a lot of blind toothless people.) True justice is when wrong things are made right. God is better at this than you are.
>
> **C. It opens the door for God's part of forgiveness:** Healing your soul: When you give up the role of being your own healer, however futile it may have been, you make room for God to do what He does best. The restoration of our souls is the real goal of forgiveness. This allows us to be who we are created to be even when we have faced real evil or real pain.[21]

Step Three: Understand the Growth and Healing Process

No one has the big picture of what God is doing, especially with the painful experiences of life. "Forgiveness is a healing process," says Bob Hamp, "but God's healing is not intended to be a substitute for the grieving process. Grieving is an ongoing process of God's healing work that reflects the value of what was lost or damaged. If you lost a loved one, or a relationship, or a possession, or a condition that was important, attempting to have no more pain at all about this loss, may rob you of the value of grieving. Jesus was a Man acquainted with grief. We should not run, or hide from it simply because we want to not hurt any more."[22]

Joseph, in Genesis 37–50, experienced painful and shameful treatment from his own family as well as others. After having been sold into slavery by his brothers, Joseph must have found it difficult to forgive his brothers and release them. But you never find him in denial about his circumstances, or second-guessing the hand of God. In fact, eventually he became a prince of Egypt, occupying a position of power where he could save his family from starvation. When his brothers approached him for food he told them, "…God sent me ahead of you to preserve for you a remnant on earth and to save your lives by a great deliverance" (Genesis 45:7).

Joseph had the foresight to know that hindsight would explain how God was involved in his life. He was on a journey of growth, and he never wavered from believing God was using all of his life experiences for good. Joseph proclaimed God's glory to his brothers when he said, "Don't be afraid. Am I in the place of God? You intended to harm me, but God intended it for good to accomplish what is now being done, the saving of many lives" (Genesis 50:19–20).

Joseph had the foresight to know that hindsight would explain how God was involved in his life.

Step Four: Make Reconciliation
If you have made the offense and are able to reconcile, make a phone call. That's what Robert did. He's a top officer in a national CPA firm. One day he was challenged to take an intentional first step toward two men in his company that he felt he had wronged. Sometimes you just have to set your emotions on the table and do the right thing without processing it over and over in your mind. An old country preacher used to say, "Get your doer doing, and your feeler will follow."

Robert got his "doer doing." He took the initiative and all was forgiven. That's when the gospel becomes very attractive—when something tangible happens.

Step Five: Express Kindness
This is the follow-up step. Follow the reconciliation with a note, a gift, an "I thought of you" event! Lovers used to add a note to the outside of an envelope, SWAK—Sealed With A Kiss. Reconciliation can also use a SWAK or two—Sealed With A Kindness. It is added evidence that you are very serious about what just happened. It also answers the question "I wonder if they feel the same today about the reconciliation as they did yesterday?"

TAKE ACTION

Read the Lord's counsel on forgiveness in Matthew 5:23–24; 6:14–15; 18:15–17; Mark 11:25; and Luke 17:3–4.
Forgiveness is letting an offender off your moral hook, releasing someone from any obligation to right a wrong done to you. Who do you need to release from your personal justice?

What are the potential ramifications of failing to forgive this person (or these people)? Consider the physical, emotional, and spiritual consequences.

When you have decided to forgive someone, say aloud, "Lord, I forgive (name) for (offenses)," and then share your decision with someone you trust. Ask him or her to hold you accountable for your choice to release your offender from any future obligations or expectations.

When negative feelings return—and they surely will—reaffirm your decision to forgive and ask the Lord to heal your emotional wounds. Rest assured, He will.

Be intentional: What are you going to do about what you've learned?

Be specific: What action will you take in the near future to begin applying what you've learned? When will you do it?

Be accountable: Pray it through. Share your plan with a friend and seek his/her prayer and counsel for your next step.

CHAPTER 13: EMOTIONAL ASSETS – DEPRESSION OR JOY

Scan here to watch the video!

An advertisement for an anti-depressant drug runs like this: "Depressed mood. Loss of interest. Sleep problems. Difficulty concentrating. Agitation. Restlessness. Life is too precious to let another day go by feeling not quite 'yourself.' If you've experienced some of these symptoms nearly every day for at least two weeks, a chemical imbalance could be to blame. And life can feel difficult ALL DAY."

According to psychiatrist Paul Meier, "About one-fifth of Christians worldwide experience enough depression to interfere with their ability to function normally." That means twenty percent of the Christians you meet experience deep struggles that can cause severe damage if not addressed in a meaningful way. The Lord was disturbed with the prophets and priests of Israel because they would not seriously address the wounds of His people. Instead, they would superficially cry, "Peace, peace . . . when there is no peace" (Jeremiah 6:14). Today's "priests" – regardless of any modern denominational title – offer little more than a superficial peace for people's emotional or spiritual pain, which is equally disturbing to the Lord. In order to deal with the wounds of depression seriously, we must have more than a superficial understanding of the problem. Such discernment would include the differences between the experience of male and female depression, as seen on the next page, by Dr. Archibald Hart in his book *Unmasking Male Depression: Recognizing the Root Cause to Many Problem Behaviors Such as Anger, Resentment, Abusiveness, Silence, Addictions, and Sexual Compulsiveness.*[23]

A classic case study on the symptoms of depression is found in 1 Kings 19, which recounts the story of Elijah fleeing Ahab and Jezebel after standing against 450 prophets of Baal (1 Kings 18). It is a classic story of going from the pinnacle to the pit, from a spiritual "high" to the dark night of depression. Woven into the narrative of 1 Kings 19 is a dialogue between the Lord and Elijah that reveals what depression looks like and how it is expressed. Some of the symptoms would make Elijah a candidate for antidepressants if they had been available at the time.

SYMPTOM #1: FEAR (1 KINGS 19:3)
"Elijah was afraid and ran for his life."
News that 450 prophets of Baal lost their lives made Elijah a prime target. Not only did he not have the time to savor the victory of the Lord over His adversaries, he was now on the run and would soon be trapped by thoughts that he would not have believed possible for a man of God.

Fears can get out of control, which would be one of those "wiles of the

MALE DEPRESSION	FEMALE DEPRESSION
→ Blames others	→ Blames herself
→ Acts out his inner turmoil	→ Turns her feelings inward
→ Needs to maintain control at all costs	→ Has trouble maintaining control
→ Overtly hostile, irritable	→ Always tries to be nice
→ Attacks when hurt	→ Withdraws when hurt
→ Tries to fix by problem-solving	→ Tries to fix by trying harder
→ Turns to sports, TV, sex, alcohol	→ Turns to food, friends, emotional needs
→ Feels shamed	→ Feels guilty
→ Becomes a compulsive timekeeper	→ Procrastinates, delays deadlines
→ Terrified to confront weakness	→ Exaggerates, obsesses about weakness
→ Tries to maintain strong male image	
→ Tries to act away	→ Disintegrates at slightest failure
→ Turns to alcoholism and other addictions	→ Tries to think through
	→ Increased appetite and weight

devil" to which Paul refers in Ephesians 6. Our enemy knows what deeply bothers us, so he hits us there. The following list contains some of the most common triggers of depression through the years.

- Fear your grades aren't good enough for the college you want to attend
- Fear you won't find a meaningful relationship with the opposite sex
- Fear of being stuck in a dead-end career
- Fear that your kids won't turn out well
- Fear of a bad medical report
- Fear that you won't have enough money for retirement

SYMPTOM #2: ISOLATION (1 KINGS 19:3–4)
"He himself went a day's journey into the desert."
Dr. Philip Zimbardo, Professor of Psychology at Stanford University, wrote, "I know of no more potent killer than isolationism. There is no more destructive influence on physical and mental health than the isolation of you from me and us from them."[24] The only thing worse than being fatigued, exhausted, and burned out like Elijah is having to go through it alone. After fleeing from Jezebel, Elijah came to Beersheba, a small town at the southern extreme of Hebrew territory, the last stop before endless miles of nothing. 1 Kings 19:3 reports, "He left his servant there, while he himself went a day's journey into the desert."

One of the dangers of depression is to turn inward and to hide from those who care the most for us. In an isolated condition, the mind starts playing games, causing you to hear voices that usually say scary things. In that kind of fog, it's difficult to know the difference between truth and a lie.

Isolation is a growing problem. Robert Putnam, author of *Bowling Alone*, discovered this after extensive research that involved 500,000 interviews over the last quarter century. He found that Americans have declining social connections where they know their neighbors less, meet with friends less frequently, and belong to fewer organizations. In the last twenty-five years, families spend increasingly less dinnertime together and forty-five percent less time having friends over to the house. This lack of connection is not good for longevity or a state of happiness. One surprising fact offered by Putnam is that joining just one social group reduces odds of dying next year by fifty percent!

SYMPTOM #3: SELF-PITY (1 KINGS 19:4)
"Take my life; I am no better than my ancestors."
Collapsing in the shade of a broom tree, Elijah declared, "I have had enough." He evaluated his condition based on the reasoning process forged in isolation and fear and succumbed to a "poor me" mentality. Millicent Fenwick said, "Never feel self-pity, the most destructive emotion there is. How awful to be caught up in the terrible squirrel cage of self."[25]

SYMPTOM #4: FADED FAITH (1 KINGS 19:4)
"I am the only one left, and now they are trying to kill me too."
The fear, aloneness, and self-pity were the prime ingredients that caused Elijah to forget God's presence and His past faithfulness. That is typical for someone who is not thinking clearly. If Elijah's servant had been there, he might have reminded Elijah about:

- The famine that he had foretold had come to pass (1 Kings 17:1, 7)
- His being fed by ravens (1 Kings 17:6)
- The widow's barrel of flour and jar of oil never running dry (1 Kings 17:16)
- The widow's son raised to life (1 Kings 17:22)
- God's fire on Mt. Carmel had consumed the soaked altar sacrifice (1 Kings 18:38)
- The rains returning at his request (1 Kings 18:45)
- His ability, with supernatural strength, to outrace the king's chariot (1 Kings 18:46)

Elijah's faith faded not only because of a poor memory, but because he had no one who could loan him faith. That's right—at times we need a loan, we need to borrow from someone else the faith and strength to put everything into perspective. Elijah's spiritual bank account was empty. Before he could return to the old Elijah, he needed emotional and spiritual assets. Eventually they would come.

SYMPTOM #5: SUICIDAL (1 KINGS 19:4)
"He came to a broom tree, sat down under it and prayed that he might die."
Psychologists say that people take their own lives when the pain of living is no longer bearable. In a physically, emotionally, and spiritually depleted condition, Elijah thought death was his only way to ease his suffering.

Abraham Lincoln felt that way at one point in his life. He wrote to his friend, John Stuart, "I am now the most miserable man living. If what I feel were equally distributed to the whole human family, there would not be one cheerful face on the earth. Whether I shall ever be better I can not tell; I awfully forebode I shall not. To remain as I am is impossible; I must die or be better, it appears to me."[26] Lincoln had moved from discouragement to despondency to despair. That's where irrationality sets in and thoughts of death become obsessive.

The five-year age span that has the highest suicide rate is the group from 80 to 84-year-olds, primarily because so many live alone. That may seem surprising, given the high rate of suicide among teens. Clearly, no one is exempt from depression, even those who maintain strong faith in Jesus Christ. Those who hit bottom and have suicidal thoughts need help. If a man finds a lump under the armpit, he goes to the doctor and immediately seeks help, and he doesn't feel guilty for doing so. Likewise, we should feel no shame in seeking the best advice for dealing with depression, which is potentially lethal. It's a universal problem that affects people from all across the globe and within every social stratum.

SYMPTOM #6: EXHAUSTION (1 KINGS 19:5)
Coach Vince Lombardi often quoted General George Patton: "Fatigue makes cowards of us all."[27] Patton stated flatly, "Staff personnel, commissioned and enlisted, who do not rest, do not last." Psychologists have given a name to the phenomenon that sidelines otherwise effective people: *vital exhaustion*. This kind of physical breakdown has three characteristics: (1) Feelings of excessive fatigue and lack of energy, (2) Increasing irritability, and (3) Feelings of demoralization.

Nothing looks right to the exhausted mind. Physical exhaustion does not necessarily lead to mental exhaustion, however. A person who puts in a day of physically taxing work can actually feel mentally refreshed yet physically worn out. Elijah had been running. He was physically tired, but his depression came from not understanding what was going on, not being able to see either a good conclusion or rescue on the horizon. His physical state contributed to, but didn't determine, his mental outlook.

SYMPTOM #7: FEELING REJECTED (1 KINGS 19:10)
"The Israelites have rejected your covenant, broken down your altars, and put your prophets to death with the sword. I am the only one left, and now they are trying to kill me too."

Elijah's rejection paralleled his self-pity. Few people have egos strong enough to withstand a constant barrage of personal rejection, especially from people who should know better or from those who matter. At this point, their rejection impacted Elijah's sense of well-being. But Elijah is not the only spiritual leader to experience depression; in fact, he shared this burden of leadership with people like Job, Moses, Jonah, Peter, and Paul. Spiritual giants centuries later also faced the dark night of the soul, including Martin Luther, Charles Spurgeon, and Vance Havener.

So the question is what to do when antidepressants aren't the right answer. The answer is simple but not simplistic. Let God heal and let the joy return. Here is how God healed Elijah.

1. God recognized that Elijah's depression was real.

Maybe it was post-adrenalin depression. Often, a walk through the valley can follow a significant victory. One day Elijah exalts his victory over Baal's prophets; the next day he wants to die. Yet God didn't scold him for his feelings. He acknowledged that Elijah needed help.

2. God encouraged Elijah to rest.

When you are worn out, you need rest. Sometimes the most spiritual thing you can do is eat your favorite meal and take a nap. It's amazing how some people have the attitude that the only way to prove your spiritual zeal is to burn out. That wasn't the pattern Jesus modeled. He would greatly exert himself meeting human needs and then withdraw for renewal. He understood that physically depleted people have a short cycle of usefulness.

3. God didn't give Elijah counsel for a while.

More beneficial than the power of well-spoken words is the power of presence. Anyone who has grieved deeply will tell you that they remember precious few words spoken to them during their hour of crisis, but they are forever grateful for the silent presence of someone they love and trust.

In 1862, during a difficult period in the Civil War, a Quaker woman and her friend found an audience with Abraham Lincoln for the purpose of prayer and spiritual support. Eliza Gurney, the widow of English Quaker Joseph J. Gurney, did not come to counsel Lincoln. Rather, in the Quaker tradition, she came to spend long moments in silence and prayer for the President of a nation engulfed by the ravages of war. Two years later, Lincoln would write to Elizabeth Gurney, "I have not forgotten—probably never shall forget—the very impressive occasion when yourself and friends visited me on a Sabbath forenoon, two years ago."[28]

God was present with Elijah, but He waited for the right time to offer His servant insight.

4. God allowed Elijah to explain the problem.
Dr. Paul Meier, co-founder of Meier New-Life Clinics, says that more important than prescription medicine as the antidote for depression is what he calls "talk therapy." After the Lord asked, "What are you doing here?" Elijah rehearsed how faithful he had been for the cause of God only to be isolated, persecuted, and abandoned by other believers. Elijah may have felt like he was the only faithful one left, but it was not true. Later the Lord would reveal, "I reserve seven thousand in Israel—all whose knees have not bowed down to Baal and all whose mouths have not kissed him" (1 Kings 19:18). For the time being, God gave Elijah time to vent, time to make irrational statements, time to unpack his frustration. God explored Elijah's heart, but first the prophet had to understand his own heart through the expression of his mouth. This exploration process is essential for anyone who wants to find healing.

5. God dealt with Elijah's false beliefs.
During World War II, the allied forces came across a concentration camp in Cologne, Germany that had an inscription scrawled on a cellar wall:

> I believe in the sun
> even when it is not shining.
> And I believe in love
> even when I do not feel it.
> And I believe in God
> even when He is silent.

God was ready to speak, and Elijah would be reintroduced to the God of Abraham, Isaac, and Jacob. God's awesome display of wind, earthquake, and fire would be impressive but the real power came to Elijah in profound words whispered in his ear. At the core of Elijah's problem was an inadequate view of God. It's understandable that he had this view, but it's not permissible to sustain that view.

Zig Ziglar likes to say that people's problems are related to "stinkin' thinkin'!" When we are refreshed enough to handle truth, God will put us in a place where we can enter "reality therapy," or the healing that comes from dealing realistically with ourselves and realistically with the truth of Scripture.

6. God gave Elijah something to do.
"Go back the way you came . . . [to] Damascus . . . anoint Hazael King of Aram . . . anoint Jehu son of Nimshi king over Israel . . . anoint Elisha . . . to succeed you as prophet."

In other words, "Elijah, get back to work." God told his faithful yet depressed servant, "Do something useful. Find someone in need and help that person. Get out of yourself and think about someone else." It's remarkable how your problems become insignificant when you serve those who need God's touch. Ask anyone who has volunteered for a short-term missionary trip. He or she returned spiritually energized though physically exhausted. Dr. Carl Menninger said this is a far better prescription for depression than visiting a psychiatrist.

It's remarkable how your problems become insignificant when you serve those who need God's touch.

7. God gave Elijah a friend.

Enter: Elisha. The story begins a new chapter with the introduction of Elijah's new attendant and friend. Elijah was no longer isolated. Elisha was a gift from God, a brother, a co-laborer, and exactly what Elijah needed.

In the end, one of the greatest weapons to fight depression is perseverance. You may not be able to stop the dark blanket coming over you, but you can choose how to respond to it. You tell the depression that it can come a hundred times, but you will never stop fighting. You will wear depression out. You may get knocked down, but you will always get up.

On October 31, 1974, a great fight took place in Kinshasa, Zaire. "The Rumble in the Jungle" featured the championship heavyweight boxing match between Muhammad Ali and George Foreman. Ali was thirty-two-years old and had lost his last two fights, one to Joe Frazier in 1971 and another to Ken Norton in 1973, who broke Ali's jaw. George Foreman was the Olympic champion who had defeated both Frazier and Norton, each in just two rounds. He was young, strong, and eager to show the world his notoriously heavy hands.

Ali knew he could not beat Foreman by exchanging blows, by matching strength for strength. At the beginning of the second round, he started backing up against the ropes and shielding his head with his forearms but occasionally taunting Foreman by waiting for him to come get him. Foreman landed body blow after body blow, pounding as rapidly as he could but also progressively losing steam. By the seventh round Ali was whispering in his ear, "Is that all you got George?" George knew it was all he had. In the eighth round Ali sprang like a cobra with left-right combinations and knocked Foreman out.

Sometimes our enemy needs to punch himself out. As you gradually realize this is happening, you know that eventually you will be the victor. This builds confidence in yourself and often shortens the amount of time depression has a grip on you.

TAKE ACTION

Read 1 Kings 19:1–18, which recounts Elijah's battle with depression. What "highs" or "lows" have you experienced that might contribute to an extended downturn in your mood?

Before attending to his emotional and spiritual needs, God took care of Elijah's physical needs, such as rest and food. We read about the importance of treating your body right—diet, rest, exercise, etc.— in Chapter 8. Have you begun implementing a plan to address your physical needs? Have you scheduled a medical checkup with your physician? When can you schedule that appointment?

While joy is a choice, we cannot ignore the powerful emotional contributors to depression. What scars from past trauma might you reexamine? How could these affect you today?

The answer to Elijah's depression was a spiritual reawakening through a fresh encounter with God. What can you do to deepen your connection with the Lord? How can your friends help you with this?

Be intentional: What are you going to do about what you've learned?

Be specific: What action will you take in the near future to begin applying what you've learned? When will you do it?

Be accountable: Pray it through. Share your plan with a friend and seek his/her prayer and counsel for your next step.

CHAPTER 14: SOCIAL ASSETS – YOU AND YOUR RELATIONSHIPS

Scan here to watch the video!

Earl Campbell, the famous running back for the Houston Oilers, won the Heisman Trophy in 1977 and went on to lead the NFL in rushing three times. Called a "one-man demolition team," Campbell was one of the toughest runners to bring down because of his tremendous lower body strength and a nasty stiff-arm. He either ran tacklers over or kept them at arm's length as he moved down the field.

Perhaps you have known someone who moves through life like Campbell ran the football. Have you ever been stiff-armed by a friend or loved one? Sometimes the relationship ends with a sudden jolt—the so-called friend disappears. Sometimes it happens gradually—the person simply fades away. Relationships turn sour for many reasons but often because one person has a blind spot. The person doesn't see the barrier he or she has erected that prevents the relationship from continuing. Unfortunately, the problem will surface again and again until it is dealt with and eliminated. The list of barriers could be lengthy, but here are a few of the most obvious. As you read them, consider how you are doing in the area of relationships.

Relationships turn sour for many reasons but often because one person has a blind spot.

RELATIONSHIP BARRIER #1: HIDDEN FEELINGS
Holding one's cards close to your chest is a good tactic in poker, but it's a fail-safe way of sending the message "I'll only give you the information I choose and when I choose." Some individuals fear that once they are truly known—the cards are revealed—they won't be liked or accepted. The woman at the well held back when talking with Jesus until He made it safe.[29] He engaged her with questions and soft answers until she was willing to be honest with Him. Jesus had an advantage, of course; He knew what cards she was holding. But anyone who is savvy about human behavior knows the most obvious cards.

Shallow relationships continue when people are afraid to reveal the hand they are dealt; they won't move beyond casual encounters and their relationships will never fully satisfy.

RELATIONSHIP BARRIER #2: RESENTMENTS
If someone has been deeply hurt by another, their relationship cannot heal or grow until the primary cause is identified and dealt with. A single offense can be great enough to end a relationship; more often than not, however, people drift apart because their association has become toxic. A relationship can become unhealthy in one of five ways.

Shallow relationships continue when people are afraid to reveal the hand they are dealt.

1. One-sided commitment

It boils down to feeling a lack of appreciation and being used. Person A puts a lot of thought and energy into a relationship with person B, trying to live out 1 Corinthians 13:4–7, which declares,

> Love is patient, love is kind. It does not envy, it does not boast, it is not proud. It is not rude, it is not self-seeking, it is not easily angered, it keeps no record of wrongs. Love does not delight in evil but rejoices with the truth. It always protects, always trusts, always hopes, always perseveres.
> (1 Corinthians 13:4–7)

This individual pours himself or herself into the relationship, only to realize later that Person B not only takes their friendship for granted, he or she is using Person A. One-sided commitments are doomed from the start. Sometimes people hang on for a while, hoping things will change or questioning how they are interpreting the situation. Eventually, the pain becomes too much and the relationship ends.

2. Competition

Maintaining a close relationship with someone perceived as a competitor can be quite difficult. For example, best friends in college can see their friendship unravel when both enter the same competitive environment in the corporate world. But it doesn't have to be that way. David and Jonathan, potential rivals for the throne of Israel, enjoyed a long-lasting and profoundly deep friendship (1 Samuel 13–31). Their love for each other could stand all tests because David didn't want to be Jonathan, and Jonathan didn't want to be David. They were truly content to be themselves and to enjoy the blessings God gave them.

Beware of envy, however. Time has a way of eroding the nobility of the one who plays second fiddle.

3. Verbal Betrayal

"What's spoken in this room, stays in this room." That is the admonition of the small group leader laying the groundwork for the safe expression of deep personal thoughts or life experiences. And it works, that is, until one person shares something outside the group that was intended to be private. Relationships cannot stand the lack of trust that follows. "The unfaithful are destroyed by their duplicity" (Proverbs 11:3).

Most people don't try to hurt the one about whom they gossip. But titillating news is hard to suppress. The humdrum of life looks for sensations or bits of information to spice it up. That's why James dedicated the third chapter in his book to explore metaphors for the tongue. He knew that more damage can be inflicted and more lives destroyed by that small instrument of power than by any other weapon. In each illustration, James shows that someone more powerful than human nature or the tongue must be in control. A bit is used in a horse's mouth to turn the animal when in the hands of a competent rider. Its pilot controls the rudder of a ship, or the vessel would be forever off course and tossed around by the waves of circumstance. Because no human being can control the tongue, it must be guarded ferociously and constantly be committed to the Holy Spirit's control.

4. Mocking and Put-downs
Mocking is another form of verbal abuse. It imitates a person for the purpose of laughter in order to show contempt or to ridicule, usually taking words or reactions out of context. Mockery is not only a barrier to relationships; it shows contempt for another, even when done in jest. "Whoever corrects a mocker invites insult; whoever rebukes a wicked man incurs abuse" (Proverbs 9:7). Sometimes friends enjoy verbal sparring, but when jokes start to get personal, the friendship can take an ugly turn. Great wisdom knows when to back off and season the conversation with encouraging words.

5. Smothering
Certain personality types are warm, caring, eager to please. They enjoy being with you, are committed to making you happy, would never do or say anything to hurt you. They also tend to become overprotective, to take on a mothering quality. A fine line stands between being concerned and being nosy— between caring and smothering. Attempts to get too close feel threatening to the other person because he or she wants space, to be able to breathe and live without every thought and action being observed and critiqued by another.

The danger is that the smothered individual can develop physical problems if he or she internalizes the stress and refuses to set boundaries with those who do more harm than good. Research shows that smothering relationships take away a person's sense of control, which can lead to a negative impact on physical health.

Another form of smothering is when one person is always right and the other is always assumed to be wrong. No matter what is said, the smothering one sees absolutely no reason to confess his or her share of responsibility in the conflict. This can lead to a barrier so wide that it will eventually destroy the relationship for both the one who smothers and the smothered.

RELATIONSHIP BARRIER #3: RISKY BEHAVIOR
Normally, risky behavior is equated with adolescence; however, adults can also sabotage a relationship by engaging in addictions or illegal behavior.

Excessive drinking, for example, is risky behavior, and most of the reasons are obvious. Not only are health, job, and other drivers at risk but also those closest to the drinker. A spouse, child, or friend will flee if threatened. Alcoholics Anonymous and other 12-step programs have saved millions who

---

Signs of an Unhealthy Relationship:

1. *One-sided Commitment*
2. *Competition*
3. *Verbal Betrayal*
4. *Mocking and Put-Downs*
5. *Smothering*

were in the process of destroying their lives. Alcoholics Anonymous claims to have over two million members in over 150 countries. Imagine how many friends and family members are affected, both those who were forever scarred by the drunk and those who were restored because help was found.

Physicians who treat alcoholics say that at some point a "psychic change" takes place when people submit to an unquenchable craving for alcohol and, though remorseful and after having made a firm resolve to never drink again, slide down the same slope. At first they think that they can drink in moderation but not be controlled by it. But alcohol is a demon they cannot control on their own; thus, part of the psychic change is feeling doomed and utterly without hope. At that point, it is as much a spiritual issue as it is physical. At the point when we are in over our heads, we cry out for help.

If your life is unraveling because of alcohol or any other addiction, get help. Call a counselor, a pastor, or a friend who has been there. Millions have seen the fortune of family and friends restored—you can too.

RELATIONSHIP BARRIER #4: CHANGES IN LIFE

Life is never static, even though it is changing at an imperceptible pace. Sometimes the change is more apparent and drastic, especially when a person comes to Christ, and the old values and way of life fall off like an old garment. Paul wrote, "If anyone is in Christ, he is a new creation; the old has gone, the new has come!" (2 Corinthians 5:17).

Not everyone is thrilled with the new values embraced by a friend or spouse, especially if those values threaten the person's worldview or lifestyle. Many relationships have not survived someone's spiritual transformation. The two come to a fork in the road and never will be on the same path again.

Other changes allow relationships to slip away. You have heard the old adage, "out of sight—out of mind." A person may move away and then try to maintain the bond that was once there, but it's nearly impossible. Aging, adversity, health issues, and other life changes have a way of changing the dynamics of a relationship. This is a natural process that we should permit to happen without remorse. But all changes have the potential to bring about sadness. Those who don't want the changes to be a barrier to a relationship need a strong, mutual commitment to work against the gravitational pull with an equal determination to stay connected. This must be intentional—no relationships survive passivity, no matter whether it is marriage or friendship.

BUILDING STRONG RELATIONSHIPS: YOU AND YOUR NETWORK

The fact is, humans work best in community. As Solomon wrote, "Though one may be overpowered, two can defend themselves. A cord of three strands is not quickly broken" (Ecclesiastes 4:12). Adding numbers to the social equation can add strength, but without an understanding of roles and purposes for the added strands, the result will be a knot. A person may have many friends and numerous acquaintances, but the quality of those relationships can be helpful or destructive.

Those who study social networks point to at least four critical links in the network chain. Dr. David Krakchardt, a leading researcher in social networks, uses the metaphor of a "Kite Network" to describe the way people are connected to one another. It is a good illustration and more understandable if we assign the letters A, B, C, and D to the four key links for a kite.

This diagram assigns these roles.

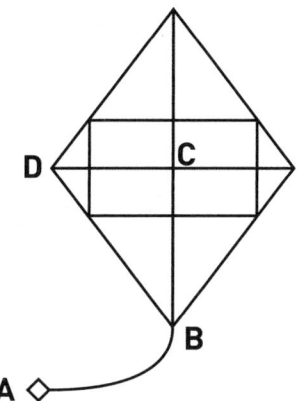

A. The A stands for ANCHOR. This is the person who steers you in the right direction and is a stabilizing influence during turbulence. This can be your mother or father, a mentor, a family member, or a friend. For the sake of memory, we will assign four characteristics that make an anchor an anchor by using the acronym "WISE."

Wisdom

Unfortunately, this is not in ample supply. A person's life anchor needs solid ideas and a Solomon-like quality of providing understanding about how the world works—what product does the world need, even if the world doesn't know it? They have a strong foundation of faith that connects both Biblical wisdom and the wisdom of the world.

Insight

Knowing how to apply wisdom takes insight. Sometimes this involves timing. That is, when is the best time to roll out a product or to tackle a major project? Who are the key players? What other products are on the market that may become a potential competition or a barrier? It is also the ability to verbalize or express knowledge. Some people have wisdom but are unable to express it.

Savvy

A person can have the wisdom to understand what products or programs are needed and the insight of when to roll them out, but he or she also needs the practical know-how or common sense of how to get the job done. This doesn't happen by just thinking wise thoughts. It takes appropriate action at the appropriate time. It also takes the persistence that is required to overcome inertia.

Experience

Nothing gives clarity to life like experience. The experienced person knows where the land mines are located. This person knows how people respond. He or she knows that good ideas often run out of steam or are undercapitalized. To have credibility, the anchor must speak from experience and not from prejudice. This person can be trusted, for experience has taught him or her that only those who are faithful can have a deep impact on another human and on the goals they seek to accomplish.

An ANCHOR may not have all four of these characteristics in equal proportion, but we know one thing for certain: We trust his or her judgment. We know that this person is willing to give us his or her time and serious thought.

B. The next link in the social network is the BROKER. A broker takes another person's wisdom, adds his or her own, and then unlocks the door of opportunity. The broker is the most critical person in the action/connection structure of the kite. We will use the word "KEY" to describe this person's role.

Knowledge

The broker's knowledge is in the area of what you need to do to get the job done and the people it will take to get moving. This person is not just a well-connected person with multiple friends; he or she is connected in the right places with the right people. Some have called this person a "deal maker" or a "rain maker" because things get done when he or she goes into action. The wheels spin very little; this person can make a couple of phone calls and connect us to people who can change our horizon.

Equity

This is relationship equity. The broker not only knows whom to call; he or she knows that the people called will answer the phone or return the call. That kind of trust is built over time. Brokers have earned the right to have access, and that makes them very special people.

The apostle Paul was a world-class broker. His spiritual office was "apostle," but his skills were as an anchor and a broker. His wisdom flowed through his pen to the churches of Rome, Corinth, Galatia, Ephesus, Colossae, and Thessalonica. He took the time to provide guidance for Silas, Barnabas, Titus, Timothy, and others.

With Onesimus, he became a broker.[30] Onesimus, a runaway slave from the household of Philemon, had somehow met Paul in Rome. Then he became a Christian and an encouragement to Paul while Paul was in chains in a Roman prison. Paul wrote a letter to ask Philemon to receive Onesimus now as a brother in Christ, not as a slave. Paul's plea for Onesimus is based upon Onesimus' spiritual transformation but also on the friendship equity that Paul had with Philemon. Paul used some of that equity when he wrote, "So if you

---

Your anchor is like the North Star, always there, always in the same place, always helping you to get your bearings for the journey.

consider me a partner, welcome him as you would welcome me" (Philemon 1:17). Philemon could not resist. The right person made the appeal. Onesimus was restored to favor and his place in Philemon's household.

Yearning Help

Paul was not reluctantly approaching Philemon. He loved Onesimus and made this a part of his appeal, "Yet I appeal to you on the basis of love. I then, as Paul—an old man and now also a prisoner of Christ Jesus" (Philemon 1:9). A broker won't use his friendship equity without a driving desire to do so. So a good case has to be developed for the course of action. We should remember, however, that not every contact made by a broker will be productive. The contact may have other pressing issues or may not be ready to respond to a specific need. But the contact respects the broker, will respond if possible, and is not put-off by the request. Just the opposite is true—the contact is honored to be in the broker's network.

C. The third link is a CONNECTOR. The connector is at the center of contact cross sections. We will use the metaphor "LINK" to describe the characteristics of this person's position.

Lots of Friends

Some people are like that—they are everyone's friends. They have been in social circulation for a long time, and people enjoy being around them. Like the broker, they have no problem having people return their phone calls or getting a foursome for a round of golf. If they receive a call from a broker and decide to spring into action, they have no difficulty in coming up with names.

In some ways, Peter was a connector. His personality and position within the Galilean fishing community gave him access to everyone associated with his trade. Eventually, the church would meet at his house—typical for someone well connected.

Ideas

Connectors are also idea people. They may not have every connection needed, but they make good suggestions about social paths not yet traveled.

New networks

One of the greatest assets of a connector is to introduce us to new networks. If our social, business, and church life all involve the same people, we will soon run thin on contacts. Life consists of a variety of communities. We have a family support community, a career community, a faith community, an investment community, a recreation community, and, perhaps, a personal growth community. If the connectors from each of these communities get to know each other, it multiplies the breadth, depth, and speed in which the word gets out about our idea, need, or project.

Knowledge

Connectors are not just social butterflies; they are also people of depth, or they won't prove to be much use in disseminating thoughtful ideas. The best connectors are known to be people of substance, not panhandlers. This whole process is not about hype and shortcuts to meet unworthy goals. If that becomes the perceived agenda, the network will quickly collapse.

D. The final link is the DOERS. The connectors launch them into action. They are the people who get the job done. The metaphor of their characteristics is "TAP."

Talented

Depending on the size and scope of the project, unique talents will be required. Almost every situation needs graphic arts and marketing. There can be a great buzz about an idea and high voltage synapses firing from connectors to the connected, but if no one has the skill to capture the public's attention, it will be dead in the water. Part of the wisdom employed by the connector is knowing what talent resources are needed and then who to call.

Available

You might find the person with the right talent, and he or she may even seem interested in the project. But availability is essential. Many projects have been brought to a halt because a "doer" with a specific talent volunteered to help but, in reality, didn't have the time. It really becomes frustrating when they won't admit this and continue to make everyone feel they are still on track to make it happen.

Productive

All projects have timelines and deadlines. A talented person who has made the commitment to be available can still create problems by delays in productivity. When a target is met, something is produced or energy is unleashed that is invigorating to all who are involved. That is absolutely necessary, especially when the project is long term, taking months and maybe years to be accomplished. In that case, periodic bursts of adrenaline are needed to keep the momentum going. The production of a talented person can provide that energy.

WHO'S IN YOUR NETWORK?

One social network does not meet all needs; a look over your shoulder will tell you that. Take a sheet of paper and list across the bottom the five categories where social networks played a role in your development:

Family Support—Career—Faith
Investment—Personal Growth

Create a kite for each of these categories, by actually drawing the kite and assigning names or resources for each of the links. Here is an example for FAITH.

SOCIAL ASSETS – YOU AND YOUR RELATIONSHIPS

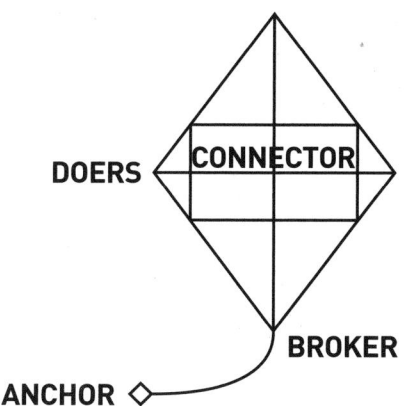

DOERS—Who provided a talent that helped produce fruit (teachers, preachers, books, people who met a special need)?
CONNECTORS—What people or resources (books, etc.) within different religious networks gave you the greatest number of contacts?
BROKER—Who introduced you to the network of people and ideas that made your faith grow?
ANCHOR—Who was your spiritual father, mother, mentor, or friend?

As you do this for the essential areas of your life, you'll not only see that the social network was engaged without your being aware of what to call it, but now have the creativity to think about the next area that needs a network.

TAKE ACTION

Read Philemon (all 25 verses).
Look closely at the words Paul uses to urge Philemon to accept his former servant and restore him to his duties.

Have you at one point acted as Paul to mediate the restoration of a broken relationship? Have you been an Onesimus who left a job undone? Are you a Philemon who is in a position of offering reconciliation? Stop and prayerfully ask the Holy Spirit to reveal your responsibility in these types of relationships. What is the Holy Spirit saying to you?

Let's return to the kite illustration. Consider what the Holy Spirit has spoken to you through the exercise above, and now prayerfully think through your relationship network:

Are you an anchor for anyone? Have you acted as a broker for another? Do you help make connections whenever possible? Are you a doer who is able to serve a faithful friend? Prayerfully ask the Holy Spirit to help you recognize opportunities to assist others and give you wisdom to know what to do.

Be intentional: What are you going to do about what you've learned?

Be specific: What action will you take in the near future to begin applying what you've learned? When will you do it?

Be accountable: Pray it through. Share your plan with a friend and seek his/her prayer and counsel for your next step.

3

PRIORITY THREE

3

"LOVE YOUR NEIGHBOR ..."

MATTHEW 22:39

A PERSONAL, PROGRESSIVE COMMITMENT TO RELATIONSHIPS

OVERVIEW

Life can become a fast pursuit of wealth and possessions, a perpetual focus on strengthening the financial bottom line, a solitary race to get ahead. Unfortunately, the price of victory could be the loss of the most valuable asset of all—personal relationships. When considering the legacy of a life well-lived, esteemed author Ann Voskamp writes,

> "I've never had a bucket list, and I'm thinking that I don't want a bucket list as much as I want a poured bucket list. I'm thinking: **The best lives don't have Bucket Lists as much as they have *Empty* Bucket lists.** *Because the thing is when I kick the bucket, I don't want there to be anything left in my bucket. When I kick the bucket, I want the bucket right empty.* I don't want my life to be how I took experiences — but that I gave exceedingly. That I gave every last drop, that I poured it all out, that I held nothing back. **Because the way to really live is not to try to fill your life up — but to spill your life out.**"[1]

When you commit to strengthening your bond with the people God has given you, you build up the body of Christ (1 Corinthians 12:12-26). Few people, however, cultivate the skills necessary to pour themselves out—to become a better spouse, better parent, better friend, or better member of the local and universal church. While we understand the value of training in virtually every other discipline of life, we tend to "wing it" when relating to others . . . until a crisis forces us to seek help.

Too many Christians discover the First Priority (a personal, progressive commitment to Jesus Christ) and stop there. They see their relationship with the Lord as a private matter that doesn't involve participation with others. If something goes wrong in a relationship, or they don't like the way things are done, they simply pack up their personal Jesus and leave. But when Christians understand that they are individual members of the body of Christ, their perspective shifts: they begin to see how vitally important they and others are to fulfilling the mission of all believers. They experience a dynamic shift from an inward "What's in it for me?" attitude to a powerful "How may I serve you?" mentality.

Once we enter into relationship with Jesus (Priority One) and allow Him to renew our minds to show us who we are in Him (Priority Two), then we begin to fulfill our purpose and calling within the body of Christ to build others up and deepen our relationships with other believers… as parents, spouses, mentors, friends, and so on. We see how powerful the body becomes when all members are working together, focused on Jesus, and not on ourselves.

In our fast-paced, highly-technical world of social media, we have never been so *connected* to one another…but so out of touch *personally*. Technology– while a great convenience– has only served to perpetuate a lack of depth and authenticity in our relationships and communications. Priority Three refocuses us on authentic, face-to-face, heart-to-heart, life-on-life human relationships, the kind that technology can't produce and that are critical to the strength of our culture.

A man who embodied Priority Three and had a profound impact on John Tolson and Larry Kreider was Jim Smith. Jim invested his final years as the head of a counseling ministry. All relationships were important to Jim, and he succeeded at all of them. His influence was so widespread that he became the focus of a lead article in *Texas Monthly Magazine*. Unfortunately, pancreatic cancer took him in mid-life.

Jim's legacy lives on in the words penned by Curtis Meadows, words now framed and displayed in one of Jim's former offices. As you read this tribute, reflect on what can happen when a person lives out Priority Three.

I HAVE A FRIEND CALLED JIM SMITH

I had a friend called Jim Smith. He greeted me as "Brother" and waved goodbye as Friend. He listened with his heart but spoke with his head. God gifted him with wisdom, yet tempered it with love. I had a friend called Jim Smith.

As Teacher, Mentor, Counselor, or Coach, he was there beside me. He was there for my family, for my colleagues, and for those I did not know. He was there for his family, for his Church, and for all who cried out. He was there because he cared and because his Master needed him there. I had a friend called Jim Smith.

His name was common but the man was not. From rough and rocky soil came this man of compassion, forgiveness, and learning. His mind always seeking, the hands always busy, the love always there, he was alive in God's service. I had a friend called Jim Smith.

"What can I do for you?" he asked. *"Do you need help?"* he called. "Oh yes," we replied. "Oh, yes, yes, yes." And he came to us and we cried with him and he loved us to life again. "Oh yes, yes, yes," we called, and he held us and laughed with us and lifted our burdens. He was God's love alive on

this earth. It really was there and it was brought even to us by this humble man. Oh my yes, I had a friend called Jim Smith.

He gave us his time, the one unique gift we can give to another. He spent his life serving others, and I was one of the others. In this hurried world of false importance, he paused to touch me, to focus his precious moments of life upon me, bringing messages of encouragement, weaving strands of hope and understanding. At those moments, he was the vessel of my Savior, pouring forth from the pages of Scripture, he was authenticating the promises, we were not alone to face our terrors. I had *more* than a friend in Jim Smith.

Now, how do we deal with his parting. How we shall miss him! So many fears yet ahead, so many hills yet to climb, so many like me, yet afraid. *"Be still,"* he calls at Christ's side. *"I'm yet with you. I'm alive in your heart; I'm alive in your mind. I'm alive in my books; I'm alive in my tapes. I've left you my wisdom; I've left you my thoughts; I've left you my love. You were my friend. I witnessed God's love for you . . . go and do the same for others. Share His love and teachings, continue the ministry and God will use you instead of me."*

Even now he is teaching, even now he is caring, even now he's alive in my life. What a friend is my living friend, Jim Smith! All thanks be to You, Lord Jesus! Amen! (Curtis W. Meadows, Jr., February 26, 1993)

What a legacy for Jim Smith! As New-York Times Best-Selling Author Andy Andrews says, "Everybody leaves a legacy, not everybody leaves a good one." How will your legacy read? Resolve today to not only continue growing in your relationship with Jesus, but also in your relationships with other believers.

CHAPTER 15: MAKING YOUR MARRIAGE SIZZLE PART 1

Scan here to watch the video!

When a man and woman come together to form a lifelong union, they enter the covenant of marriage with a set of expectations. Some expectations take the form of vows in the marriage ceremony; most, however, are unconscious, unspoken desires and dreams that may or may not be realistic. Soon after the honeymoon, reality intrudes upon the fantasy, and the couple must decide which marriage they want to nurture: the marriage of their dreams or the marriage they have. Sadly, many cling to their fantasy marriage and become increasingly disappointed and disillusioned. As one older gentleman quipped, "Marriage is like a three-ring circus. First comes the engagement ring, then the wedding ring, followed by suffer-ring." His wife said, simply, "The sizzle has fizzled."

The truth is, good marriages don't just happen. A good marriage is built over time as husband and wife work in partnership to take what they have and then create something mutually satisfying. Each marriage will have its own unique challenges, but all have at least one in common: gender differences. Here are a few significant differences worth noting.

HOW MEN AND WOMEN COMMUNICATE

Generally speaking, women tend to focus on specifics in a conversation while men tend to talk in generalities. Women want details; men get straight to the bottom line. For example, if a man goes on a trip, he returns home to a series of questions from his wife: "Where did you stay? What kind of room was it? Where did you eat? What did you eat?" She wants details because she enjoys the *process* of communicating as a way to feel connection with her husband. The man may not remember the details of his trip because he didn't consider them important at the time. For him, the *content* of communication is primary. Consequently, he may see her questioning as nagging or fishing for useless information. He can't understand why the Cliffs Notes version doesn't satisfy her; she can't understand why he's holding back.

For women, the process of communication is primary, and it comes naturally to them. For men, however, talking is an acquired skill that takes effort and energy. So, if a wife hits her husband with thirty questions the minute he walks in the door, when he is tired and ready to unpack and unwind from the trip, he may appear agitated. She may take his desire for a little space as a rejection.

When a couple comes to terms with their fundamental differences in communication, she will learn how to time her questions well and he will learn how to express his need for space without rejecting her. He will discover how to spell out in detail the things she wants to know and she will make allowances for his bottom-line style of expressing himself. These are gifts each partner gives the other to build a strong marriage.

HOW MEN AND WOMEN DEAL WITH EMOTIONS

Generally speaking, the bundle of nerves connecting the hemispheres of the brain is much larger for women than men. As a result, women tend to be in touch with their feelings and their thoughts simultaneously. Men, on the other hand, tend to process thoughts first, and then, maybe, their feelings. This has nothing to do with intellectual capacity but the manner in which they process experiences. Beyond the physical differences, however, we are shaped by cultural expectations of masculinity and femininity. As David W. Smith writes,

> He shall not cry.
> He shall not display weakness.
> He shall not need affection or gentleness or warmth.
> He shall comfort but not desire comforting.
> He shall be needed but not need.
> He shall touch but not be touched.
> He shall be steel not flesh.
> He shall be inviolate in his manhood.
> He shall stand alone.[2]

With this cultural voice shouting in his ear, the man stoically goes through life responding to a woman's expressed feelings as though they were thoughts, saying something like, "You shouldn't feel that way." And, in response, a woman might assume that her man has no emotional needs or that he is somehow inferior for losing touch with his feelings.

By understanding how God created men and women to deal with emotions differently, a husband and wife can learn how to meet one another's needs without criticism. That's a critical first step in building a partnership based on mutual respect. Each can say to the other, "You are not better or worse, but different. How can I be a better partner for you?"

HOW MEN AND WOMEN APPROACH SEX

A couple had been fighting with each other, and the woman was overheard to say indignantly, "How can you think of having sex when we're not even speaking?" The man replied, "I thought we could do it without talking."

Their conversation illustrates how differently men and women approach sex. Some social scientists say that men tend to give emotional warmth so they can have sex, while women will have sex in order to have a shared relational encounter. For all the hype about whether women experience an earth-moving physical experience during the sexual act, the response to an

---

By understanding how God created men and women to deal with emotions differently, a husband and wife can learn how to meet one another's needs without criticism.

Ann Landers question on the subject puts it in perspective. Out of 100,000 responses, 70,000 women said what they enjoy most about sex with their mate is the feeling of being close, nurtured, safe, warm, and connected.

Scripture is clear that the physical relationship is for the expression of love, commitment, and unity. It exists because of the need for a partner (Genesis 2:18), the need to multiply and be fruitful (Genesis 1:28), and the need for sexual fulfillment (1 Corinthians 7:3–5).

HOW MEN AND WOMEN BUILD FRIENDSHIPS

Men build friendships around activities. They fish, hunt, play golf, and go to sporting events together. Sometimes they center their friendship around projects, like working together on a home, rebuilding a car, or, if they live near a ranch, helping build a barn or branding cattle. Women, however, build relationships more directly by sharing with one another. They talk, share their stories, describe their feelings, and empathize with one another. If they need to plan an event together like a women's retreat, they will meet three times as often as men, not out of necessity, but because a planning meeting is an opportunity to connect.

When a husband and wife understand their differences, they can learn how to leverage their combined strengths.

A man often has a difficult time building long-lasting, meaningful relationships because he sees other men as competitors. He may have an array of business friends or recreational buddies, but few close confidants.

Former chaplain of the U.S. Senate, the late Dick Halverson, told the story of having lunch one time with a man who owned one of the largest construction companies in Los Angeles. After spending time in conversation over a wonderful meal, the man finally looked at his watch and asked Dick, "What is it that you want?" In other words, "What is the purpose of our getting together?" Dick responded, "I don't want anything. I just want to be with you." Dick knew that relational dynamics change when you don't have an agenda but want to get to know people on a deeper level.

When a husband and wife understand their differences—the advantages and challenges of each perspective—they can learn how to leverage their combined strengths and compensate for one another's weaknesses. This partnership encourages closeness; closeness leads to intimacy, and it's intimacy that makes a marriage sizzle, behind closed doors and outside the bedroom.

THE SIZZLE

Before we examine actions that will make a marriage sizzle, we need to make several observations.

> **1. We change as we get older.** The person you married is not the same today as he or she was at the altar. We find that difficult to believe and refuse to become proactive in helping our partners and ourselves recognize critical changes and then deal with them. It may be true that we can't teach

an old dog new tricks, but you aren't an old dog. God gave you the capacity to change by allowing Him to change your attitude and your heart.

2. Two people living together do not automatically grow together. We are like emotional bank accounts in which we are either making deposits or withdrawals by the way we speak to, and treat, one another. All of life's experiences either add or subtract until one day we realize how satisfied and fulfilled we are, or sadly, that our account is nearly depleted.

3. No matter how challenging or poor a marriage becomes, it can change. God has given us a reset button for relationships— it's called repentance, learning how to say, "I'm sorry." These two words are difficult to say, especially as the first one to say them, but they are powerful. If you refuse to say, "I'm sorry," you will add layer upon layer of resentment and wake up one day wondering what happened.

4. Any relationship, even a good one, can be improved. A special touch, an encouraging word, an engaging conversation, a timely gift, time to be away alone—just the two of you—can keep the bloom on the rose.

5. We can't avoid the importance that God plays in marriage. Marriage is an instrument to shape and direct our lives. A faulty relationship with your partner will affect your relationship with God, and a faulty relationship with God will always affect your relationship with your partner.

It looks like this:

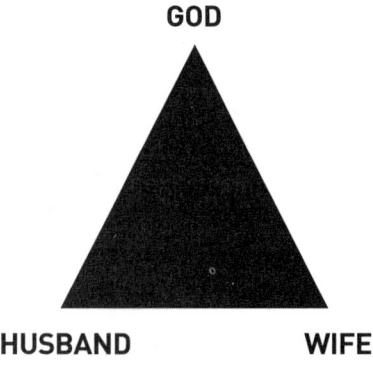

> *God gave you the capacity to change by allowing Him to change your attitude and your heart.*

The closer a man or woman comes to God, the closer they come to each other because it creates depth in their relationship. In shallow marriages, each is concerned with having the stuff of life without going to the *source* of life. Marriage, then, is like a megaphone to get your attention that God wants you to grow together and to become all He has in mind for you as you come closer to Him.

So now we examine four actions that will make a marriage sizzle—two in this chapter and two in the next.

SIZZLE #1: COMMITMENT

When it's all said and done, wealth, possessions, social status, beauty, or even warm and fuzzy feelings cannot make a marriage work. All of those things are like shifting sand, too unstable to support anything permanent. The key is commitment, the choice of each partner to remain devoted to the other regardless of circumstances.

In the last book of the Old Testament, God's messenger, Malachi, tells Israel why God was displeased, why He no longer paid attention to their prayers: "The Lord is acting as the witness between you and the wife of your youth, because you have broken faith with her, though she is your partner, the wife of your marriage covenant" (Malachi 2:14). In Malachi 2:16 we read that God hates divorce. He hates this act that contractually ends a marriage, thus breaking faith with your marriage partner, because it cheapens the covenant made before Him and wreaks havoc on the family. Make no mistake, however; God doesn't hate people who get divorced. *Grace abounds!*

God views marriage as a life-long commitment.

There is no doubt God views marriage as a life-long commitment. You stood at an altar before your partner, your family, friends, and God and committed to your marriage, "For as long as we both shall live." Whatever your marriage state is today, remember God never fails to meet you where you are and to bring you into right standing before Him. If your marriage fails beyond restoration, God stands ready to forgive any of your faults and failings, if you will repent. Admit your failings and avoid rationalizing away any poor choices by you or your spouse. Get real with God and get the help you need to do what's necessary to reach restoration.

Commitment to the marriage is more important than the feelings of love. If you are committed to a person, you will work at making the relationship work when things get tough. Family Counseling Director Jim Smith said, "Love is constructive behavior, doing what is best for your partner regardless of how you feel toward him or her at the moment." It's learning to serve the one to whom you are married. As the old country preacher said, "Get your doer doing, and your feeler will follow." Make an unconditional commitment to do the right thing to build your marriage and the feelings of romance will return in time.

All marriages have problems, even those that appear perfect. Yet, even when facing what seem to be insurmountable odds, they survive and many

He has sent me to bind up the brokenhearted, to proclaim the year of the Lord's favor, to comfort all who mourn, to bestow on them a crown of beauty for ashes, the oil of gladness instead of mourning, and a garment of praise instead of a spirit of despair. They will be called oaks of righteousness, a planting of the Lord for the display of his splendor.
Isaiah 61:1-3 paraphrased

times, become stronger. Why? Because these couples decided before they were married that divorce would not be an option after they were married. As they entered into this covenant relationship before the Lord, they determined to rely on Him to heal their hurts, look to His Word and Godly counsel to teach them how to serve each other, and commit to remain together while they waited for the Lord to restore what was lost.

SIZZLE #2: COMMUNICATION

Marriage counselors say that these are the most prevalent problems:

(1) expectations are not met; (2) lines of communication have broken down. Pastor, author, and master communicator Charlie Shedd once told about a woman who said, "You heard of the sphinx? I married it! I feel like I'm living with a total stranger. Our marriage has never been very good, but lately it's been getting worse. Do you know how barren it is to exist with someone who makes guttural sounds and that's only when he wants something like sex or food, or to change the channel?"

God refers to your spouse as a "partner" (Malachi 2:14). It's difficult to partner with someone without clear communication. One man said, "I know we don't communicate, but it's one of my few pleasures." That's not a marriage; that's a domestic cold war. It's doubtful their legal union will survive, especially if that husband faces a significant difficulty and his wife doesn't know it. Take the case of George for example.

George, a man in his late 50s, was about to be laid off from work, which would mean personal bankruptcy if he didn't find another job soon. His wife had no clue about the difficulties he faced because he refused to talk about it. One weekend, she decided to fly to Texas to spend time with her daughter and family. It had "perfect" written all over it—go shopping, enjoy eating out, spoil her grandkids. Little did she know she would receive the most horrifying phone call of her life. George had cleaned the house, typed a note, taped the note to the windshield of the car, and then took his own life with a borrowed shotgun. Bankrupt, distraught, and isolated, George couldn't bear the thought of telling his wife. He was unwilling to communicate and, therefore, unable to involve his partner in finding a solution to their crisis.

If George had been able to work through these levels with his wife, she undoubtedly would have done everything in her power to encourage him and to help him find a solution. He could have benefitted from her intuition and perspectives to resolve their financial issues, to say nothing of the intimacy gained by enduring hardship together.

It's impossible for a couple to avoid all communication, at least at some level–even if they do little more than bark out instructions or argue over trivial matters. John Powell in his classic book, *Why Am I Afraid To Tell You Who I Am*, identifies five levels of communication. The further a couple goes in this process, the more meaning their relationship enjoys.

Level 5: Cliché conversation
This level represents the weakest response to the human dilemma and the lowest level of self-communication. On this level, we talk in clichés, such as "How are you? . . . How is your family? . . . Where have you been?" We say things like: "I like your dress very much." "I hope we can get together real soon." "It's really good to see you." In fact, we really mean almost nothing of what we are asking or saying.

Level 4: Reporting facts about others
On this fourth level, we do not step very far outside the prison of our loneliness into real communication because we expose almost nothing of ourselves. We remain contented to tell others what so-and-so has said or done. . . . We seek shelter in gossip items, conversation pieces, and little narrations about others. We give nothing of ourselves and invite nothing from others in return.

Level 3: My ideas and judgments
On this level, there is some communication of my person. I am willing to take this step out of my solitary confinement. I will take the risk of telling you some of my ideas and reveal some of my judgments and decisions. My communication remains under a strict censorship, however. As I communicate my ideas, etc., I will be watching you carefully. . . If you raise your eyebrow or narrow your eyes, if you yawn or look at your watch, I will probably retreat to safer ground.

Level 2: My feelings (emotions) – "Gut Level"
The things that most clearly differentiate and individuate me from others, that make the communication of my person unique knowledge, are my feelings or emotions. If you really want to know who I am, I must tell you about my stomach (gut-level) as well as my head. . . . If I tell you only the contents of my mind, I will be withholding a great deal about myself.

Level 1: Personal disclosure of fears and struggles
This is peak communication. All deep and authentic friendships, and especially the union of those who are married, must be based on absolute openness and honesty.[3]

Unfortunately, communication is not always as straightforward as it seems. First of all, communication involves more than the use of words. You may think you are communicating a message of concern and compassion, but your fidgety body language indicates you want out of there. According to A. Barbour, author of *Louder than Words: Nonverbal Communication*, inflection and tone makes up thirty-eight percent of communication, body language (mostly facial expressions) makes up fifty-five percent, and the actual words spoken are responsible for seven percent.

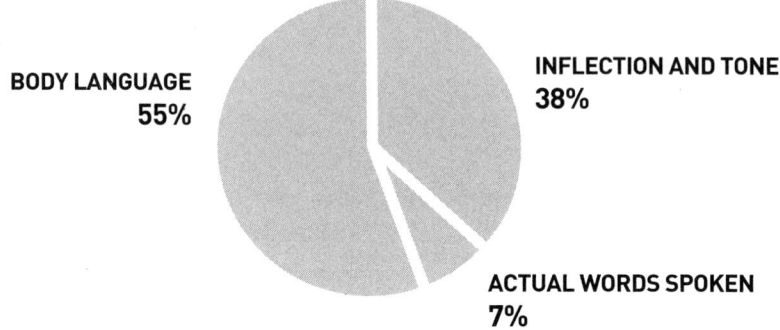

But even the actual words get lost in the fog. Every time you talk, there are six possible messages:

1. What you mean to say
2. What you actually say
3. What the other person hears
4. What the other person thinks he hears
5. What the other person says about what you said
6. What you think the other person said about what you said

Communication is especially difficult for men, who not only fear the complexity described above, but generally avoid activities in which they do not feel competent. Rather than risk making things worse by talking, many men take refuge in silence, hoping difficult issues will resolve themselves, or that a solution that doesn't involve talking will present itself. Unfortunately, they often fail to realize that avoiding communication does more damage to the relationship than communicating poorly. Talking may, indeed, cause more pain for both partners in the short term, but it offers greater potential in the long term for improving the quality of the relationship.

Think of it this way. If you're lost in a strange city without a map, pulling into a parking lot and just sitting still accomplishes nothing. Better to consult a map or ask directions (even if you're a man!) than to do nothing. In fact, driving in the wrong direction offers a greater chance of discovering the right course than sitting still. When one partner clams up, the relationship remains in limbo. There's no risk of failure, but each silent moment wastes an opportunity for growth.

TAKE ACTION

Read Philippians 2:1-4 from the J.B. Phillips paraphrase:
"Now if you have known anything of Christ's encouragement and of his reassuring love; if you have known something of the fellowship of his Spirit, and of compassion and deep sympathy, do make my joy complete–*live together in harmony, live together in love, as though you had only one mind and one spirit between you. Never act from motives of rivalry or personal vanity, but in humility think more of each other than you do of yourselves.* None of you should think only of his own affairs, but consider other people's interests also" (emphasis mine).[4]

The Biblical concept of marriage is that husbands and wives should *complete* each other, not *compete* with each other.

As you consider the differences between men and women (or, if you are married, your mate in particular), which difference presents the greatest challenge to marital happiness? Why?

In what ways can this challenge become an asset if each partner were to understand and empathize with the other? Think of a real-world, practical example.

What personal behavior or tendency keeps you from communicating effectively with your spouse or another significant person?

If you were to explain this behavior or tendency, how can this person use the information to improve communication?

When you are with your spouse or another significant person, ask these two questions:
"What makes communication on a deep level most difficult for you?"
"How can I make honest, vulnerable communication with me less difficult?"

Be intentional: What are you going to do about what you've learned?

Be specific: What action will you take in the near future to begin applying what you've learned? When will you do it?

Be accountable: Pray it through. Share your plan with a friend and seek his/her prayer and counsel for your next step.

CHAPTER 16: MAKING YOUR MARRIAGE SIZZLE PART 2

Scan here to watch the video!

In the last chapter, we discovered two of the four actions that make a marriage sizzle were commitment and communication. The two additional actions build on this solid foundation: caring and courtship. Take note, however, that caring and courtship have little meaning apart from an unconditionally committed marriage kept strong through good communication.

SIZZLE #3: CARING

Malachi 2:13–16 reminds us that God has little regard for the worship of men who treat their wives poorly. In fact, the prayers of a lousy husband carry little weight with the Lord. When the Israelites complained that their dutiful worship in the temple and their prayers for God's help did no good, the prophet Malachi wrote,

> You flood the Lord's altar with tears. You weep and wail because he no longer pays attention to your offerings or accepts them with pleasure from your hands. You ask, "Why?" It is because the Lord is acting as the witness between you and the wife of your youth, because you have broken faith with her, though she is your partner, the wife of your marriage covenant. Has not the Lord made them one? In flesh and spirit they are his. And why one? Because he was seeking godly offspring. So guard yourself in your spirit, and do not break faith with the wife of your youth. "I hate divorce," says the Lord God of Israel, "and I hate a man's covering himself with violence as well as with his garment," says the Lord Almighty. So guard yourself in your spirit, and do not break faith.
> (Malachi 2:13–16)

Our culture places undue emphasis on the romantic attraction between women and men. Furthermore, we believe compatibility somehow translates into longevity. The fact is, after the initial thrill of attraction has passed, our sinful, selfish natures will overlook compatibility and find fault in the smallest differences. When the first flush of infatuation gives way to real life—warts and everything—romance doesn't just happen. Romance occurs when two people who have the potential of living together for the rest of their lives decide to cultivate an enduring *friendship*. A spouse is a partner. A spouse is a loyal friend and, hopefully, a best friend.

Many try to kindle romance with superficial expressions of love. Expensive gifts. Bouquets of roses. Jewelry. Dinner for two in a dark restaurant. These can be wonderful tokens of love, but romance begins much simpler. A romantic relationship is the result of each partner asking and answering a simple question each day: "What kind of friend will I be today?" Rather than asking, "How will he or she meet my needs today?" a faithful partner makes friendship an intentional, deliberate act of the will. If friendship isn't your daily goal, forget about romance. Without friendship, your spouse will either be hurt or never edified in the way God intended.

So what are the characteristics of a caring friend that need to be understood and embraced? There are at least four.

1. Mutual Acceptance and Respect

When a man and woman commit themselves to each other in marriage, they commit to forsaking all others to establish this exclusive relationship. They leave their fathers and mothers (Ephesians 5:31) to focus on this primary relationship. They remain meaningfully engaged in all their existing relationships with family and friends, but they give first place to their marriage relationship; all other associations take a back seat. Each partner devotes himself or herself to Jesus Christ, who strengthens their marriage bond as they faithfully serve one another for the rest of their lives (1 Corinthians 7:3–4, 10–11). When mutual understanding and respect become core values in the home, faithfulness becomes as natural as breathing. Respect comes when the spouse is patient and understanding (Colossians 3:19) and when each honors the other (1 Peter 3:7). As the apostle Peter admonished husbands,

> Be considerate as you live with your wives, and treat them with respect as the weaker partner and as heirs with you of the gracious gift of life, so that nothing will hinder your prayers. (1 Peter 3:7)

Take note of the key words in Peter's admonition to husbands. He calls for the same kind of consideration expected of wives in 1 Peter 3:5–6. He also calls for husbands to "respect" their wives. The Greek term conveys the idea of treasuring something. In the same way we would give extra care and attention to a priceless Stradivarius,[5] Peter urges husbands to give extraordinary consideration for their wives. That means husbands should be considerate and respectful at two times—*when they feel like it and when they don't.*

A high profile TV actor married a woman he deeply loved and adored, a professional woman who had established a reputation as a rising star in the marketing department of her corporation. The wedding had all the glamour expected when two people of this stature joined together in marriage. They planned to exchange vows on the lawn of a resort, overlooking the Pacific

---

When mutual understanding and respect become core values in the home, faithfulness becomes as natural as breathing.

Spouses should be considerate and respectful at two times—when they feel like it and when they don't.

Ocean at sunset.

Prior to the ceremony, the couple met with the minister for counseling and to talk about their dreams, expectations, and eventual challenges. When asked why they were attracted to each other, they didn't answer with typical superficial responses because they had become good friends, despite their position, wealth, fame, and physical qualities. They *liked* each other as much as they loved each other. Their commitment seemed unshakable and their communication constant, meaningful, and fun. So they declared their intention to do whatever was necessary to both demonstrate and maintain their respect for one another.

Then the first test arrived. The wife realized that even though her husband wanted her to continue her career (if that is what she desired), she could not be a super executive and a super wife at the same time, especially at the beginning of their marriage. Out of consideration for him, she took the initiative and submitted a letter of resignation to the corporation. Together they agreed to start a similar business that could be run from their home. Regardless of whether the business succeeded, their marriage started on a solid foundation of mutual respect.

2. Mutual Responsibility

At times one partner can see the other struggling. A person who cares remains aware, sensitive, and ready to help.

A wife can feel overwhelmed when the children are young and require nearly twenty-four hour supervision, especially when she must work outside the home. The pressures of career and home invariably collide, taking a physical and emotional toll on a working mother and putting her on a collision course with a meltdown. The last thing the beleaguered wife needs is a lecture; she desperately needs a husband who will provide practical, hands-on help. Not advice. Not guidance. Not a new plan. Personal involvement. Assistance. That leads to a third characteristic.

3. Concerted Initiative

The word "concerted" is very important. It brings to mind the image of a concert with the brass, percussion, woodwinds, and string instruments blending together to create a moving piece of music. "Concerted" means "jointly arranged, planned, or carried out; coordinated," or "mutually contrived or agreed on; performed in unison."[6] A concerted effort draws upon all available energies and resources to get the job done.

A very faithful and talented man in ministry was at a low spot in his career. Out of energy and feeling unappreciated—even exploited by those he thought were friends—he began to lose his grip on hope. His wife sensed his struggle and picked up the conductor's baton. She planned a party. She called friends from out of town to put it on their schedule, and she arranged a location, catering services, and entertainment. She had committees organized to divide his load and multiply the output. People jumped on the bandwagon and each contributed what they could to the cause. After this concerted initiative, the man went home singing another tune. His marriage gave him not merely a wife, but a faithful friend.

4. Unconditional Love

At some point, every married person behaves in unlovable ways toward his or her spouse. We will mess up, foul our nests, and behave like jerks. Some will even break the hearts of their partners. We live in an age of seduction and exhaustion, two volatile ingredients that frequently prompts one partner to dishonor the other. When this happens, a marriage falters and divorce may follow. But it doesn't have to. Unconditional love says, "I abhor your sinful behavior, but I choose to love *you* regardless. I will not tolerate your sin, but I choose to forgive you and will respond to your efforts to rebuild trust. When you behave unfaithfully, I will not retaliate, but remain faithful."

Unconditional love doesn't require one to become the doormat of the other. On the contrary, true love seeks the highest, greatest good of another, which may call for firm boundaries and a demand for sinful behavior to end. Consequently, unconditional love sometimes requires a tough-love confrontation. Unconditional love does not respond to offences with retaliation, but with firm compassion and a call to do what is right. Unconditional love "is not rude, it is not self-seeking, it is not easily angered, it keeps no record of wrongs. Love does not delight in evil but rejoices with the truth. It always protects, always trusts, always hopes, always perseveres" (1 Corinthians 13:5–7). In the face of wrongdoing, love encourages another to put aside wrongdoing and expresses belief in his or her ability to do good.

This kind of love is humbling. This kind of firm, compassionate, steadfast love doesn't make you want to take advantage of your spouse; it inspires respect. This kind of unconditional love makes you want to avoid any behavior that disappoints your spouse, to avoid any circumstance that might cause him or her to ask the anguished question, "How could you do this?"

SIZZLE #4: COURTSHIP

All too often, courtship lasts a very short time. In the beginning, the promise of possibilities keeps the man and woman on their best behavior: kind, courteous, generous, fun, entertaining, spontaneous, creative, and understanding. As each begins to take the other for granted, however, and the novelty wears off, couples find little reason to put their best foot forward. After the wedding ceremony, the challenge is gone; the once-inseparable pair begins to drift apart from each other and away from the ideal people they once presented.

At some point, the couple must make a conscious decision to reenergize their romance by reengaging their courtship skills. Originally, he proactively pursued her, using his creative skills to show his interest and to receive her favor. In the beginning, she graciously responded and made him feel like a

---

Unconditional love "is not rude, it is not self-seeking, it is not easily angered, it keeps no record of wrongs. Love does not delight in evil but rejoices with the truth. It always protects, always trusts, always hopes, always perseveres."
1 Corinthians 13:5–7

superhero. They pursued and responded to deepen their bond and, hopefully, make it permanent. Once they said "I do" and exchanged rings to memorialize their lifelong commitments, the motivation must change. They no longer pursue and respond to gain what they desire; they must pursue and respond for the sake of unselfish love!

This means etching into the schedule specials night out and weekends away. It means an occasional call to home or the office to "just check in" and to say, "I love you." It means feeding your romance a steady diet of tiny kindnesses—opening her door, expressing gratitude, admiring his integrity, telling her she's beautiful, giving him respect, overlooking minor faults, praising successes, doing whatever might make his or her day a little easier or a little more pleasant. It means bringing unexpected gifts, just to say, "You were on my mind." It means discovering what makes one another feel loved and then following through.

Courtship is the fire that makes a marriage sizzle. But *courtship* must be the product of *caring*. After all, courtship without caring is manipulation. No one gets turned on by exploitation. *Caring*, in turn, depends upon effective *communication*—Level One talking in which we share our ideas and judgments, thoughts and emotions, fears and struggles. We can only give effective care to someone we know. The formula is simple:

Superficial Knowledge = Superficial Care
Intimate Knowledge = Deep Care

Of course, communication, care, and courtship must build upon a solid foundation of commitment. Without commitment, nothing else has any lasting meaning.

When a couple engages all four factors, their marriage offers a kind of satisfaction that can only be experienced. Words fail to describe the fulfillment of a healthy one-flesh bond. Moreover, a strong marriage becomes a gift to later generations of children and grandchildren. Take, for example, the case of Brenda, who came from a healthy family. Not perfect, but a functional and loving home with parents devoted to one another.

She went away to college, and during her freshman year, started dating a young man who met the approval of both her parents. They were actually quite fond of him. One long weekend, the couple went to meet the boy's parents.

The following week, Brenda called home, in tears and confused. She thought her affections for her boyfriend were real, but when she saw how his father treated his mother, she was frightened. *Is this the way Kyle could end up treating me?* she wondered. She would never find out because the thought blocked her emotions, causing her to back away from the relationship.

While it might not seem fair, she couldn't deny the emotional impact of seeing how Kyle's parents treated one another. Certainly, every young man

Courtship is the fire that makes a marriage sizzle. But courtship must be the product of caring.

Courtship without caring is manipulation.

> *Remember, caring and courtship have little meaning apart from an unconditionally committed marriage kept strong through good communication.*

who comes from a dysfunctional home should not be penalized for what "may happen" because of family history. Even so, Brenda refused to ignore what she perceived to be the seeds of abusive behavior in Kyle's mannerisms. Whether you call it woman's intuition or paranoia, the fact remains: Kyle's parents had an unattractive marriage that stood in stark contrast to the bond shared by her mom and dad. The prospect of committing herself to a lifetime of unkindness quenched whatever love she may have had for Kyle.

We should take that as a warning. After we're married, backing away from the relationship isn't an option. Even so, unkindness kills romance. The good news, however, give us good reason for hope. Commitment, communication, caring, and courtship make marriages sizzle, and it's never too late to start.

TAKE ACTION

Let's read again Philippians 2:1-4 from the J.B. Phillips paraphrase:
"Now if you have known anything of Christ's encouragement and of his reassuring love; if you have known something of the fellowship of his Spirit, and of compassion and deep sympathy, do make my joy complete–live together in harmony, live together in love, as though you had only one mind and one spirit between you. Never act from motives of rivalry or personal vanity, but in humility think more of each other than you do of yourselves. *None of you should think only of his own affairs, but consider other people's interests also"* (emphasis mine).[7]

As you have come to know your spouse or other significant person in your life, what causes him or her to feel cared for? If you aren't certain, ask. (If you are single, consider your close friendships. Do you know how your close friend feels cared for?)

If you are married, think back to the days of your courtship. List the ways you expressed interest in your future mate. In those early days, what behavior encouraged him or her to desire more of your time? Turn your list of actions and behaviors into a "to do" list and get busy!

Consider learning the Five Love Languages taught by Dr. Gary Chapman. Whether you are single, married, parents, or a youth, go to 5lovelanguages.com and take the free online assessment. What did you learn about yourself?

Be intentional: What are you going to do about what you've learned?

Be specific: What action will you take in the near future to begin applying what you've learned? When will you do it?

Be accountable: Pray it through. Share your plan with a friend and seek his/her prayer and counsel for your next step.

CHAPTER 17: THE PARENTING GIFT OF PROTECTION

Scan here to watch the video!

The Peace Corps used to have a slogan that applies perfectly to the responsibility of parenting: "It's the toughest job you'll ever love." God could have perpetuated the human species by any number of means. Just look at nature and you'll see a stunning diversity of methods. Nevertheless, no other creature can rival the intimacy and longevity of human procreation and rearing. Nine months for gestation is among the longest in creation and no other creature comes close to the eighteen years required to prepare a child for complete independence. Even after "launching," the bond between child and parents can—and should!—remain strong for a lifetime.

With the permission of authors Dave Veerman and Chuck Aycock, let's begin our examination of the parent-child relationship with three gifts every mom and dad has to offer. The three gifts are: Protection, Identity, and Confidence, which we will examine in the course of three chapters.[8]

It's quite possible that you are not a physical parent – you may not have birthed, adopted, or fostered a child. If, after completing this book you decide to continue to disciple others with *The Four Priorities*, then you will become a type of *spiritual parent* for a young-in-their-faith believer. No one knows what the future might hold, but this we know for certain: You are someone's child. What we will describe in chapters 17-19 may not immediately apply to you as a parent, but rather than skip these chapters or lightly skim the material, try reading this content from the child's perspective. We will examine three gifts a parent can give his or her children. Perhaps you may not have known these gifts existed because they were never given to you. Some gifts you may have received in great abundance, if not from a parent, then from another significant adult. Knowing about these gifts and their implications will be helpful in two respects. First, you will have something for which to thank the important adults in your early years. Second—and vitally important to good emotional and spiritual health—understanding these gifts helps to explain why we think, respond, feel, and behave as we do. That knowledge, in turn, tells us where to find healing.

A FATHER'S ROLE

Before we look at these gifts, we must understand the critical role our fathers played in our development. We focus on fathers at this point for two reasons. First, more people had absentee fathers than estranged mothers, and the struggle to overcome the resulting issues is immense. Second, we hope to engage this generation of fathers by reminding men of their importance in the lives of their children.

According to Eddie Staub, the founder of Eagle Ranch near Gainesville, Georgia, who has provided group homes for troubled children for many years, "The impact of mothers on a child is essential, but the impact of fathers is magical." When the father is not around, all kinds of problems stack up. One shocking yet revealing statistic is that eighty-five percent of youths in prison grew up in fatherless homes – twenty times the average.[9]

Most men and women carry the imprint of an absentee father into their own parenting arena. This imprint was created by a dad who was either present or absent; engaged or detached; loving, abusive or indifferent; accommodating or domineering. Like it or not, parents cannot be ultimately effective if they do not come to terms with the expressed or unexpressed feelings toward their fathers. The pain can run deep and the scars are forever obvious. No dad is perfect, but if he hurt you, healing will not take place unless you have the courage to live with the loss of an "idealized" father, and grieving may be a natural part of the process.

> *A father's drifting in and out of his child's life causes more harm than good when he merely teases his child with fleeting possibilities of a healthy relationship.*

One cold January morning, a video production crew flew to Atlanta and then traveled to Gainesville to interview some children who were living in a group home at the Eagle Ranch. All of them had riveting stories about their past and gripping ways of expressing how they felt about their fathers. One boy, his blond hair shining with all the production lighting, looked like a poster child for white suburban America. The interviewer posed a question that caused the child's countenance to drop. "If you could tell your father anything, what would it be?" The boy gazed at the floor. Six or seven seconds passed in silence. Then he looked up with a blank stare and responded, "I'd tell him . . . (he paused again) . . . I'd tell him never to come back."

When the child of an absentee parent becomes an adult, how does he or she cope with the loss? How can the abandoned or neglected child find healing for his or her wounds as an adult? It's not easy, but four steps can help.

Step 1: Express Your Feelings

Children generally cope by stuffing their unwanted feelings or by channeling them into an activity. Sometimes that activity takes the form of unhealthy behavior. A healthy response to sorrow begins by acknowledging and expressing the pain of loss. Speaking to the parent in person is preferred, but may not be possible. If the missing parent isn't available, place an empty chair across from you and visualize him or her as you speak.

If you have the opportunity to discuss this with your absentee or neglectful parent, go easy. Seek to understand before you hope to be understood. You might start with a question that shows interest in his or her childhood: "What was life like when you were a kid?" This may offer an opportunity to explain—without making accusations—how you felt when he or she behaved in certain ways. Regardless of how poor the relationship, find something good he or she did and affirm the positive where possible.

Step 2: Confess Your Faults
No one is perfect. Everyone has been guilty of hurting others. Acknowledge your faults and failures. Be specific, where possible. This requires courage. Be brave enough to offer this vulnerability, not only out of compassion, but to model for your parent the response you hope to receive.

Step 3: Forgive Your Parent
Forgiving doesn't require you to condone or excuse the wrongdoing of another. Forgiveness merely lets the other person off your moral hook. You agree to let the offense go without expectation of justice or retribution or even reconciliation. You can hope for reconciliation or restoration, but you release your offender from all expectations. Forgiveness is the first step in recovery from loss. It may take several meetings before all the cards are on the table, but it can be liberating to finally deal with the painful past and then create a better future. Healing will take time. You may have to revisit your painful past repeatedly with the help of a counselor, a wise friend, or your small group. With time and focused effort, grieving will give way to healing... starting with the choice to forgive.

Step 4: Commit to the Relationship Going Forward
As a son or daughter, you can honor your parent by healing from the past and charting a new course for your relationship. A close, healthy relationship may or may not be possible depending upon the willingness or stability of your parent. Building a relationship requires trust on the part of both people. Trust requires a good-faith investment of kindness on the part of each person. If your parent remains untrustworthy, you may have to be contented with a limited relationship. If so, grieve and move on. (Easier said than done, but it's possible.)

Once you have made the necessary steps to settle unresolved issues with your parent, you can make a commitment to your own children and the priority they play in your life. With that kind of commitment in mind, we proceed to the first gift that all parents can give their children: *Protection*.

A PARENT'S GIFT OF PROTECTION
To protect means to create an environment in which the child can thrive without external threats. This occurs most productively in a home that is open, loving, communicative, fun, interesting, and that emphasizes personal growth and redemption. Such an environment provides protection in four ways, which we have expressed as four imperatives.[10]

Provide a Sense of Belonging
Every child craves a sense of home. A familiar culture of "home" comes as the child experiences routine sounds, aromas, and other sensations. Hopefully, these accompany pleasant memories, such as the smell of cookies baking,

---

How can the abandoned or neglected child find healing for his or her wounds as an adult?
Step 1: Express Your Feelings
Step 2: Confess Your Faults
Step 3: Forgive Your Parent
Step 4: Commit to the Relationship Going Forward

> *To protect means to create an environment in which the child can thrive without external threats.*

the squeak and creak of a rocking chair, laughter over a child's sharp wit, or the feeling of being hugged often. The feeling of belonging also comes from a sense of family heritage. This could include telling family stories, creating traditions and rituals by taking family vacations, or having special meals on regular occasions. When children are given a place in the routines and special occasions of family life, they feel protected. Those who lack these childhood moorings suffer the agony of feeling unimportant, unloved, unworthy, and unwanted. The gift of belonging protects children from the fear that they must earn love or prove their worth. The gift of belonging assures children that a solid core of people will be there for them and will do whatever they can when all else fails.

Provide Appropriate Boundaries

A child without boundaries is a fearful child. A child without freedom is an exasperated child. Children need a healthy balance of both freedom and boundaries (Ephesians 6:4). Freedom to express creativity, to discover their uniqueness, and to become fully accepted individuals. Boundaries are essential to establish safe limits. Some parents don't want to stifle their children's creativity by setting a bunch of rules, but they fail to realize that children need fences in order to feel free.

Many years ago, a young man walked with his family across a bridge over the Royal Gorge in Colorado. A sturdy, wire-mesh barrier protects visitors from a deadly 1,053-foot plummet to the Arkansas River below, but to a young boy, the railing appeared transparent—barely there at all. So, he crossed the bridge in the very center, petrified of what should have been a magnificent view.

Boundaries provide reasonable discipline and rules, allowing us to enjoy freedom with the assurance of safety. Children may complain about chores, homework, manners, curfews, and rules, but deep inside, they derive a strong sense of value when parents care enough to establish standards of conduct. When a parent expresses reasonable expectations, the child hears, "I believe in you."

> *Some parents don't want to stifle their children's creativity by setting a bunch of rules, but they fail to realize that children need fences in order to feel free.*

Having established reasonable expectations, parents must, however, distinguish between childish irresponsibility and a spirit of defiance. Not all wrong behavior is the result of deliberate disobedience. A kid needs to be able to breathe without fear that every step he takes will bring punishment. Furthermore, children entering adolescence will test boundaries, but this is not defiance; this is their trial-and-error manner of learning which boundaries are firm and which are appropriately flexible. With consistency without severity, the parent must determine which issues are non-negotiable and which are open to discussion. As children mature, they need to know the rationale behind certain boundaries. Their questions become the parents' opportunity to instruct, to help the child learn how to think. "Because I said so" not only exasperates a child, it squanders an opportunity to train a naturally curious mind.

As children grow, wise parents learn to rely less upon punishment and more upon the natural consequences of decisions. For example, most schools limit extracurricular privileges when a student's grades fall below a certain average. Wise parents allow the impact of poor decisions to change future behavior. Wise parents know that punishment for childish irresponsibility merely distracts a child from learning how to make good decisions. Ironically, when a parent heaps punishment on top of negative consequences, the child not only fails to learn the lesson, he or she learns to resent the parent. Counselors report that as many as thirty percent of twenty-year-old adults are estranged from their parents because of excessive punishment during childhood. They are the exasperated ones. They play the victim, resenting what they perceive to be unfair treatment by life and never learn how to adjust their behavior to achieve success. Moreover, they don't want to hear anything of the Lord's instruction from their parents.

You must be a protector for your children, yet you must also allow the negative consequences of bad choices to impact them. How do you maintain that balance?

Provide a Moral Framework

Famous UCLA basketball coach, John Wooden famously said, "Be more concerned with your character than your reputation because your character is what you really are, while your reputation is merely what others think you are."[11] Children who grow up with a greater concern for reputation than character will become the victims of any guiding principle that appeals to their self-interest or prurient desires. The basis of character is a moral framework, without which they cannot decide what priorities are essential for living. Wise parents know that character is cultivated through constant emphasis and reinforcement of moral principles. These help children shape their attitudes about money, how to treat people, the value of honest work, priorities, and the ultimate importance of spiritual matters.

Provide an Emotional Connection

Psychologists conducting research in the aftermath of mass murders on high school campuses discovered that most offenders never bonded with a parent or other meaningful adult. The children often grew up in middle to upper middle class neighborhoods. They had the good "stuff" of life—plenty of money and possessions—but they lacked the most important stuff: caring guidance from a trusted adult.

Quality time is good. Quantity time is essential. You can schedule quality time; but it also should be a natural and regular occurrence. Make yourself available for those rare and precious moments as you spend copious amounts of unstructured time with your children. Make yourself available for emotional connection in at least five ways:

1. Be there at bedtime. Tell stories, pray together, read together, and laugh together. Let the children go to sleep with the

How much time do you spend with your children each week—not merely in the same room, but with them?

emotional warmth of the last fifteen minutes of the day.
2. Be there when they hurt. When they are sad, be aware of their countenance and take them aside for a conversation. Your genuine concern will speak volumes about their importance to you.
3. Be there when they make mistakes. Don't cover for them when they blow it, but let them know that we are all flawed and that we can all recover from our stupidity and our sin.
4. Be there when they have special activities. Dad and Mom on the sidelines, in the grandstand, in the audience, is a nutrient to emotional health.
5. Be there to listen with understanding to either their pain, their joys, or their overly long narrative about some mundane subject that is important to them but is boring to you. Resisting the urge to yawn, look away, or glance at your watch.

In this chapter, we discussed four imperatives for the gift of protection. Think of them as building four walls of a fortress, each strong enough to ward off threats and to provide a safe enclosure for young people to grow and thrive. In review, the walls of protection are:

A Sense of Belonging
Appropriate Boundaries
A Moral Framework
Emotional Connection

TAKE ACTION

Throughout this week, begin building your fortress by focusing on these foundational scriptures for each "wall of protection." Prayerfully read and re-read each scripture, asking the Holy Spirit to give you fresh insight and understanding to what the Word of God is saying. Then, ask the Lord what you should do in response to each scripture.

A Sense of Belonging: *Provide comfort, establish "home" environment and routines, communicate family heritage and memories, and encourage self-worth.*
- Deuteronomy 32:7
- Joshua 24:15
- Psalm 78:1-7; 139:13-16

Appropriate Boundaries: *Enforce reasonable discipline and rules, enjoy freedom with the assurance of safety, and allow natural consequences to play out.*
- Deuteronomy 4:9-10
- Proverbs 3:11-12; 13:24; 22:6
- Hebrews 12:5-11

A Moral Framework: Establish Godly character over a manmade reputation, and model values to demonstrate what is really important in life.
- Deuteronomy 6:4-9; 11:18-21
- Psalm 112:1-2
- Proverbs 10:9
- Matthew 22:37-40
- James 1:26-27

Emotional Connection: Be available, listen with understanding, and spend quality as well as quantity time with your children.
- Psalm 103:13
- Proverbs 3:21-24; 15:1; 17:27-28
- 1 Corinthians 13:4-6
- Colossians 3:21
- James 1:19

Be intentional: What are you going to do about what you've learned?

Be specific: What action will you take in the near future to begin applying what you've learned? When will you do it?

Be accountable: Pray it through. Share your plan with a friend and seek his/her prayer and counsel for your next step.

CHAPTER 18: THE PARENTING GIFT OF IDENTITY

A mirror can be a painful device. Nearly everyone has looked in the mirror and thought, *If only my nose weren't so big . . . If only I could lose weight . . .* or *If only I didn't have bags under my eyes . . .* Our relationship with the mirror begins early in life. We shape our concept of self as we see our own images reflected and then evaluate what we perceive. It's a continual, unconscious process that involves more than one kind of mirror. We see ourselves not only in the "looking glass," we also see our reflections in the responses of the people we value. Psychologists call this relational process "mirroring."

To illustrate this concept of mirroring, imagine a man singing before an audience. With each note, the people scowl and cringe. Some wear the expression of someone overtaken with the smell of rotten eggs. At the end of his song, he notes relief on many faces as they offer a smattering of polite applause. They have, in fact, mirrored a message about his singing ability: "You're a terrible singer!"

As children, we depend almost completely upon the responses of others to learn who we are, what talents we possess or lack, what value we hold as people, and for what purpose we exist. Whether they realize it or not, parents play a critical role in shaping their children's identities, primarily in how they respond to what they see. They help build strong identities by accepting, affirming, acknowledging, and appreciating the uniqueness of each child. Parents can also leave children with fragile identities through negativity and criticism. If parents do nothing, our culture will mirror the child with distorted images. Movies, TV, radio, and commercials constantly celebrate beauty, brains, bucks, and brawn as the measure of personal worth. These distorted images of worth scream the message, "You don't measure up!"

So what can parents do to help their children have healthy identities? They know their kids aren't perfect and act horribly at times. They also realize that their kids are fragile and need a steady stream of encouragement. Over time, each child must come to terms with two facts: first, he or she is the apex of God's creation (Psalm 139); second, he or she is a sinful creature living in a fallen world (Romans 3:23); third, God affirmed their value, despite their sinfulness, by sending His Son to save them (John 3:16). Parents begin this physical, emotional, and spiritual journey by helping their children discover their God-given identities.

A PARENT'S GIFT OF IDENTITY
When a parent provides protection from outside threats, this creates an opportunity for a child to discover and develop his or her God-given identity. Early in life, children seek out mirrors to help them discover who they are and for what purpose they exist. Parents are the first mirrors children encounter.

Scan here to watch the video!

When a parent provides protection from outside threats, this creates an opportunity for a child to discover and develop his or her God-given identity.

We can mirror a healthy identity by committing to at least four actions.[12]

Love Them Unconditionally

The psalmist says with delight, "I praise you for I am fearfully and wonderfully made" (Psalm 139:14), and again "What is man that you are mindful of him, and the son of man that you care for him? You have made him a little lower than the heavenly beings and crowned him with glory and honor" (Psalm 8:4–5). God has given each child a unique fingerprint and a special touch; therefore, no child should be compared with brothers and sisters or expected to develop at anyone's pace except his or her own. Moreover, each child gives and receives love uniquely.

Gary Chapman has identified no less than five "love languages" that define how a person expresses love and feels loved.[13] They are:

Words of Affirmation

Verbal compliments, or words of appreciation, are powerful communicators of love. They are best expressed in simple, straightforward statements of affirmation, such as:
"You look sharp in that suit."
"Do you ever look nice in that dress! Wow!
"You must be the best potato cook in the world. I love these potatoes."

Quality Time

Giving someone your undivided attention. I don't mean sitting on the couch watching television together. . . . What I mean is sitting on the couch with the TV off, looking at each other and talking, giving each other your undivided attention. It means taking a walk, just the two of you or going out to eat and looking at each other and talking.

Receiving Gifts

A gift is something you can hold in your hand and say, "Look, he was thinking of me," or, "She remembered me." You must be thinking of someone to give him a gift. The gift itself is a symbol of that thought. It doesn't matter whether it costs money. What is important is that you thought of him. And it is not the thought implanted only in the mind that counts, but the thought expressed in actually securing the gift and giving it as the expression of love.

Acts of Service

By acts of service, I mean doing things you know your [loved one] would like you to do. You seek to please [this person] by doing things for him or her. Such actions as cooking a meal, setting a table, washing dishes, vacuuming, cleaning a commode, getting hairs out of the sink, removing the white spots from the mirror, getting bugs off the windshield, taking out the garbage . . . They require thought, planning, time, effort, and energy. If done with a positive spirit, they are indeed expressions of love.

Physical Touch
We have long known that physical touch is a way of communicating emotional love. Numerous research projects in the area of child development have made that conclusion: babies who are held, hugged, and kissed develop a healthier emotional life than those who are left for long periods of time without physical contact.

Can you show love to your child without first understanding their love language? Sure. But, many of your efforts would probably be lost in translation. It would be like expressing your depth of love and commitment to someone in Swahili when they only understand English. Some gestures may be grasped and understood, but most of what you hope to communicate would be meaningless to them. Just like adults, each child has a love language and needs to receive love in that manner. We have a responsibility to observe children to determine the "love language" they comprehend.

Affirm Their Worth
We know that our children are extremely valuable, but they do not. Every child needs to be reminded that he or she is special.

Every child needs to be reminded that he or she is special.

David, a man in his mid-fifties, was walking down a church hall one day and stopped to make way for a line of eight or nine children who were going from recess in their day care routine back to their home room. At the end of the queue was a three-year-old girl who looked up at David and began to hit his leg. David knelt down in an attempt to make a connection, but the girl continued to hit him with her little fists. The day care leader looked back and noticed what was going on, stepped in to pick up the child, and followed up with an apology. "I'm sorry, but Shannon has no father or any other man in her life, and from time to time, she acts out in this way."

Little Shannon had a spontaneous reaction of frustration that stemmed from a hole in her heart with no meaningful male to fill it. She couldn't verbalize her needs, but all children have four basic desires.

1. Children crave affection. Counselors will explain that adults can damage a child's identity as much by withholding praise as by shouting criticism. Children need to hear adults say often, "I love you," "I'm proud of you," "You're good at so-and-so," "What a great job you did!" Negativity

> Negativity and criticism come most naturally to children, so look for reasons to compliment, affirm, reassure, and encourage. Be their biggest fan!

and criticism come most naturally, so look for reasons to compliment, affirm, reassure, and encourage. Find excuses to praise children.

2. *Children want to be wanted.* Children know when adults enjoy being with them. They love when an adult gets down on their level to wrestle, play, or just have a talk. Parents can also make a child feel welcome by including him or her in conversation with adults. A child feels wanted and significant when adults take him or her seriously. When a child tells silly stories, go along with it and ask questions; invite the child to elaborate.

3. *Children want to be hugged.* In her book, *Love at Goon Park*, Deborah Blum reveals the tragic consequences of depriving children of love in her examination of stories from orphanages. In the middle of the 18th century, the Hospital of the Innocents in Florence, Italy, received more than 15,000 babies over two decades. Ten thousand of those children died before they reached their first birthday. A 1915 study stated that in nine of the ten orphanages surveyed, no child survived past the age of two. The prevailing wisdom of the time blamed infections spread by touch. In order to prevent the opportunity for a baby to be exposed to germs, special boxes with inlet sleeves were used to allow a nurse or staff person to change diapers without skin-on-skin contact with the child. In addition, popular psychology publications declared that infants have no capacity for relationship and therefore have no emotional needs; only physical demands until they develop the capacity for recognition and communication. All of this nonsense was called to intellectual accountability when psychologist Harry Harlow revealed the terrible results for those deprived of physical affection.

Harlow's experiments, supported by Blum's stories, made an irrefutable case for the significance of physical contact. Touching is not merely important; it is essential for human wellbeing.

4. *Children want to be appreciated.* Children need to feel they are making a contribution to the family. Enlisting their help with household chores or work projects teaches them discipline and gives them a sense of accomplishment. Their self-worth blossoms when adults express appreciation for their contributions. The happiest adolescents on the planet are those who have grown up playing on a team—the family team. Every home has needed yard work, repairs, or some other face-lift, and an "attaboy" is a wonderful compensation for those who pitch in and work hard.

Acknowledge Their Uniqueness

Finding and celebrating each child's uniqueness is critical because if the parents don't identify it, the child will look for it the rest of his or her life. This task becomes easier when you have a little Mozart on your hands. Most children, however, don't appear exceptional as preschoolers. Parents of non-prodigies can gather clues from a child's motivated pattern, activities they enjoy and do well. A child who spends hours working with Legos or creates a complex design with other materials is sending a message. Children also display behavioral patterns. Some are extremely loyal; some are courageous and some compassionate. Some play the role of peacemaker. A parent trying to discover a child's identity can help him or her identify, celebrate, and develop a latent talent.

Appreciate Their Presence

A public school survey in Maryland revealed that parents spend an average of fifteen minutes a week in meaningful dialogue with their children—not much time for bonding or guidance. Time pressures allow little time for relaxation, so laziness takes over. Before long, the unwary parent wakes up and wonders where the time has gone. Time is short, so we must make the best use of our time.

Make eating dinner together as a family a high priority. And make it fun. For example, you could play the "what if" game. "What if you had $1,000—what would you spend it on?" or "What if you could go anywhere—where would you go?" or "What if you could have a conversation with someone from history—who would that be?" Adding fun to the equation is a way to make children feel wanted and appreciated. You can even have fun with spiritual questions. The father could state: "Tonight we are going to have a family discussion on whether we really believe the story about Jonah and the big fish is true." Everyone is allowed to chime in, give his or her opinion, and then defend it.

In his book, *Parenting: From Surviving to Thriving*, Chuck Swindoll states, "The job of a parent is to help his or her children come to know themselves, grow to like themselves, and find satisfaction in being themselves."[14] Basically, this is the gift of identity.

> Make a list of the strengths, interests, aptitudes, and motivations you have observed for each of your children. Over the next few weeks, make a habit of affirming each child with your positive observations.

TAKE ACTION

Throughout this week, focus on these foundational scriptures for each area of identity. Prayerfully read and re-read each scripture, asking the Holy Spirit to give you fresh insight and understanding of what the Word of God is saying. Then ask the Lord what you should do in response to each scripture.

A parent's gift of identity to their children is to:
Love Them Unconditionally
- Malachi 4:6
- 1 Corinthians 13:1-13
- Mark 9:36-37
- Romans 8:38-39
- 1 John 4:7-12

Affirm Their Worth
- Genesis 1:26-28
- Psalm 139:13-18
- 1 Thessalonians 2:11-12
- James 3:7-12

Acknowledge Their Uniqueness
- Psalm 139:14
- Acts 10:34-35
- Romans 12:4-8; 15:7
- Ephesians 4:10-13

Appreciate Their Presence
- Psalm 127:3-5
- Proverbs 17:6; 31:28
- Matthew 19:14-15
- 2 Corinthians 12:14

Be intentional: What are you going to do about what you've learned?

Be specific: What action will you take in the near future to begin applying what you've learned? When will you do it?

Be accountable: Pray it through. Share your plan with a friend and seek his/her prayer and counsel for your next step.

CHAPTER 19: THE PARENTING GIFT OF CONFIDENCE

Scan here to watch the video!

con•fi•dence \ kän-f -d n(t)s, - den(t)s\ *noun*
14th century
1   **a** : a feeling or consciousness of one's powers or of reliance on one's circumstances (had perfect *confidence* in her ability to succeed) (met the risk with brash *confidence*)
     b : faith or belief that one will act in a right, proper, or effective way (have *confidence* in a leader)[15]

A PARENT'S GIFT OF CONFIDENCE

If a parent has created a safe environment through protection, and an encouraging environment where a child can discover his or her identity, the third gift should come easily: confidence.[16] Monty Roberts knows something about the important role confidence plays in the development of a happy child. His book, *Horse Sense for People*, explains how shy, skittish horses can become serene saddle horses in thirty minutes, and how his technique can help people develop healthy relationships with others—especially children. He knows what he is talking about—he helped to rear forty-seven foster children.

The kind of confidence we are talking about is where a child has a firm enough foundation to test his or her ideas, values, and relationships in a nurturing environment. The child feels the freedom to fail without negative reprisals from parents and other significant adults. Confidence develops as the result of someone releasing a child from fears or insecurities to discover—usually through trial and error—how to succeed and to discover his or her full potential.

There are a number of effective models to help children build upon strengths, develop confidence, and then develop new strengths. Psychologist Flip Flippen has taught public school teachers for years a model of transformation that can capture a kid's heart. As a result of the EXCEL program, thousands of children have found a liberating confidence because of the deliberate involvement of teachers who care about them. It's built upon an education model known as the 5Es: Engage, Explore, Explain, Empower, Encourage. This and similar programs are well worth exploring as an effective method of giving children the gift of confidence.

ENGAGE

Monty Roberts illustrates engagement by stepping into the trainer's ring with the horse and approaching the animal in a nonthreatening manner.[17] With his history of studying horses and how they respond to various circumstances, he studies each particular horse to understand its unique idiosyncrasies. Then, using this knowledge, he indicates to the horse that he intends no harm, only relationship. He calls this "joining up."

This is the first step in building confidence in children. We take the time to observe how children perceive the world and how our child is unique. Then we lower ourselves to their eye level by stooping or kneeling. We communicate nonverbally that we have no other agenda than to connect, to engage person-to-person.

EXPLORE

After joining up, Monty Roberts illustrates exploration by rubbing his hands over the horse's body to find where muscles vibrate or where contact causes the horse to back away, lift its head, or avoid touch. Monty calls this "finding the story." He's able to discern where the horse has been kicked, whipped, or abused. He then removes the leash and encourages the horse to run—to be free—to discover that he has no intention of dominating. While Monty remains in control of the situation and takes the initiative to form a bond, he does so by building trust, not by asserting control.

Before long, the horse stops running and then moves to the center of the ring to connect with Monty. His method works because horses want connection as long as they don't have to sacrifice the dignity of autonomy.

The illustration is clear enough. People, like horses, want relationships, but we generally avoid domination. Once we have the child's undivided attention and she knows she has ours, we ask questions to better understand her world. Not every conversation with a child will be deep and profound, but all conversations are meaningful. When you show genuine interest in a child's stories, he will want to hear yours.

Through observation and trust-building, we provide opportunities to help children discover and unleash their potential.

EXPLAIN

Having engaged the horse, Monty can begin training. In a spirit of relationship, he indicates what he wants from the horse; because he has earned the animal's trust; the horse complies. Roberts is careful not to press the illustration too far. A horse is a horse, and a child is a person. Nevertheless, he highlights the fact that the horse gains something from the relationship. It discovers how to fulfill its God-given purpose more effectively than if left in the wild. The horse and rider are mutually fulfilled by the relationship.

When rearing a child, we discover through engagement what motivates him and what aptitudes he possesses. Through observation and trust-building, we provide opportunities to help him discover and unleash his potential. When we guide the child toward his own destiny rather than what we hope he might become, he finds fulfillment in our instruction. He doesn't see training as another nagging session, but as a time to learn, grow, succeed, and celebrate accomplishment.

EMPOWER (OR EXTEND)

When we deeply touch another person, we empower him or her to attempt and accomplish things never before imagined. The point of empowerment occurs when someone perceives the world in a new way. Old fears fall away and new possibilities become excitingly clear. Training must continue to keep the student on course and to avoid picking up unproductive habits, but the source of motivation shifts from teacher to student, from parent to child. When she discovers the joy of achievement, an internal drive for success takes over.

ENCOURAGE (OR EVALUATE)

Once a child is directed and empowered, he or she flies toward the intended target (Proverbs 22:6). Again, the target is not what we desire for our children to become, but the purposes established for each one by God (Psalm 139:13–16). Our role shifts again from trainer to mentor. Having released the child, we encourage him or her. We make ourselves available for evaluation and advice *when called upon*. If we have successfully established a relationship of trust, nurtured through the years, our children will seek out the advice of their parents.

While the 5 Es guides the eighteen-year process of childrearing, it also plays out many, many times in smaller ways throughout the years. Tying shoes. Telling the truth. Riding a bike. Obeying rules. Mastering an instrument. Making friends. Playing sports. Respecting others. Earning good grades. Cultivating a work ethic. Driving a car. Taking responsibility. Each challenge becomes an opportunity for the parent to engage, explore, explain, empower, and encourage.

While Jesus neither devised nor taught a specific system of training and development, we can, nevertheless, see the 5 Es illustrated in His encounter with the Samaritan woman (John 4:7–43). He engaged the woman with the simple request, "Will you give me a drink?" (v. 7). Both understood it to be an unprecedented invitation to connect. She acknowledged her reason for suspicion. "You are a Jew and I am a Samaritan woman. How can you ask me for a drink?" (v. 9). The Gospel writer, John, notes, "Jews do not associate with Samaritans." Moreover, men did not associate with women, and important rabbis did not associate with peasants.

Jesus eventually won her trust by conversing with her, hinting that a relationship with Him held the promise of meeting her deepest needs. He then explored her life with a challenge.

> He told her, "Go, call your husband and come back." "I have no husband," she replied. Jesus said to her, "You are right when you say you have no husband. The fact is, you have had five husbands, and the man you now have is not your husband. What you have just said is quite true." "Sir,"

the woman said, "I can see that you are a prophet."
(John 4:16–19)

She tried to change the subject, moving away—as it were—when Jesus touched a sensitive area of her life, a place bruised by repeated abuse (v. 20). The Lord didn't give chase or try to control her. He, instead, drew her toward Himself by explaining His true identity as the Messiah . . . her Messiah . . . her Savior (v. 21–26). She responded by bringing her community to meet Jesus (v. 28–30). Note how confidence replaced her shame. Feeling empowered by Christ, and utterly unselfconscious, she urged her community to follow her to the well. "Come, see a man who told me everything I ever did. Could this be the Christ?" (John 4:29).

Having released the woman from her shame and having filled her with confidence, Jesus launched a powerful advocate for the gospel.

> Many of the Samaritans from that town believed in him because of the woman's testimony, "He told me everything I ever did." So when the Samaritans came to him, they urged him to stay with them, and he stayed two days. And because of his words many more became believers. They said to the woman, "We no longer believe just because of what you said; now we have heard for ourselves, and we know that this man really is the Savior of the world." (John 4:39–42)

While our role as parents involves education—playing a vital role in God's program of salvation and transformation—the job requires much more. Parents have other opportunities to pass along the gift of confidence.

Confidence from Predictable Parents

It's nearly impossible for a child to develop confidence if his or her parents respond inconsistently when rules are violated. Imagine sitting in traffic court watching a judge determining fines for speeding violations. Three men stand before the bench, each charged with the same infraction. One man gets a $100 fine; another receives a ten-year sentence; a third goes free. Now it's your turn to answer for the same charge. How would you feel? Remorseful or confused?

When a child can't predict his or her parents' response to wrongdoing, confusion interferes with any lessons that might be learned. The same is true for hard work. Predictably rewarding or praising a job well-done boosts confidence.

Confidence in Boy/Girl Relationships

Every boy and girl wonders, even frets, over how to handle dating. Hallway talk at school can make it appear that some students have mastered the dating game. Most, however, struggle with a deep sense of insecurity and self-doubt. Mom and Dad can help build confidence in this area by taking an adolescent on a "practice date."

Roger did that with his daughter, Kathy. They went to a nice restaurant. Roger opened the door of the car for her and politely sat her at the table—he showed her how a young lady should be treated. He helped her with ideas from the menu, carried on a light conversation with the waiter, and used his best manners, but always with an eye on how he could make Kathy feel comfortable while enjoying the meal and the ambiance of this special evening. Roger opened the subject of what to look for when she was on a date with her special someone. The topic was a little awkward because he had to reveal the more prurient side of a boy's thoughts and intentions. After several "practice dates," Kathy not only learned what to expect from a decent young man but also to spot red flags.

Boys learn by watching how dad treats mom, and they can build confidence with a few practice dates.

Confidence to Become Independent

Our goal, as parents, is to help our children learn how to live independently, to care for themselves, make wise choices without our oversight, protect themselves from harm, and cultivate their own relationships with God. This doesn't happen suddenly at age eighteen; we help them grow into their independence by creating what family therapist, Dr. Rod Cooper, calls an "Open System."

In a "Closed System," those in authority (the parents) govern with rigid, autocratic efficiency. They expect others to obey rules without questions or independent thought. "Because I said so" is the response to all questions "Why?" or "Why not?" The atmosphere in a closed family system is often tense, tight, defensive, and negative. People laugh when the leader is happy, and tremble when the leader is not. Consequently, children in a closed system are well behaved, but don't prefer to be at home. They learn what to think, how to conform, and how to maintain the family reputation, but struggle to make good decisions apart from the oversight of the leader.

In an "Open System," the leaders (parents) establish firm rules and define clear boundaries, and they place greater emphasis on why than on what. The goal of the open system is to help everyone internalize the group's values rather than simply conform to the leader's will. Questions are encouraged and given thoughtful response. Accountability is mutual. Discipline is instructive, not merely punitive. Consequently, those who eventually depart an open system carry the values of the group with them, and frequently try to replicate the environment wherever they go. They emerge competent to face challenges and confident in their ability to succeed.

If every parent successfully gave their children the gifts of protection, identity, and confidence, imagine how the world would change for the better!

Imagine the reduction in crime and the increase in prosperity for everyone. Within two or three generations, we wouldn't recognize planet Earth.

Alas, we can't change the world. So, let's concentrate on our little corner of it, beginning at home with a commitment to parenting well.

TAKE ACTION

Read John 4:7–43, which describes the Lord's encounter with the Samaritan woman and illustrates several principles of disciple training. Jesus did not ignore the woman's sinful past. Rather than using it to shame and condemn her, He used it to win her trust. How did He accomplish this? How can we apply this to childrearing?

The Samaritan woman spoke with confidence despite her sinful past. In what ways did the Lord's encounter facilitate this transformation?

For each child in your care, write his or her name on a note card. Describe his or her most troubling challenge or limitation. Then, list specific ways you can help him or her achieve success in something despite this difficulty. (By the way, never reveal this exercise to any child!)

Be intentional: What are you going to do about what you've learned?

Be specific: What action will you take in the near future to begin applying what you've learned? When will you do it?

Be accountable: Pray it through. Share your plan with a friend and seek his/her prayer and counsel for your next step.

CHAPTER 20: SMALL GROUPS – FROM ISOLATION TO CONNECTION

Scan here to watch the video!

It seemed like everyone was talking about First Church. Jim, Pete, and John were pastors at this amazing church. Even though it was a congregation that met in an old building in the heart of the city, it was vibrant and alive. Literally overnight, First Church had experienced exponential growth, mostly because of some controversial remarks Pete had given in an open-air rally not far from the church building. The former commercial fisherman turned associate pastor stated openly that Jesus is the only way to God. When some objected, he challenged those who were offended by the bottom line of Christianity to evaluate the source of their objections. The reaction had been unexpected. Scores of people confessed their sins, accepted God's gift of eternal life, and began following the Son of God.

Weekly services were filled to capacity. Word spread throughout the community. Visitors showed up to see what was going on. Old and young sat side by side in celebrative worship. The music wasn't fancy. The lyrics were quite simple. Many of them came straight out of the Bible. Each service culminated in practical teaching from God's Word. The pastors who took turns speaking gave heavy emphasis to application.

It soon became obvious to the staff that a church of five thousand couldn't meet the individual needs of its members without breaking the huge congregation down into smaller settings. The most obvious way of doing this seemed to be the creation of home groups. In these small groups the big family "did church" between weekly gatherings. They took turns hosting fellowship dinners in each other's homes. Following dessert they enjoyed long conversations about the pastors' sermons from the previous Sunday. It wasn't uncommon for them to also celebrate the Lord's Supper before having a time of extended prayer.

These small group gatherings allowed First Church members to connect with each other on an authentic level. Individuals shared personal needs such as health concerns, financial challenges, and relationship difficulties. They admitted to issues in their marriages or ethical dilemmas at work. Men of the group began to meet together to hold each other accountable. Women did the same. Members didn't let their informal small group involvement take the place of their more formal public worship. They knew they needed both.

THE REST OF THE STORY
Would it surprise you that the church just described is not one that was started in the past ten years? Actually, it is one mentioned in the New Testament. In Acts 2:42–47, we read,

> They devoted themselves to the apostles' teaching and to the fellowship, to the breaking of bread and to prayer. Everyone was filled with awe, and many wonders and miraculous signs were done by the apostles. All the believers were together and had everything in common. Selling their possessions and goods, they gave to anyone as he had need. Every day they continued to meet together in the temple courts. They broke bread in their homes and ate together with glad and sincere hearts, praising God and enjoying the favor of all the people. And the Lord added to their number daily those who were being saved.

From the very beginning of Christianity, small groups have been essential to healthy spiritual growth. Large public gatherings were common, but individuals depended upon regular small gatherings for meaningful connection with other believers. The temple continued to be the primary place of worship and Bible teaching, but these first Christians gathered in homes for accountability, encouragement, and fellowship.

In his candid evaluation of the human experience, King Solomon celebrated the life-saving nature of community. He wrote,

> Two are better than one, because they have a good return for their work: If one falls down, his friend can help him up. But pity the man who falls and has no one to help him up! Also, if two lie down together, they will keep warm. But how can one keep warm alone? Though one may be overpowered, two can defend themselves. A cord of three strands is not quickly broken. (Ecclesiastes 4:9–12)

What a graphic portrait of our common need for other believers. God never intended that we attempt the Christian life solo. We were created for community. Reaching our God-given potential depends upon interaction and introspection with others, preferably a small group of people regularly inquiring about our personal well-being and progress can keep us from desperate, or even diabolical, behavior.

A CASE STUDY IN ISOLATION

The lack of meaningful interaction played out tragically for one young man. His mother was a domineering woman who had married three times. His father—her third husband—died before he was born. Their home offered no love or discipline. When this young man was a teenager, girls would have nothing to do with him, and he continually fought with his male classmates. Despite a high IQ, he dropped out of high school. He enlisted in the Marine Corps, only to be dishonorably discharged. Friendless and shipwrecked, he moved to a foreign country but was rejected there as well. In an attempt to latch on to love, he married a beautiful girl in that foreign place, but soon she wanted nothing to do with him. He couldn't please her. After one fight in particular, she locked him in the bathroom of their home. Later he tried to make it on his own, but failed. He proceeded to crawl back to his wife who only ridiculed his series of failures. If that wasn't bad enough, she made fun of his sexual impotency in front of her friends. As you might guess, he felt utterly isolated and extremely lonely. He was drowning in despair.

The person just described was Lee Harvey Oswald.[26] He lived in isolation, never forming a network of individuals to extend unconditional love, accept his shortcomings, challenge his thinking, forgive his faults, and encourage personal growth. In isolation, he withered as a human being. Imagine how history might have changed if Oswald had received the benefits of a small group of Christ-following men.

THE BENEFITS OF BELONGING

Can you identify with these struggles?

- The pressures of mid-life make it nearly impossible for you to keep pace with demands. You're becoming more realistic about your chances for grasping those upper rungs of the corporate ladder. Your strength isn't what it used to be and your own mortality has never seemed closer.
- You're concerned about your aging parents who live several states away. At the same time you wonder where you'll find the mountain of money needed for college tuition.
- The life you dreamed of having has become a nightmare after divorce demolished your family. Everyone's hurting but you are powerless to ease their suffering.
- A devastating diagnosis from your family doctor has brought life to a screeching halt. The future you planned has been set aside to focus on surviving this crisis. You're scared. Your faith is worn down. You find it easier to imagine a worst-case scenario than the potential of a successful outcome.
- You are the parent of a prodigal. Your child has rejected the values of your home, and has declared unequivocally that he or she wants nothing to do with you or your God. You wonder what you did wrong and you fear for his or her safety—in this life and the life to come.
- You're a new Christian. You don't know Genesis from Jeremiah. You understand that God has promised you a place in heaven with Him, but struggle to answer the question, "What now?" In truth, you have more questions than answers.

If you identify with any of the above scenarios, you need a small community of people with whom you can unload your deepest worries and fears while finding encouragement as you verbalize your heartfelt hopes and dreams. You need a refuge from a world that wants to beat you down. You need a place where others can bandage your broken heart, where you can feel the compassion of those who will strengthen you with understanding and prayer.

The author of the letter to the Hebrews cautioned his readers not to neglect gathering together small home groups. He knew that in a godless culture like his (and ours) we can't afford to go it alone. He wrote, "Let us not give up meeting together, as some are in the habit of doing, but let us encourage one another—and all the more as you see the Day approaching" (Hebrews 10:25). The Greek verb translated "give up" is better translated "abandon" or "desert." If we don't make an effort, busyness will cause us to abandon community. And, if we don't make this a priority, we will inevitably succumb to the deadly effects of isolation.

> *Let us not give up meeting together, as some are in the habit of doing, but let us encourage one another—and all the more as you see the Day approaching. Hebrews 10:25*

HOW DO YOU MOVE OUT OF ISOLATION?

Like most wise decisions, getting involved with a small group begins with an honest recognition of need. A look in the mirror may signal the need for better eating habits and regular exercise. A toothache prompts a trip to the dentist. An unflinching examination of one's own emotional and spiritual life should highlight the need for meaningful connection with others. The fact is, God never intended for anyone to go through life alone. One writer says there are fifty-five "one another" verses in Scripture. "Serve one another." "Love one another." "Encourage one another." The New Testament stresses the importance of being there for another person as a crucial part of building and maintaining the body of Christ.

God's plan involves a relationship with a small band of like-minded brothers or sisters who share our journey through life. While Paul traveled around the Roman Empire spreading the gospel and planting churches, he rarely traveled alone. He assembled a team of other men to disciple and welcomed the friendship of married couples, not only for their assistance but for their company. In one letter Paul wrote, "I think it is necessary to send back to you Epaphroditus, my brother, fellow worker and fellow soldier . . . whom you sent to take care of my needs" (Philippians 2:25). He wrote to Titus, "Do your best to come to me at Nicopolis, because I have decided to winter there (Titus 3:12). Near the end of his life, the apostle wrote his friend, Timothy, "I long to see you, so that I may be filled with joy" (2 Timothy 1:4). He urged him, "Make every effort to come to me soon," and again, "Do your best to get here before winter" (2 Timothy 4:9, 21). Paul needed friends as well as fellow workers. And so do we.

> *We often have a lot of fellow worker and fellow soldier relationships, but few, if any brother relationships.*

THE REQUIREMENT OF A DYNAMIC SMALL GROUP

There must be a commitment to one another as firm as your commitment to

Christ. You didn't seriously follow Christ until you became intentional about it. The same is true for the relationships developed within a small group. You intentionally commit to the wellbeing of the brothers or sisters within your group.

True fellowship consists of honesty to the point of vulnerability. The discussions move beyond superficiality to honest dealing with the messy side of life. At this point, they address difficult "what if" questions: "What if I lose my job?" or "What if my wife moves out?" or "What if I fail?" That's when conversation enters a new level and brotherhood/sisterhood adds a new dimension to life.

True fellowship involves accountability to one another. Every week you need to "report in" and tell how Christ is working in your life, or how you struggled with staying on track. Each person in the group can be both an encouragement and a challenge to the others.

True fellowship means expressing our dreams and aspirations. The collective wisdom of the group plus their contacts might supply what is needed to send that dream toward fulfillment.

True fellowship involves accountability to one another as well as expressing our dreams and aspirations.

So How Do You Get Started?

1. Start by praying for a few good friends to join you.
2. Take the initiative and ask them to meet together for eight weeks.
3. Model unity and watch how others observe what is going on and long for the same experience.
4. Use the following schedule during your time together and watch your small group grow into a *supportive team*.

- Share the Scripture. Each person should talk about what they've learned on their own in private study. More is caught in this environment than listening to seminars.
- Share your schedule. What will you be doing over the next couple of weeks? How will the Four Priorities be reflected in that schedule?
- Share your relationships. Who will you spend time with? Where will it be? What do you expect to happen?
- Share where you are now. Are you excited? Let's hear about it! Are you struggling? Let your team share the load.

5. Close the session by praying for one another. Keep a record of prayer requests and note God's responses. As the Lord works through everyone's life over the next few weeks, highlight His faithfulness.

Jesus said, "A new command I give you: Love one another. As I have loved you, so you must love one another. By this all men will know you are my disciples, if you love one another" (John 13:34–35). The small group experience is perhaps the best way to be intentional about obeying God's command.

ONE PERSON'S EXPERIENCE

Psychologist Henry Cloud discovered the power of connection early in life. As a young man, he aspired to become a professional golfer. When a hand injury derailed those dreams, he fell into a deep depression. As a young Christian, Henry became disillusioned with God, wondering why He didn't instantaneously make him better. Over time, however, as he engaged in a meaningful relationship with a Christian couple and committed himself to a small group of fellow strugglers, Henry experienced release from depression. He realized that God usually accomplishes His work in us through the people in our lives. God not only healed Henry's depression, He gave this future psychologist a means of avoiding relapse and a resource to experience greater joy. He discovered through experience the truth of an old Swedish proverb: "A shared joy is a doubled joy and a shared sorrow is half a sorrow."

You can discover that truth for yourself by involving yourself in a small group.

TAKE ACTION

Read 1 Peter 4:10–11, which instructs Christians on their duty to one another, and Romans 12:4–8, which compares a community of believers to a human body.
What do you think it means to "administer God's grace in its various forms?"

In both passages, the grace of God is practical in that it meets the needs of people. What forms can grace take within a small group?

You already belong to one or more informal small communities, such as a department at work, a circle of close friends, a sports team, parents of your children's friends, etc. Think of three specific practical needs you can meet with your own resources.

If you are not part of a small group of other Christians—formally organized or informally bonded—find one. Start by getting information from your pastor or your Christian friends. Then get involved. Make this a priority.

Be intentional: What are you going to do about what you've learned?

Be specific: What action will you take in the near future to begin applying what you've learned? When will you do it?

Be accountable: Pray it through. Share your plan with a friend and seek his/her prayer and counsel for your next step.

CHAPTER 21: CHURCH – YOUR BODY

Scan here to watch the video!

Every four years, athletes from around the world gather to compete in the most-watched athletic event in the world: the Summer Olympics. What part of this global gathering do you think the majority of spectators say they enjoy most? Track and field? Swimming? Diving? Gymnastics? Undoubtedly, the part most people declare as their favorite is the opening ceremony. The parade of nations is a microcosm of the world. Six billion people represented by several thousand Olympians. Competitors with different skin colors, speaking different languages, representing a broad diversity of cultures and governments have this in common—they are members of the Olympic family.

THE CONTENDERS FOR THE FAITH ON PARADE

Have you ever thought of the Church that way? No, not the congregation where you hang your spiritual hat—that's just a small expression of a much larger whole. The worldwide body of believers has more in common with the parade of nations at the opening Olympic ceremony than you might initially think. In every country of the world, Christians gather week after week to worship the same God. While some make their way to a suburban multi-purpose auditorium to sing songs projected on a wall, others assemble in a gothic stone cathedral to become enveloped by the majestic music of a pipe organ. Some believers gather in storefront buildings with cardboard-covered windows. Some sit on split-log pews under thatched grass roofs. Others huddle in single-family homes; fearing persecution or interrogation, they congregate under the cover of darkness. Still others who have come to faith in Christ while serving life sentences in prison find creative ways to "do church" behind bars. In all these settings and more, the church of Jesus Christ gathers to sing hymns, profess faith, read Scripture, absorb teaching, celebrate communion, draw strength, offer prayer, and enjoy fellowship.

Each year, followers of Christ gather to celebrate the Savior's birth in their own unique ways. On Palm Sunday they remember Jesus' triumphal entry into Jerusalem. Each Good Friday, Christians on every continent recall the cruel cross on which our Lord was crucified. Then on Easter, praise songs in every imaginable language proclaim God's power over death.

Pause for a moment and think about it. Broaden your horizons. Redefine your working definition of those who are your brothers and sisters in the faith. Can you fathom it? Those who claim Christ as Savior and Lord and who welcome His rule in their lives can be found in virtually every nation on the earth. Like the Olympic athletes, they represent diversity united by a single cause.

THE UNIVERSAL CHURCH PORTRAYED IN SCRIPTURE

The Scriptures picture this family portrait of all God's children in the last book of the Bible. Revelation allows us to look at a page of heaven's family album. Even though it's a snapshot of the future, what we see corresponds to the reality of a multi-ethnic inter-continental Church here and now. The apostle John describes the scene: "After this I looked and there before me was a great multitude that no one could count, from every nation, tribe, people and language, standing before the throne and in front of the Lamb" (Revelation 7:9). By the time the apostle Peter wrote his letters to the first-century Christians scattered across the Roman Empire (1 Peter 1:1), the universal church had become a movement that transcended all locations, governments, ethnicities, and cultures. Even in the Old Testament, the prophets predicted how the people of God would be found in every imaginable nation: "Arise, shine, for your light has come, and the glory of the Lord rises upon you. See, darkness covers the earth and thick darkness is over the peoples, but the Lord rises upon you and his glory appears over you. Nations will come to your light, and kings to the brightness of your dawn" (Isaiah 60:2–3).

According to David Aikman, the author of *Jesus in Beijing: How Christianity Is Transforming China and Changing the Global Balance of Power*, the church has grown to an estimated eighty million people despite ongoing persecution and other significant difficulties. David is not given to exaggeration. He is the former senior foreign correspondent for Time Magazine and bureau chief in Beijing. He could not ignore the explosive growth from just four million Christians in 1949. Aikman declares, "It is possible that Christians will constitute twenty to thirty percent of China's population within three decades."[18] This will have a profound impact on the universal Church and on the ethnic makeup of that Church in the years to come. Chinese Christians believe they are called to evangelize the nations between China and Israel. Aikman said such numbers and intensity of mission could change the global balance of power. Isaiah was right; "Nations will come to your light."

IN LIGHT OF THAT, THIS

Statistics are fine. They help us to see things in objective terms. Now let's get real. We have brothers and sisters who struggle to survive outside the comfortable community in which we worship. More Christians suffer persecution for their faith right now than at any other time in history. Pastors in Pakistan are being gunned down in their pulpits. Husbands are being carted off to prison, separated from their wives and children. Women are tortured in an attempt to get them to renounce their faith. These are members of our eternal family, so we have to get past our petty complaints and find ways to become tangibly involved with those forced to worship in secret.

Ministries like Voice of the Martyrs (VOM) connect Christians and churches in North America with the challenge facing believers in countries where Christianity is denounced. The statistics provided by VOM are staggering. There were more martyrs for Christ during the twentieth century than during the previous nineteen centuries combined, and the number of martyrs exceeds all battlefield deaths of the combined wars of the twentieth century. These facts demand a response. Through organizations like VOM, contributions can be channeled to provide tangible encouragement and support to brothers and sisters struggling to survive daily persecution.

MISSIONS REDEFINED

Years ago, North American congregations took the lead in sending out missionaries. We would learn the language of those we were trying to reach. We would translate the Bible into the indigenous tongue. We would explain that Jesus died to save them. We would start churches. Our missionaries would spend a lifetime establishing and training local leaders. And all the while, the church supported these frontline warriors with money, encouragement, tangible supplies, and prayer.

As more and more churches became established in previously unevangelized countries, it became obvious that Christians in those nations made the best missionaries. They knew the language and the culture and were more easily accepted by their peers. But in most cases these Christians live in parts of the world where the per capita income is a fraction of ours. Giving to missions through World Vision, World Concern, Wycliffe Bible Translators and the denominational mission agencies is a way we can "be" the worldwide church.

MISSION POSSIBLE

While the paradigm of missions has changed over the years, North Americans have never enjoyed more opportunities to cross cultural borders and to serve in person. Continue to give. Continue to pray. Continue to send. But don't overlook the opportunity to go! A short-term mission trip offers the best means of seeing the power of the gospel at work abroad and to experience the breadth, depth, and diversity of Christ's global family. Chances are your local church provides opportunities throughout the year for volunteers to spend a week or two assisting believers in a country you've only heard about.

An example of this is Mission Emanuel, a ministry of The Gathering/USA in the Dominican Republic. Over the past two decades, teams of men, women, and children have served the villages of Nazaret and Cielo, building schools, clinics, churches, homes, baseball fields, and a youth center. They also provide clean water and sponsor children who need help with education expenses. As a result, a spiritual awakening has taken place in these villages; many have come to Christ and the churches are at capacity. The impact comes from dedicated people who have decided to put the Scriptures into action, not only by sending money and praying, but by going.

THE KIND OF CHURCH FAMILY GOD INTENDS

God intends for all believers to participate in dynamic fellowship with other Christians, to join together in regular worship, ongoing service, consistent instruction, and unbroken fellowship. He wants us to become interdependent as we sort through the issues of life. Normative Christianity assumes that the church operates as a family of imperfect-yet-forgiven people who are committed to each other and involved in each other's lives. If a believer has no desire to make involvement in a local church a priority, something is out of whack. As someone once put it, "If your relationship with God doesn't overflow into caring relationships with other Christians, you aren't as close to God as you think you are."

Consider this description of the first gathering of believers in Jerusalem:

> They devoted themselves to the apostles' teaching and to the fellowship, to the breaking of bread and to prayer. Everyone was filled with awe, and many wonders and miraculous signs were done by the apostles. All the believers were together and had everything in common. Selling their possessions and goods, they gave to anyone as he had need. Every day they continued to meet together in the temple courts. They broke bread in their homes and ate together with glad and sincere hearts, praising God and enjoying the favor of all the people. And the Lord added to their number daily those who were being saved. (Acts 2:42–47)

The first century church was more organism than organization. They "devoted themselves" to each other. The first Christians took part in activities at the temple and in homes, but they considered "being the Church" a matter of relationships, not programs or buildings or budgets or hierarchy. They called their mutual bond *koinonia*, a Greek terms that means "fellowship, brotherly unity, generosity." It's based on the concept of sharing something in common. That "something" was a personal relationship with Jesus Christ that bonded them at the soul level.

NO LONE RANGER CHRISTIANITY

In too many churches, individuals discover the First Priority (a personal, progressive commitment to Jesus Christ) and stop. They see their relationship with the Lord as a private matter that doesn't involve participation with others. If something goes wrong in a fellowship, or they don't like the way things are done, they simply pack up their personal Jesus and leave. Their union with God, made possible by the Savior, doesn't translate into *koinonia*. This kind of privatized piety smacks of American individualism and not Biblical Christianity. It's what we might call "Lone Ranger" Christianity.

You may have encountered Lone Ranger Christians. Oh sure, they smile

---

If a believer has no desire to make involvement in a local church a priority, something is out of whack.

and perhaps offer a superficial greeting. Perhaps they comment about the weather or a sports score, but no in-depth conversation occurs. And like the Lone Ranger, they wear a "mask" that protects them from letting people at church know who they really are.

To the first Christians in Jerusalem the idea of a Lone Ranger Christian was literally unthinkable. Years later, when individuals began to reject the fellowship of the Christian community, the apostle John stated plainly, "For anyone who does not love his brother, whom he has seen, cannot love God, whom he has not seen" (1 John 4:20). He remembered the early days of the movement, which Luke described in Acts.

> All the believers were one in heart and mind. No one claimed that any of his possessions was his own, but they shared everything they had. With great power the apostles continued to testify to the resurrection of the Lord Jesus, and much grace was upon them all. There were no needy persons among them. For from time to time those who owned lands or houses sold them, brought the money from the sales and put it at the apostles' feet, and it was distributed to anyone as he had need. (Acts 4:32–35)

THE TELLTALE SIGNS OF FELLOWSHIP

The willingness to commit to the local Body in dynamic fellowship has three observable results. First and foremost, when our union with the Father spills over into communion with His other children, that kind of fellowship results in *unparalleled joy*. If you've tasted that favor of authentic inner fulfillment, you know all about it. Being committed to others and sharing the highs and lows of life with them exposes you to a joy factor you didn't even know existed.

Being committed to others and sharing the highs and lows of life with them exposes you to a joy factor you didn't even know existed.

The apostle John wrote a postcard length letter to some early believers. He was convinced of the fact that authentic union with the Lord naturally results in communion with His people. John was also aware of the direct correlation between the amount of joy a believer experiences and that believer's level of intimacy with fellow Christians. In the first chapter of 1 John, he wrote: "We proclaim to you what we have seen and heard, so that you also may have fellowship with us. And our fellowship is with the Father and with his Son, Jesus Christ. We write this to make our joy complete" (1 John 1:3–4).

In addition to experiencing the kind of joy God intends for us, dynamic fellowship with other believers also results in a *sense of unity*. We will not be guilty of turning away wounded souls and unlovable people if we consciously seek to know people and celebrate what makes them unique. What is more, we bear one another's burdens, accept the faults we find, we forgive the failings we encounter, and we urge one another to rise above our faults, failures, and burdens. Like mountain climbers, we're tied to the same safety line and we ascend together.

And, finally, dynamic fellowship is a means by which we capture the attention of those who look at the church and scratch their heads in amazement. In other words, when we are sharing a level of life that is transparent, intimate, and engaging, the source of our common life becomes extremely attractive. Jesus said, "By this all men will know that you are my disciples, if you love one another" (John 13:35).

TAKE ACTION

Read Acts 2:42–47 and 4:32–37, which describe the first congregation of Christians.
Using these two passages as the measure of healthy church membership, how would you rate yourself as a member on a scale of one to ten?

Devoted to Teaching (2:42)

|—|—|—|—|—|—|—|—|—|—|
    2   4   6   8

Devoted to Communion (2:42)

|—|—|—|—|—|—|—|—|—|—|
    2   4   6   8

Devoted to Prayer (2:42)

|—|—|—|—|—|—|—|—|—|—|
    2   4   6   8

Generous Giver (2:43–45)

|—|—|—|—|—|—|—|—|—|—|
    2   4   6   8

Joyful (2:46)

|—|—|—|—|—|—|—|—|—|—|
    2   4   6   8

Sincere (2:46)

	2		4		6		8		

Openly Grateful to God (2:47)

	2		4		6		8		

Enjoy the Favor of the Community (2:46)

	2		4		6		8		

Advocate of Unity (4:32)

	2		4		6		8		

Bold Proclaimer of the Gospel (4:33)

	2		4		6		8		

Unselfish (4:34–37)

	2		4		6		8		

In what ways do you think your church will be impacted if you improve your personal church-building skills?

Be intentional: What are you going to do about what you've learned?

Be specific: What action will you take in the near future to begin applying what you've learned? When will you do it?

Be accountable: Pray it through. Share your plan with a friend and seek his/her prayer and counsel for your next step.

PRIORITY FOUR

"WHEN HE SAW THE CROWDS, HE HAD COMPASSION ON THEM, BECAUSE THEY WERE HARASSED AND HELPLESS, LIKE SHEEP WITHOUT A SHEPHERD. THEN HE SAID TO HIS DISCIPLES, 'THE HARVEST IS PLENTIFUL BUT THE WORKERS ARE FEW. ASK THE LORD OF THE HARVEST, THEREFORE, TO SEND OUT WORKERS INTO HIS HARVEST FIELD'"

MATTHEW 9:36-38

A PERSONAL, PROGRESSIVE COMMITMENT TO THE WORK OF CHRIST IN THE WORLD

OVERVIEW

In A.D. 313, Emperor Constantine legalized Christianity. Not long after this historic edict, he began to call himself a Christian, which, of course, made going to church very fashionable. The resulting influx of superficial converts disgusted many devout believers, who retreated from public life to worship God in the seclusion of monasteries. These cloistered communities, separated from the world by stone walls or vast stretches of wilderness, allowed Christ-followers to pursue "a personal, progressive commitment to Jesus Christ" to the exclusion of all other concerns. But Jesus didn't say, "Seek his kingdom *only*." He said, "Seek his kingdom *first*" (Matthew 6:33).

The fact is, we cannot love God without loving and serving the people He made (1 John 4:20). To become fully formed followers of Jesus Christ, we must not neglect His command, "Go and make disciples of all nations" (Matthew 28:19). John tells us, "God so loved the world that he gave his one and only Son" (John 3:16). The opening line in Rick Warren's *The Purpose Driven Life* states, "It's not about you," and that's true. Our focus needs to be outward, toward God and others.

As a Christian you have a new identity according to 1 Peter 1:9. This includes being a part of a new group of people called a "holy nation," which is made up of believers from all over the world. With this new identity comes a new perspective, the way you view the world. You no longer see your neighbor down the street as just another stranger, but as a person who needs Christ, someone with whom you can build a relationship. You no longer examine your lifestyle based on your desires but on how it impacts those around you. You no longer see social problems as someone else's responsibility, but from the desire to bring a godly solution. When you see suffering, it brings you pain. When you see the earth, you see a wonderful creation that needs protection. You now see everything through God's eyes.

This doesn't mean you can right every wrong or solve every problem. But as you live out **Priority Four**, you will seek to find God's call on your life so you know where to focus your attention and energy. As a believer you will be intentional about touching the world by touching your world. To do less will fall short of both your potential and God's expectations.

> *If anyone boasts, "I love God," and goes right on hating his brother or sister, thinking nothing of it, he is a liar. If he won't love the person he can see, how can he love the God he can't see? The command we have from Christ is blunt: Loving God includes loving people. You've got to love both.*
> 1 John 4:20-21 MSG

CHAPTER 22: A WORLDVIEW

Scan here to watch the video!

Everybody has one. We usually acquire it by inheritance, we work hard to pass it on to our children, we hope everyone will want to copy ours, and nearly everyone dies with the one he or she received early in life. It determines how we experience the world and it guides our every decision. Even so, very few people know they have one of these, and fewer still take the time to examine it. As you have undoubtedly surmised from the title, this universal possession is called a "worldview."

A worldview is the sum total of our values, beliefs, preference, and prejudices that determine how we view life, process information, form judgments, and make decisions. It is the mental lens through which we view the world. Like a contact lens for the mind, it can clarify or distort what we see. This lens can be tinted or clear. It can warp our perspective or allow us to see sharper details. According to George Barna, an astute observer of North American culture, "Your worldview is the product of all the information, ideas, and experiences you absorb to form the values, morals, and beliefs that you possess."[1] He contends it largely defines who you are and how you behave.

With that as a foundation, consider the worldview of someone who does *not* believe in the existence of God. That person does not approach his or her personal behavior with any sense of ultimate judgment or reward. If someone believes in a higher power but does not subscribe to the concept of life after death, that person will likely operate on the notion that whatever he or she does has no eternal consequences. Because this worldview limits a person from looking for ultimate retribution when injustice is done, he or she must either live with the fallout of an unfair world or take matters into his or her own hands.

A person who does not believe in absolute truth has a view of the world that results in gut reactions and flying by the seat of the pants. Everything is relative for that individual. Depending on who stands to benefit, or what others might think, or what currently is considered politically correct, this person's perspective on what is "right" or "true" will change from one set of circumstances to another.

Conversely, a person who acknowledges the existence of God and believes that the Bible is nothing less than God's revealed knowledge will come at life differently. Unlike those who look to themselves for moral authority, people with a biblical worldview measure popular opinion against God's immovable standard of right and wrong.

It might seem reasonable that those who view themselves as Christ-followers would maintain a different worldview from those who do not profess belief in the God of the Bible. But this assumption is not necessarily true.

A BIBLICAL WORLDVIEW OUT OF FOCUS: A CASE STUDY

Sherm Douglas was raised in Oklahoma and educated in Texas, his upbringing very much a product of the Bible belt. His dad owned a very successful hardware store in a suburb of Tulsa. His mom devoted herself to volunteer work with several praiseworthy groups in town. This faithful family never missed a church meeting. A large family Bible graced the living room coffee table, which Sherm's mother dusted each week without fail.

Sherm always believed in God. "After all, doesn't everybody?" he would ask when questioned about his beliefs. He knew, by heart, old-time hymns like "Amazing Grace" and "How Great Thou Art." Often the family would gather around the piano in the den on Sunday afternoon to sing church songs in four-part harmony. When the pastor and his wife were guests for Sunday dinner (a common occurrence), the evening wasn't complete without a good, old-fashioned hymn-sing. The Douglas family was also big on singing the "Doxology" before every dinner. A plaque of the Lord's Prayer hung in the entryway of their large colonial-style home.

Although church attendance was a guarded core value, the choices of Douglas family members were not necessarily consistent with sermons they heard from week to week. For example, at tax time, Sherm's dad failed to report the income he received in cash payments. The family liquor cabinet was stocked with whiskey, vodka, brandy, and wine, which Mr. Douglas drank to excess and suffered a hangover most Saturday mornings. When Sherm's sister got pregnant in junior high school, her daddy drove her to the clinic and paid for the abortion. And Sherm's two brothers chose not to marry their girlfriends, opting to live with them after graduating from college.

Sherm graduated with honors from Baylor University and then proceeded to get his MBA at the University of Texas. It was during graduate school that he exchanged his nominal churchianity for a deeply personal Christianity. A campus ministry leader convinced Sherm to join a weekly Bible study with sharp, intelligent grad students who loved the Lord. In this small group of other CEOs-in-training, Sherm realized that he treated Jesus like a mascot or a lucky charm, not a Master with whom he could have a relationship. So, he decided to discard the superficial religion his parents and siblings had followed, and he embraced the Word of God as his guide for life. As a result, everything changed. When he accepted the Scriptures as absolute truth inspired by his Creator, he began to cultivate new attitudes about compassion, interpersonal conflict, the use of alcohol, and stewardship of the environment. He also gained a completely new perspective on the commitment his wedding vows entail. No longer did Sherm march to the cadence of what culture deemed appropriate. Instead, he based his conduct on the answers to two questions: "What does the Bible say about this issue?" and "What would Jesus do?"

After earning his MBA, Sherm returned to Oklahoma where he went to work for an oil company. He married the attractive daughter of the company's president, and within ten years he was vice president. Ten years later he replaced his father-in-law as top man with a salary that he was embarrassed to mention at MBA class reunions. He wasn't embarrassed, however, to talk about Jesus. Sherm was an outspoken Christian who kept a dog-eared copy of his Bible on his desk. It wasn't for the sake of maintaining a good Christian image like his parents; he kept it handy because he referred to the Word of God often. He consulted Scripture with every decision and referred to it often in weekly staff meetings.

At the age of sixty-two, Sherm was blindsided with a devastating diagnosis. Doctors told him that an inoperable brain tumor would take his life in nine months. When Sherm shared this news with his small group at church, they rallied around him and prayed, asking God for healing. One of Sherm's best friends in the group attempted to comfort him with verses concerning the brevity of life and the confidence we have as Christians that death is not to be feared but welcomed.

Sherm could give mental assent to the fact that Christians should not fear death but accept the end of physical life as a transition to the presence of Christ. Even so, it was difficult to embrace that reality in his heart. He and his wife began to fly to Mexico and Europe seeking alternative treatments. Sherm died eleven months after his initial diagnosis. He did everything he could to find a cure but in the end, cancer ended his life.

A CONFLICT OF WORLDVIEWS

This case study illustrates two important principles.

First, sometimes there is a great gap between our *declared* worldview and the worldview that actually guides our decisions. Jesus called this hypocrisy, a mask we wear for the sake of others to hide our true face. This tendency kept Him in perpetual conflict with the religious leaders of His day.

Second, even a sincerely held worldview can be difficult to apply when challenged by the difficulties of life. Sherm's choices in life after grad school remained consistent with his sincere Christian belief. When it came to accepting death as a transition that promotes Christians to the presence of Christ, Sherm struggled with a dilemma. He echoed the words of Paul, who wrote, "I am torn between the two: I desire to depart and be with Christ, which is better by far; but it is more necessary for you that I remain in the body" (Philippians 1:23–24).

This is not sinful. This is normal. Jesus predicted that the tension between the Biblical worldview and the way of the world would stretch Christians to the point of breaking (John 15:18–21; 16:1–4). Fortunately, the Bible assures us, "We do not have a high priest who is unable to sympathize with our weaknesses, but we have one who has been tempted in every way, just as we are—yet was without sin. Let us then approach the throne of grace with confidence, so that we may receive mercy and find grace to help us in our time of need" (Hebrews 4:15–16).

Society (what Jesus called "the world") exerts enormous pressure for us to take our cues from what the media suggests is appropriate behavior or what the current prophets of tolerance in our culture consider acceptable. According to George Barna's research, the percentage of Bible-professing Christians who view the world from a non-Christian perspective is astoundingly high. From his vantage point, he sees several popular perspectives that account for this belief-action disconnect.

Barna contends, for example, that among professing born-again adults, only six out of ten follow a set of specific principles or standards that serve as behavioral guidelines. Two out of ten committed believers do whatever feels right or comfortable in a given situation. One out of ten of those who call themselves "born-again Christians" do whatever they believe will make the most people happy or will create the least amount of conflict with others.

Barna goes on to say that a lesser number of believers—about one out of ten—make moral decisions based on whatever they think will produce the most personally beneficial outcome, whatever they believe their family or friends would expect them to do, or whatever they think other people would do in the same situation.

In his book *Think Like Jesus*, Barna writes,

> Among those who say they rely on Biblical standards and principles as their compass for moral decision making, only half believe that all moral truth is absolute. The rest either believe that moral decisions must be made on the basis of the individual's perceptions and the specific situation, or they haven't really thought about whether truth is relative or absolute.
>
> That means the bottom line is that only fourteen percent of born-again adults—in other words, about one out of every seven born-again adults—rely on the Bible as their moral compass and believe that moral truth is absolute. While these perspectives are not, in themselves, the totality of a Bible-based worldview, they form the foundation on which such a life lens is based. Very few born-again Christians have the foundation in place.[2]

Barna's research reveals several alarming statistics. Ninety-one percent of all born-again *adults* do not have a Biblical worldview; ninety-eight percent of all born-again *teenagers* do not have a Biblical worldview. In 2003, the United States adult population stood at 210 million. Roughly 175 million of them claimed to be Christian, eighty million professing to be "born-again" Christians. About seven million of them had a Biblical worldview. That was less than one of every thirty adults in America.[3]

Based on that data, is it any wonder the divorce rate among Christians is rising? It helps to explain why Christian teens are not much more inclined to abstain from premarital sex than their non-Christian peers. Given what you now know, are you surprised that young people reared in Christian homes increasingly prefer cohabitation to marriage? If the worldview— the basic assumptions—of most church-going adults and teens barely differs from the worldview of popular culture, we cannot expect their behavior to be any different.

PIECING TOGETHER A MOSAIC WORLDVIEW

While Moses served as the human author of the first five books of the Old Testament, he also composed an epic psalm. According to Bible scholars, Psalm 90 was written by the same person who brought down the Ten Commandments from Mt. Sinai. In addition to offering a sobering reflection on the brevity of life, Psalm 90 presents a candid picture of the realities of living in an imperfect world subjected to the pain, suffering, and consequences of sin. Moses writes,

> We are consumed by your anger and terrified by your indignation. You have set our iniquities before you, our secret sins in the light of your presence. All our days pass away under your wrath; we finish our years with a moan. The length of our days is seventy years—or eighty, if we have the strength; yet their span is but trouble and sorrow, for they quickly pass, and we fly away. (Psalm 90:7–10)

But Moses' perspective was not limited to what he saw around him. While his peers became jaded and let the injustices and hardships of life derail their hopes and dreams, Moses remained steadfast in his outlook. He wrote,

> Satisfy us in the morning with your unfailing love, that we may sing for joy and be glad all our days. Make us glad for as many days as you have afflicted us, for as many years as we have seen trouble. May your deeds be shown to your servants, your splendor to their children. May the favor of the Lord our God rest upon us; establish the work of our hands for us—yes, establish the work of our hands. (Psalm 90:14–17)

Moses doesn't write like someone overwhelmed by the world. He hasn't given up, even though it appears people or circumstances have let him down. His words drip with hope in what God has promised to do. The reason? His worldview exceeds the confines of his difficulties. Look at the first two verses of Psalm 90: "Lord, you have been our dwelling place throughout all generations. Before the mountains were born or you brought forth the earth and the world, from everlasting to everlasting you are God."

Despite what occurs in the world, Moses remained steadfastly convinced that God is sovereign and all-powerful and that God has a plan to which every life can contribute. Seeing the Almighty as Creator and Lord was the lens through which the prophet looked at the world. For him, this life-defining perspective demanded submission and obedience. Consequently, Moses drew a direct correlation between his worldview and his decisions. One informed the other. Therefore, he appealed to God, "Teach us to number our days aright, that we may gain a heart of wisdom" (Psalm 90:12).

That's what a Biblical worldview calls each of us to do as well. Having the mind of God revealed in Scripture and living within us in the person of the Holy Spirit, we must seek His guidance so that we make wise choices and put that divine knowledge into practice.

Moses remained steadfastly convinced our God is sovereign, all-powerful, and has a plan to which every life can contribute

BASIC ASSUMPTIONS

So what are your assumptions about the world? That people are inherently selfish? That there is no direct correlation between integrity and success? Hey, don't be too daring! But given the fact that you are reading this book, you probably also have some assumptions about the world based on what you've heard at your church or read in your Bible. Is it safe to say that your basic assumptions include the following?

- God is the all-knowing, all-powerful Creator of the universe who still rules the universe today.
- When Jesus Christ was on earth, He lived a sinless life.
- Satan is not just a symbol of evil but is a real, living entity.
- A person cannot earn eternal salvation by being good or doing good things for other people; salvation is the free gift of God.
- Every person who believes in Jesus Christ has a personal responsibility to share his or her faith in Him with people who believe differently.
- The Bible is totally accurate in all that it teaches.

PRACTICING WHAT WE PREACH

Believing the truth and actually allowing the truth to guide our behavior are two different matters. That has been the case for more than two millennia. Back in the first century, a church leader by the name of James wrote a letter to a group of Christians whose "orthopraxy" (practice) did not reflect their orthodoxy (beliefs). He charged them,

> Do not merely listen to the word, and so deceive yourselves. Do what it says. Anyone who listens to the word but does not do what it says is like a man who looks at his face in a mirror and, after looking at himself, goes away and immediately forgets what he looks like. But the man who looks intently into the perfect law that gives freedom, and continues to do

this, not forgetting what he has heard, but doing it—he will be blessed in what he does. (James 1:22–25)

TAKE ACTION

Read John 15:18–16:4, in which Jesus describes the Christian's tension with those who do not embrace a biblical worldview.
What hot-button issues will likely cause a believer to suffer rejection or mistreatment today?

If you were to be brutally honest with yourself, in what ways has your behavior run contrary to what you say you believe?

What do you most fear if you put a biblical worldview into consistent practice at work or among people who reject the authority of the Bible?

If you are part of a small group, or have a trusted Christian friend, confess your fears and failures, and ask for support in living out your biblical worldview.

Be intentional: What are you going to do about what you've learned?

Be specific: What action will you take in the near future to begin applying what you've learned? When will you do it?

Be accountable: Pray it through. Share your plan with a friend and seek his/her prayer and counsel for your next step.

CHAPTER 23: THE NEED FOR EVANGELISM

Scan here to watch the video!

On a beautiful Saturday afternoon, Larry was enjoying a family picnic on Casper Mountain with his parents and siblings. As any normal twelve-year-old boy, he loved to explore the rocks and crevices. So, weaving in and out of the tall Rocky Mountain pines, Larry searched the landscape hoping to find an abandoned miner's cabin or perhaps an abandoned mine. Unfortunately, he forgot two important principles of wilderness survival during his afternoon exploration.

>Rule 1: always know the time of day.
>Rule 2: always know the way back to camp.

Around 4 p.m., Larry realized that he had better head back to camp, but he had lost his bearings. He ran down the most recent ridge he had climbed and stood in a familiar-looking meadow. As he glanced at the sky and noticed the sun sinking below the pine trees, he swallowed his first gulp of fear. He was lost. He didn't know which way to turn next. "All right, don't panic" he told himself. "Just think calmly and try to retrace the steps that got you here." But no matter which direction he walked, he couldn't find familiar terrain. With darkness closing in and the evening chill surrounding him, Larry felt a growing sense of desperation.

Then, he thought he heard a voice in the distance. He strained every nerve to see if his mind was playing games or if he really heard a voice. A moment later, a woman's voice, far in the distance, called, "Laaarrrrryyyyy!" Immediately he recognized his mother's voice. He yelled back, but he didn't think she could hear him, so he kept walking through the darkness, weaving through trees and brush, trying to head in the direction of the voice. Soon two voices were calling—his mother and his father. Before long he approached his parents, who fell on him with hugs like the father of the Prodigal Son. Like any self-respecting twelve-year-old, Larry acted as though nothing significant had happened and chided them for worrying. Deep down, however, he was turning somersaults of joy. He had never been so happy to hear the voices and feel the embrace of his parents.

WHY PEOPLE FEEL LOST

Jesus often referred to people in need of Him as "lost" (Matthew 10:6; 15:24; 18:10–14). It's a fitting word picture. Think of the last time you were lost—hopelessly turned around, panicked by disorientation, and helpless to find your way. You may have to reach back into the discarded memories of childhood, but try. Then imagine living your life that way—morally turned around, unable to find the right ethical path leading to your Creator.

Everyone is born lost into the confusing landscape we call the world. And we stay lost for several reasons.

The world is dark.

As the ancient writer, Chrysostom, writes, we are "like men with sore eyes—they find the light painful, while the darkness, which permits them to see nothing, is restful and agreeable."[4] Not only do they shun the light, they remain hopelessly enslaved to darkness until someone seeks them, finds them, and leads them. Like our opening story of Larry, lost on Casper Mountain, he found his way back to camp because his mother and father searched for him. Their voices led him to safety. This theme shows up repeatedly in Scripture. God relentlessly cups His hands around His mouth, calling "Follow My voice. Come home!"

The world is fallen.

God sovereignly designed the world to sustain our physical lives and to facilitate our ongoing, intimate relationship with Him. When Adam and Eve sinned, the world fell from its original purpose and became distorted. Now, there's something wrong with everything. Disasters, diseases, death, and decay rule the creation God once pronounced "good." Unfortunately, this Fall was not limited to creation. Human nature became distorted as well. We are born relentlessly selfish and stubbornly prideful, and therefore slaves to sin.

Ironically, God gets a lot of bad press. When bad things happen, we ask, "Where was God?" or "How could God let this happen?" when, in fact, the majority of all pain and suffering are caused by people. We act like people with darkened minds—totally foolish—because we are fallen people living in a distorted creation. When addressing the Romans, Paul said that God has revealed Himself to humanity through His creative acts, but humankind's "thinking became futile and their foolish hearts were darkened" (Romans 1:21). He declared that people can't look at a sunset over a beautiful mountain range and then sing praises to God because we are born spiritually dead. "You were dead in your transgressions and sins, in which you used to live when you followed the ways of this world" (Ephesians 2:1–2). Dead people can't respond. A doctor can shine a light directly on the dead person's pupil and he or she will see nothing.

Paul describes spiritually dead people as "darkened in their understanding and separated from the life of God because of the ignorance that is in them due to the hardening of their hearts" (Ephesians 4:18). These are not the kindest words you can say about a person, but a spiritual physician must be truthful. People who are lost without Christ have three characteristics; they are dead, blind, and ignorant. And because they have no power to respond, no ability to get themselves out of their darkness, they need the intervention of an outside source. They need life given to them by grace, the unmerited favor of God. Paul calls this salvation a "gift" (Ephesians 2:8).

The world is relativistic.

Dr. Francis Schaeffer was a physically small man with a great intellect and a heart as big as the world. He and his wife, Edith, moved from St. Louis, where he served as a seminary professor and pastor, to establish L'Abri (French for "the shelter), a philosophical community in Switzerland. Dr. and Mrs. Schaeffer used their alpine home as a retreat for lost souls crisscrossing Europe in search of the truth. The sixties and seventies were decades where college students were searching deeply for the meaning of life and any guru who could shed light on their paths.

As people found their way to L'Abri, they would sit and listen for hours as Dr. Schaeffer gave lectures on the direction of western civilization as reflected in philosophy, art, architecture, cinema, and popular culture. He lamented the intellectual direction of society, saying, "We live in an age of synthesis and relativism; men don't believe truth exists."[5] In other words, people do not believe in absolutes; truth is relative. This chapter is not the place for a thorough debunking of this thought process, only to acknowledge that according to Dr. Alan Bloom, author of *The Closing of the American Mind*, "There is one thing a professor can be absolutely certain of: almost every student entering the university believes, or says he believes, that truth is relative."[6]

The world is hurting.

Every person, Christian or not, experiences pain. Suffering is class-blind, race-blind, gender-blind, denominationally blind, and age-blind. Pain comes in a variety of options—psychological, emotional, physical, and relational, and can show itself in anything from harsh words to addictions to suicide.

The Genesis account of creation explains that pain and suffering first began when Adam sinned. His moral fall brought the world down with him so that all living creatures experience pain. The apostle Paul declares, "Creation was subjected to frustration, not by its own choice, but by the will of the one who subjected it, in hope that the creation itself will be liberated from its bondage to decay and brought into the glorious freedom of the children of God. We know that the whole creation has been groaning as in the pains of childbirth right up to the present time" (Romans 8:20–22).

GOD'S PLAN FOR THE LOST

There's a story told that after Jesus finished His thirty-three years of ministry, died on the cross, rose from the dead, and ascended into heaven, He was met by a great host of saints who had gone before. They asked Him about the wonderful plan laid out before time and how His death and sacrifice would result in salvation for all who would respond to His invitation of new and eternal life. Then one of the angels asked, "But if people don't respond, what is your plan?" Jesus responded, "There is no other plan."

While God is ultimately responsible for the salvation of lost souls, He does not have a "Plan B." The Bible states plainly,

> If anyone is in Christ, he is a new creation; the old has gone,

the new has come! All this is from God, who reconciled us to himself through Christ and gave us the ministry of reconciliation: that God was reconciling the world to himself in Christ, not counting men's sins against them. And he has committed to us the message of reconciliation. We are therefore Christ's ambassadors, as though God were making his appeal through us. We implore you on Christ's behalf: Be reconciled to God. (2 Corinthians 5:17–20)

On the eve of His crucifixion, Jesus told His disciples, "I am the way and the truth and the life. No one comes to the Father except through me" (John 14:6). No one else is qualified to save humankind. Jesus lived a perfect life. He alone can forgive sins. He alone meets the deepest needs of the human heart. He alone meets the need for significance. He alone can wipe away all guilt. He alone is the One who can find us in the dark and lead us to safety.

Johnny Cash and June Carter starred in a TV special titled, "Is There a Family in the House?" This telethon helped raise funds for the ministry, Youth for Christ. During one segment of the production, Johnny told the story of a little girl from Kansas who went missing one day. Her distraught parents looked frantically around the house and farm for her but to no avail. Soon friends and neighbors from that part of the state showed up to help in the search. State troopers joined the effort while helicopters hovered over cornfields, but there was no sign of the missing girl.

Eventually, someone suggested that everyone hold hands and form a human chain that would stretch from one end of the farm to the other. Step by step they moved forward, eyes straining for any hopeful signs. Finally, they came upon her lifeless body. Out of the agony and heartbreak of the situation, someone asked, "Why didn't we join hands sooner?"

That is the ultimate question for evangelism. Why don't we join hands to find those who are lost, who desperately need a Savior, and cannot find their way out of the darkness?

TAKE ACTION

Read 2 Corinthians 5:17–20, which describes our role in God's plan to seek and to save the lost.

- On a scale of 1 to 10, rate your confidence in sharing the core message of the gospel in two minutes. Why did you give yourself this score?

What is the primary reason you don't tell more people how to receive God's forgiveness and His gift of eternal life?

This week, check with your church or ask your pastor how you might receive evangelism training to become more competent and more confident in helping the lost find Christ.

Be intentional: What are you going to do about what you've learned?

Be specific: What action will you take in the near future to begin applying what you've learned? When will you do it?

Be accountable: Pray it through. Share your plan with a friend and seek his/her prayer and counsel for your next step.

CHAPTER 24: METHODS OF EVANGELISM

Scan here to watch the video!

Once upon a time, a man from a far off country purchased an apple orchard and hired hundreds of workers to live and work on his property. Each worker was issued a tent by the owner and instructed to pick the apples around his own tent in exchange for free lodging.

In the early years, everyone faithfully picked the apples and very few fell to the ground and rotted. Eventually the owner had to return to his own country, and so he left a detailed book of instructions and asked a few people to act as supervisors. For several people, picking apples and guiding others in picking required their full time attention. The other workers, who earned income from outside jobs, contributed to their support.

As time passed, some of the workers started saying about their supervisors, "He's such a good apple-picker. He gets paid to pick apples. I'll have him come pick my apples."

In a surprisingly short time, no one picked apples except the paid apple-pickers. A few volunteers would occasionally help with the picking, but everyone considered apple-picking to be the supervisor's job. Once or twice a week, special apple picking services would be held. All the people of the orchard would gather to watch the supervisor climb his stepladder and pick apples. Many people invited the supervisors to pick apples in their sections of the orchard. But with so few people actually working, apples throughout the orchard kept falling to the ground and rotting.

To encourage and motivate everyone, the leaders built a special hall and gave wonderful lectures about picking apples and explained the latest harvesting techniques. They tried to foster a culture of apple-picking by hosting special festivals and brought in musical groups to lead everyone in singing apple-picking songs. Everyone loved to sing about picking apples, and the motivational films were very inspiring. Famous apple-pickers from other parts of the nation regaled the crowds with stories and lessons about the importance of the harvest. They even had everyone fill out commitment cards, pledging to attempt regular apple-picking, but apathy took over within a couple of weeks.

Building and maintaining the lecture hall, bringing in great apple pickers and purchasing special apple picking machinery cost money. A lot of money. Many special meetings were held to discuss all the money spent on picking apples. Wasn't there some less expensive way to get this work accomplished? They kept detailed records of every apple picked and the attendance at apple-picking ceremonies. Everyone felt successful if attendance at apple picking meetings increased, especially if expenses were kept to a minimum and more apples were picked this year than last.

And yet . . . and yet . . . there were those that had a disquieting concern about all those rotten apples. No count was ever taken of unharvested apples. But there were millions of them. In front of almost every tent; all throughout the orchard. People leaving the lecture hall couldn't help tripping over them! All those rotten apples caused complications for everyone. Rotten apples in the school building, rotten apples in the town hall, rotten apples on the neighbor's tent. Some people even had rotten apples falling on their own tents! You would think if the supervisor couldn't handle the job, at least the owner of the orchard would do something . . . maybe even call for a new supervisor.

Then an amazing thing happened! One day, two men discovered some pages from the apple-picker's guide that must have fallen out of the book years before. They were old and wrinkled and lodged inside the hollow trunk of an ancient apple tree. They immediately brought the pages to the supervisor (since everyone believed that only the supervisor could understand the true meaning of the apple-picker's guide). He read these words: "The job of the supervisor is to exhort the people to do their work of picking apples. Everyone has special gifts to pick the apples from the trees around his own tent. Only in this way can all the apples be picked."

Some of the people were angry. "It can't say that! Everyone knows it's the supervisor's job to pick the apples." Others were excited. "Why, that makes sense!" they said. "If we each just pick the apples around our own tents, almost all the apples could be picked, and very few would fall to the ground and rot. The supervisor would still have enough to keep himself busy, as he helps us and guides us as we pick the apples." And so the people did as the apple-picking guide suggested. As a result, they harvested more apples than they ever thought possible! When the owner in the far off country heard of it, he was very pleased![7]

Surveys show that ninety-eight percent of Christians never lead another person to Christ, even though the Word of God provides specific instructions to all believers and commands them to "go and make disciples of all nations" (Matthew 28:19).[8] Acts 8:26–39 describes a life-changing encounter and an effective pattern for communicating your faith. Take some time to read this passage now.

If you want to be faithful, if you love people and you want them to know about Christ, yet you are reluctant because you lack confidence, this chapter contains six keys to sharing your faith.

SIX KEYS TO SHARING YOUR FAITH

Key 1—Sensitivity to the Lord's Leading (Acts 8:26–27)
Philip was highly attuned to God. After the martyrdom of Stephen, believers in Jerusalem began to feel the fire of persecution, prompting many to flee Judea for Samaria. Of course, they brought the gospel with them, sparking a great spiritual awakening among the Samaritans. Philip played a significant role in bringing many to Christ and never intended to leave. God, however, had other plans. An angel of the Lord sent Philip to an isolated road between

Jerusalem and Gaza.

Philip was familiar with the Old Testament, so he didn't struggle with the idea of receiving divine instructions from an angel. Even so, he could have doubted or denied this leading. He could have argued that remaining in Samaria gave him greater opportunity to reach thousands with the good news of Jesus Christ; what could he do on a deserted road in persecuted territory? Regardless, Philip obeyed. As a devout follower, he remained sensitive to God's wishes.

Sensitive people are available people. This kind of sensitivity develops over time as people walk closely with the Lord. He is like the person described in Psalm 1:1–2: "Blessed is the man who does not walk in the counsel of the wicked or stand in the way of sinners or sit in the seat of mockers. But his delight is in the law of the Lord, and on his law he meditates day and night."

Key 2—Availability to Move (Acts 8:27–29)
Philip was available because he had prepared himself. While Philip ministered among the crowds in Samaria, God saw an Ethiopian official—a man holding high office in his native country—reading a portion of Scripture that he didn't understand. The Ethiopian was a Gentile known as a "God-fearer," a non-Jew who worshiped the God of Israel. He had undoubtedly visited the temple and was returning home. While in Jerusalem, he had encountered Christians and heard their stories about Jesus, the Messiah. So, he consulted the prophetic writings of Isaiah to learn more about this long-promised King, and how He would suffer the penalty of death for the sins of His people.

God wanted someone who knew the Scriptures, who was sensitive to this man's position and questions, and could help the Ethiopian see Jesus Christ as the fulfillment of Isaiah's promises. So, He chose Philip.

When young Henry Kissinger was the Secretary of State, he talked about the political and intellectual preparation needed to serve the President of the United States. When summoned to the White House and asked his opinion on a conflict in some remote part of the globe, he couldn't respond by saying, "Let me go get my map and see if I can find where that is, and I'll get back to you." The President needed cabinet members who had already done their homework and had the intellectual capital necessary to advise him promptly and reliably. Philip had that kind of capital and was available to move.

Key 3—Initiative (Acts 8:30)
Philip ran up to the chariot and heard the Ethiopian reading from Isaiah. In one verse, we learn a lot about this extraordinary man. He used a combination of skills to engage him in a way that would lead the Ethiopian to the most important discovery of his life. He combined patience with zeal and intelligence. He was bold but not brash. He knew how to explore the man's soul with a penetrating question: "Do you understand what you are reading?"

It's one thing to take the initiative; it's another to do it effectively. Philip was on a mission, and he didn't have to determine whether it was the right mission. God had prepared the opportunity and Philip seized it. But, let's face it; it's unlikely we will ever receive audible instructions from a divine messenger. Still, we can learn from Philip's example as we meet strangers in need along the road of life.

First, Philip made a habit of going where people needed to know about Christ; first in Samaria and then to this lonely spot where God had sent him. As some seasoned ministers have stated, "Half of ministry is simply showing up." Whether it is selling a product or building a relationship with a potential believer, it will not happen without being where we need to be. And we need to be there consistently. Business studies show that most deals are sealed after a fifth visit. Most believers who came to Christ as an adult report hearing the gospel several times before making their decision to believe.

Second, Philip listened for an opportunity to engage the man. He didn't say, "God sent me to talk to you" or "You're a sinner and you need Christ." He listened to the Ethiopian, discovered his need, and then engaged the man by offering to supply what he lacked. Taking initiative doesn't require us to become pushy. It calls for us to be available for service and then proactive in serving the needs of those we hope to reach.

Key 4—Tactfulness (Acts 8:31)
Philip joined the Ethiopian in his chariot, but not before he was invited. He listened as the man confessed his need for explanation. Philip didn't make him feel foolish but rather showed genuine concern. He was courteous and honored the dignity of this seeker.

Too often a person moves from witnessing for Christ to arguing against the seeker. No one can be argued into God's kingdom. When a person genuinely is seeking the truth, when his or her heart has been prepared by God's spirit, any messenger who can tactfully and inoffensively declare the content of the good news can be used to lead another to Christ.

Key 5—Precision (Acts 8:34-35)
After the Ethiopian read the passage from Isaiah 53, Philip focused the light of Scripture on Jesus like a laser. The account in Acts states, simply, "Beginning from this Scripture he preached Jesus to him" (Acts 8:35). The "suffering servant" in the passage describes Jesus, who had been crucified not long before the Ethiopian arrived in Jerusalem. Because the heart of the Ethiopian had been prepared, and because Philip taught with clarity and precision, the man believed in Christ without delay. In fact, when the chariot came upon a body of water, he asked, "What prevents me from being baptized?"

That day, he became a part of the family of faith.

Key 6–Decisiveness (Acts 8:36–39)
Throughout this encounter, Philip acted decisively. He obeyed God without

---

Taking initiative doesn't require us to become pushy. It calls for us to be available for service and then proactive in serving the needs of those we hope to reach.

argument. He went to where God sent him immediately. He approached the Ethiopian without hesitation. He listened with deliberation. He seized the opportunity to engage the man promptly. And he preached Christ with clarity and precision. He wasn't pushy. He wasn't obnoxious or offensive. But he wasted no time waffling or deliberating. He proceeded with competence, and therefore confidence. All of this started with a decision to obey the command of Christ.

HOW TO WITNESS EFFECTIVELY

Earlier in Chapter 2, we discussed the Christian life and used Lane Adams' analogy of the beachhead. We illustrated how Christ establishes a foothold in a person's life and then progressively conquers more territory that is held by the Enemy for the rest of that person's journey. Now we want to use the same illustration as a model for sharing your faith with someone in a private conversation. This involves a five-step process. We will write as if we are speaking to a non-believer as we lay out the plan for inviting Christ into his or her life.

1. Go back to the beginning.

When God created the universe, He also created humans to be in fellowship with Him. The world was perfect; God and His creation enjoyed harmony, until the humans decided to violate His command not to eat of a specific tree. In that one act of disobedience, man and woman found themselves cut off from God and, as a result, cut off from their own sense of well-being and fulfillment, and also cut off one from another. That act of disobedience is called SIN.

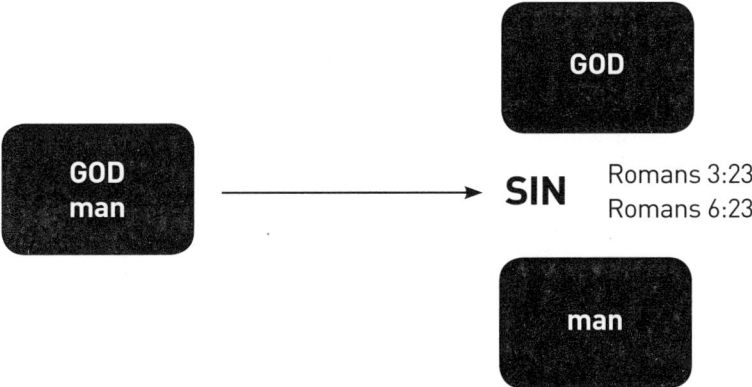

2. People try to get to God on their own.

Knowing that things are not right, humans yearn to have a relationship once again with their Creator. They know they have messed up and that they have done things that make them ashamed, so they attempt to reconnect by going to church, doing good deeds for others, giving money to charity, or creating philosophies and religious rules to appease their conscience. Some people (under the domination of scary religious teaching) even cut or beat themselves in order to gain God's favor. But Scripture teaches that no one can earn his or her way into God's favor; it can only be received as an act of God's grace (Ephesians 2:8–9).

3. God provides a way to reconnect.

God could've left humans in the state they created: fallen, broken, and disconnected from Him. Before time began, before God created mankind, He knew He would redeem us (Ephesians 1:4). God provided a way to reconnect Himself to mankind through His Son, Jesus Christ (John 3:16-17). Jesus came to earth (Matthew 1:18-25), lived among mankind, and sacrificed Himself for our sin (Matthew 27:32-56). With the death, burial and resurrection of Jesus, our sin was atoned for and we have a way of being reconnected to God…by trusting His Son, Jesus Christ (Romans 10:9-10).

4. Christ establishes a beachhead.

Once someone trusts Jesus as Savior, they often wonder why they still struggle with bad habits or old addictions. The beachhead illustration helps outline:

During World War II, the Allies banded together to reclaim a chain of islands in the South Pacific. Aircraft carriers moved in and planes were sent for aerial reconnaissance to find the strengths and the weaknesses of the enemy. Other aircraft were then sent in to bomb the island in order to drive back the enemy so the Allied forces could establish a beachhead. Just as this invasion was critical to the outcome of the war, so, too, an individual needs to be invaded by Christ.

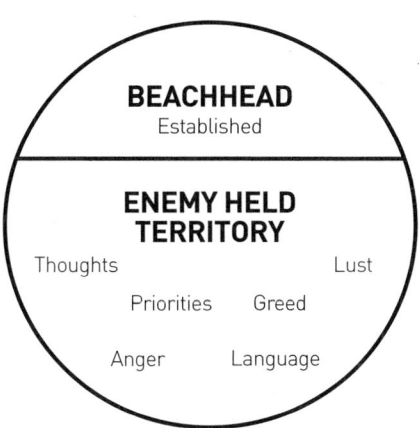

Christ invading a person's life does not end the conflict. Enemy-held territory remains. Once a person becomes a Christian, he or she still has areas of life that create problems: lust, greed, anger, selfishness, pride, etc.

5. The Invasion comes by personal invitation.

I need to tell you my story. There was a time I was lost and confused. I saw that I was in serious trouble. I had sinned and I tried every trick I could find to get to God, but it didn't work. Then someone showed me this illustration, and I did what it says in John 1:12. I received Christ into my life. As a result, Christ took up His position in my life.

I am by no means perfect. I still struggle, but I know Christ is there. Why? Because He said so. That's the beauty of John 1:12. Now when I fail and disappoint both God and myself, I do two things: I confess and I obey. I confess my sin and ask for forgiveness. First John 1:9 states, "If we confess our sins, he is faithful and just and will forgive us our sins and purify us from all unrighteousness." I then turn my back on the thing that tripped me up and go the other way. I obey God and His Word. John 14:15 says, "If you love me, you will obey what I command."

I know Christ's position in my life is permanent (1 John 5:12–13), but by the power of the Holy Spirit, He forgives those temporary failures where I do what I don't want to do (Romans 7:15). He continues to claim more territory in my life, and He will do the same for you.

See "How to Begin a Relationship with Jesus Christ" in the Resource Appendix for more support.

If you would like for Christ to invade your life, do what Jesus asks in Revelation 3:20. He said, "Here I am! I stand at the door and knock. If anyone hears my voice and opens the door, I will come in and eat with him, and he with me." Having Christ enter your life is as close as your willingness to ask Him in. He doesn't beat the door down. He doesn't try to manipulate you to open the door. He simply knocks. The question is, WILL YOU INVITE HIM IN?

THE CHRISTIAN LIFE IS A PROCESS:

THE INVASION   John 1:12: "Yet to all who received him, to those who believed in his name, he gave the right to become children of God."

John 3:36: "Whoever believes in the Son has eternal life, but whoever rejects the Son will not see life, for God's wrath remains on him."

THE POSITION   1 Corinthians 1:8-9: "He will keep you strong to the end, so that you will be blameless on the day of our Lord Jesus Christ. God, who has called you into fellowship with his Son Jesus Christ our Lord, is faithful."

1 John 5:12-13: "He who has the Son has life; he who does not have the son of God does not have life. I write these things to you who believe in the name of the Son of God so that you may know that you have eternal life."

THE CONDITION   Hebrews 10:14: "because by one sacrifice he has made perfect forever those who are being made holy."

TAKE ACTION

Read Acts 8:26–39, which describes Philip's encounter with a potential believer.
Of the six keys to sharing your faith, which two present the greatest challenge to you personally?

- Key 1—Sensitivity (Acts 8:26–27)
- Key 2—Availability (Acts 8:27–29)
- Key 3—Initiative (Acts 8:30)
- Key 4—Tactfulness (Acts 8:31)
- Key 5—Precision (Acts 8:34–35)
- Key 6—Decisiveness (Acts 8:36–39)

Why do you think you struggle in these areas?

Many churches offer instruction in evangelism, including on-the-job training with an experienced witness, who will allow you to shadow him or her until you feel competent and confident. You can also gain valuable training via online courses with ministries like EvanTell (**evantell.org**). Be sure to ask your church leadership for information.

Be intentional: What are you going to do about what you've learned?

·

Be specific: What action will you take in the near future to begin applying what you've learned? When will you do it?

Be accountable: Pray it through. Share your plan with a friend and seek his/her prayer and counsel for your next step.

CHAPTER 25: YOUR CULTURE AND YOUR CALLING

Scan here to watch the video!

If you look carefully at *evangelism*, you'll discover an angel at the heart of the word. Not a dazzling celestial being dressed in white and radiating light. Not that kind of angel. The word evangelism is based on the Greek term, angelos, which means, simply, "messenger." An "evangelist" is someone who brings good news.

In recent years, Christians who give priority to the work of evangelism have called themselves evangelicals. Generally speaking, evangelicals affirm the Creator came to earth in the form of a sinless human being who died for the sin of the world and then rose from death as proof He had accomplished His purpose. We believe the Bible is an infallible revelation of God, transcending time and culture and remaining applicable to life. Furthermore, we claim to have experienced a life-changing encounter with Jesus Christ and believe faith alone is required for one to be reconciled to God and to receive His gift of eternal life. As such, we are motivated to share our faith and to discover effective methods of evangelism.

Sadly, however, if you were to ask most non-believers their opinions about evangelicals, they don't paint a flattering picture. Many think of evangelicals as obnoxious hypocrites who constantly harp on others about prayer in school or rally for the Ten Commandments to be posted in a courthouse lobby. Many now define "evangelicals" as combative or disengaged extremists who continually complain about the loss of moral values, yet offer few solutions to the world's greatest problems. Even so, the Lord's personal approval numbers remain high. If you were to conduct your own research, go to a shopping mall, and ask passersby what they think of Jesus, chances are good the majority will identify Him as an inspiring moral leader, an authentic prophet, a loving leader, and a winsome teacher. Ask those same shoppers what they think of evangelicals you will likely hear words like intolerant, judgmental, hypocritical, and arrogant.

Generally speaking, people in the United States don't have trouble with Jesus; they simply don't like His wife. The Bible calls the church, "the bride of Christ," and we often reflect poorly on our husband. Jesus predicted that the world would hate His followers "for My name's sake" (John 15:21), and history has certainly borne out His warning. However, much of the hatred directed against the church is, unfortunately, earned and, in some ways, justified.

To be fair, walking the tightrope of "being in the world but not of the world" isn't easy. Striking the right balance of engagement with our culture while upholding Christian values has been, and continues to be, an ongoing challenge. History has seen several approaches to resolving this tension.

A REJECTION STRATEGY

The Amish have historically viewed themselves as a movement within society whose members are called to eschew the contamination of culture. Unwilling to compromise with a secular mindset that could dull the edge of their fundamentalist faith, they have closed themselves off from technology. In an Amish community you will see no power lines connected to the homes because electricity is not permitted. They drive horse-drawn buggies, not cars. They plow with teams of horses, not tractors. They wear dark clothing without accessories. The men wear beards and the women avoid makeup.

Not only do the Amish reject modern conveniences, they avoid engaging anyone outside their community. They take the Apostle Paul's admonition to the first century Corinthians quite literally. "Come out from them and be separate" (2 Corinthians 6:17). They strictly apply Paul's instruction, "Do not conform any longer to the pattern of this world" (Romans 12:2), by rejecting the technology of the world and by isolating themselves from society.

While those who are part of the Amish community are a vanishing minority, millions of others embrace a similar mindset. These include Christians who drive cars, light their homes with electricity, use computers, and watch televisions, but limit their association with non-Christians. Some choose to home-school their children or enroll them in private Christian institutions with the specific intent to limit contact with nonbelievers.[9] Rather than run for a position on the local school board, participate in the PTA, or give leadership to the band booster club, they opt out of the system. They are either unconvinced their voice will be heard, or they fear their children will be contaminated by alternate worldviews.

When it comes to friends, these Christians tend to socialize only with those who share their perspectives on life and faith. Mark and Cindy Hanson illustrate this tendency. They are far from Amish in their manner of living. They wear only the latest trends. Their palatial home is smartly furnished and boasts Mark's success as a print salesman. The Hansons both drive late model SUVs. They actively participate in a church fellowship that prides itself on upholding sound doctrine and not accepting as members any who do not agree with every article of belief. Their son and their daughter have attended parochial schools since they were preschoolers.

When Mark and Cindy first moved into their home, neighbors invited them over for barbecues. After several rejections, the neighbors got the message. Mark once told his prayer group that he felt he should avoid fraternizing with his non-believing neighbors as a matter of witness. Their neighbors served beer with their burgers. Because he and Cindy didn't drink alcohol, he thought showing up would be interpreted as their endorsing an ungodly lifestyle. As a result, Mark and Cindy maintained a superficial relationship with their neighbors. They socialize only with people from their church and entertain only Christians in their home.

Mark and Cindy were deeply troubled by the moral decay they observed in society. They realized that people all around them need the Lord, and they hoped their neighbors and business associates would see their lifestyle and then want to know about their Savior. They regularly asked God to keep them unstained by the world around them.

ACCOMMODATION STRATEGY

Another common response to a non-Christian or even hostile culture is to "go with the flow." This strategy seeks to accept opposition as a given, adopt a low profile, make friends with all, and avoid conflict.

Heidi and Grant Barth serve as excellent examples. The Barths met and fell in love at a Midwest university. Thanks to a campus outreach, they also received Christ as students. Neither had grown up in a church-going family, so they were quite thrilled to discover the assurance of salvation and freedom in Christ. When Grant took a job in New York City following graduate school, he and Heidi moved to a high-rise apartment uptown. As best as they could tell, they were the only Christians in a building comprised mostly of Jewish, Muslim, East Indian, and Korean families.

The Barths read their Bibles and prayed regularly, but rarely went to church. Because they relied on public transportation to get around and the nearest evangelical church was five miles away, faithful attendance on Sundays was a challenge. In time, lack of regular fellowship with other believers began to take its toll. Heidi and Grant spent most of their time with non-believing business professionals who partied hard and drank plenty. Longing for friendship, the young couple compromised their code of conduct. Soon they found themselves going along with their friends' secular viewpoints and in so doing, lost their Biblical worldview.

If you were to ask Heidi and Grant today if they were committed followers of Christ, they would assure you they are. In the same breath, however, they would tell you they do not feel obligated to foist their beliefs on others. Christianity is their personal choice of religion and, since we live in a nation that celebrates diversity and tolerance, Jesus' words about being salt and light don't apply today (at least not in North America).

The trouble with simply accommodating culture is that you are quite likely to be changed by it. This occurred repeatedly in the Old Testament. The children of Israel were instructed not to marry those who worshiped other gods. They ignored the Lord's advice and, before long, those who claimed to worship the one true God were sacrificing to pagan deities. Instead of living by the commandments Moses had given them, the Israelites simply went along with the majority and, eventually, became just like their pagan peers.

The trouble with simply accommodating culture is that you are quite likely to be changed by it.

CREATIVE TENSION

Perhaps it would be better to avoid these extremes to pursue another course that might be termed, "creative tension." Rather than avoid contact with our culture, we engage it directly. Instead of accommodating anti-Christian beliefs to get along, we let our manner of life create a wholesome tension, an environment that facilitates constructive change. This occurs when a Christian remains engaged with others without personal compromise. And the best way to do that is for each believer to pursue his or her personal calling.

The word "called" often causes confusion because people believe a divine calling necessarily leads to full-time Christian work. Os Guinness in his compelling work, *The Call*, writes, "Calling is the truth that God calls us to himself so decisively that everything we are, everything we do, and everything we have is invested with a special devotion, dynamism, and direction lived out as a response to his summons and service."[10] This often does present as a divine redirection of a life away from other pursuits to serve God as a vocation. Even so, *everyone* has a primary call from the Lord: "Follow Me." Then, believers have a secondary call to live out our created purpose, what God intended us to do when He fashioned us in our mother's womb. As David considered his own created purpose, he marveled at God's genius.

> You created my inmost being; you knit me together in my mother's womb. I praise you because I am fearfully and wonderfully made; your works are wonderful, I know that full well. My frame was not hidden from you when I was made in the secret place. When I was woven together in the depths of the earth, your eyes saw my unformed body. All the days ordained for me were written in your book before one of them came to be. (Psalm 139:13–16)

According to v. 14, you were "fearfully and wonderfully made" by God. The term, "fearfully," means that He holds great respect for the gifts, talents, skills, and passions He placed within you. He also "ordained" a destiny for you. The term means "to form, to fashion" in the same manner an artisan uses his skill to bring his imagination into reality. He put great thought and skill into making you who you are and outlining your role in His plan for the world.

Our divine purpose may or may not lead us to a specific career. Some are created with gifts that equip them for work in medicine, which they make their primary vocation. Others take any job that will put food on the table while living out their calling in other ways. Andrea is an excellent example. Her accounting career paid the bills, but her heart belonged to underprivileged children. She devoted much of her time to "Clothe a Child," a program designed to provide needy children with clothes for school. She also led others in support of underprivileged children at Landry Elementary School near her home.

Andrea discovered her calling after examining three clues, three aspects of a divine calling: passion, giftedness, and role preference.

PASSION

We make finding our calling more difficult than it has to be. The starting point is to ask about one's interests and concerns. For example, when you receive the daily newspaper, what sections do you read first (not including the comics)? When you go to a bookstore, what topics do you check out? When you sit in front of the television, which of the 500 channels on cable or satellite do you tune in?

If you have passion for a topic, you can spend hours reading about it and find you still have an appetite for more. Hints of this passion show up in early childhood. The child who spends hours in his or her room working with Legos or other building toys has a God-given desire to build. It's the way that person is wired, and an attentive parent would recognize this and create more opportunities to expand the child's abilities.

Another indication of one's passion is daydreams. So when you are alone, what consumes your thoughts? And whom do you envy because they are doing what you would like to do? It was obvious that Labri didn't belong in the administrative assistant role. She had many of the necessary skills, especially proficiency on the computer and with PowerPoint and the ability to interact with clients. She did a good job, yet sitting at a desk most of the day felt to her like sitting at a perpetually red traffic light. She dreamed of teaching musical arts to children. That's what she dreamed about, talked about, and prayed about.

She was like Nehemiah, who served faithfully as the cupbearer to King Artaxerxes in Babylon, yet thought continually of Jerusalem. He had received word that the walls of the city were in great disrepair (Nehemiah 1:1–11) and his passion burned to do something about the problem. The king sympathized with Nehemiah's burden and gave him a leave of absence to follow his dream.

If you are not sure about your passion, ask others to observe you. What do they hear you talking about? Your friends may see things that are not obvious to you and make suggestions that can help you discover what is apparent to everyone but you.

GIFTEDNESS

Dick Hagstrom (Hagstrom Consulting, Inc.) says we learn more about our passions and gifts from our positive experiences than we do from our failures. Everyone who comes to Dick for career counseling receives instruction on how to list positive experiences. Dick tells the person to divide his or her life into two time frames. If the person is thirty-years-old, he or she should list experiences for the first fifteen years on the left side of the page and the second fifteen years on the right side.

These experiences should include meaningful events and accomplishments the person recalls most vividly. These positive experiences help to highlight areas of talent or skill. Of course, not every skill points directly toward one's calling. For example, someone with great cooking skills shouldn't necessarily become a chef. The idea is to find patterns of giftedness, such as creativity, organization, leadership, service, or team-building. Those whom God calls, God equips.

While giftedness can be an indicator of one's calling, it is not determinative. God called Moses to speak before Pharaoh, yet Moses stuttered. He called Moses to lead His people, yet Moses had led nothing but sheep for forty years. Giftedness is helpful, but lack of talent, skill, or experience should not deter someone from following a clear call from God. As Paul wrote, "[God] said to me, 'My grace is sufficient for you, for my power is made perfect in weakness.' Therefore I will boast all the more gladly about my weaknesses, so that Christ's power may rest on me" (2 Corinthians 12:9).

No matter what skill you possess, you need God's grace and strength because any true calling faces opposition and you will soon realize victories cannot be won without His presence and His power.

ROLE PREFERENCE

Many people choose the right pursuit but fill the wrong role. They are passionate about their calling but feel burnt out. As an example, consider Richard's experience. As a gifted architect enthusiastic about his craft, Richard's reputation gained him more work than he could handle. With expanded opportunities came employees, increased overhead, and greater leadership responsibilities. Instead of spending the majority of his workday at the drafting table, doing what he loved, he dealt with banks, solved personnel problems, and contended with government regulations. Miserable and exhausted, he questioned whether he should continue his career in architecture. Richard was in the right field, but he had assumed a wrong role.

Bobb Biehl knows something about the roles people play within organizations. He has spoken to thousands of people and introduced them to his "Team Profile," formerly called the "Role Preference Inventory." He begins with the assumption that one role isn't superior to another. Like positions on a football team, one role cannot function without the others in place. Furthermore, the roles are complementary; the talent of one player enhances the performance of the others. Because some roles are more glamorous, gain more attention, and garner higher pay, most people aspire to those positions, only to fail or become disillusioned.[11]

With your new understanding of living in "creative tension" with the world, and with the tools of *passion*, *giftedness*, and *role preference* to discover your calling, let's return to evangelism and your role in it.

ENGAGE

Most people think of evangelism as a proactive seeking of lost souls and the direct presentation of the gospel, carried out much like a well-trained sales force. That is, indeed, one very important and highly effective means of evangelism. But it is only one method among many—an infinite variety, in fact. God has called all of His followers to participate in the great task of "making disciples of all nations" (Matthew 28:20); we cannot relegate the job to so-called "professionals." Even so, your role may not involve frontline activity in preaching, door-to-door visitation, or street evangelism. God may have equipped you for a different kind of disciple-making.

The Lord has called you and equipped you for a role on His kingdom-building, world-redeeming team. Your responsibility then is to determine how your calling—as evidenced by your passion, your giftedness, and your role preference—can be used to bring others into a relationship with Christ. For example, Andrea discovered that her calling to meet the physical needs of underprivileged children put her in the perfect position to share the gospel with families in need of Christ. Her provision of tangible help gave her opportunities to meet spiritual needs like no other kind of evangelist.

Andrea's calling engaged her culture, and the result—to her own great surprise—was evangelism. Moreover, her choices have produced a creative tension among her non-Christian friends, who then struggled to criticize her beliefs while admiring her selflessness. Her Christian friends also began to feel a creative tension. By putting her faith to work, she silently stirred the conscience of her fellow-believers.

TAKE ACTION

Read Psalm 139:13–16, which describes how God endows each individual with gifts and ordains his or her purpose before birth.
If you know your calling, how do you engage the world with your gifts, talents, skills, and passion? How does this activity create opportunities to share the gospel?

If you do not know your calling, determine now to make this a priority. Consider the following resources:

> *The Call:* Finding and Fulfilling the Central Purpose of Your Life. Os Guinness. (Thomas Nelson Publishers, 2003).

> *Team Profile.* Bobb Biehl. (bobbbiehl.com, 2010).

Be intentional: What are you going to do about what you've learned?

Be specific: What action will you take in the near future to begin applying what you've learned? When will you do it?

Be accountable: Pray it through. Share your plan with a friend and seek his/her prayer and counsel for your next step.

CHAPTER 26: WORK

Several years ago, a man was driving his car at a snail's pace along a crowded freeway, only half listening to the music on the car radio. He was jolted out of his daydreaming by a song that didn't make sense. He instantly recognized the tune, "Whistle While You Work," as sung by the famous seven dwarfs of Snow White fame. Only this time the lyrics were in Japanese.

A voiceover confidently stated, "Americans work to live; the Japanese live to work." He didn't remember much about the commercial after that. He pondered the statement and whether it was true. And if it were true, who had the better philosophy, Americans or the Japanese?

Scan here to watch the video!

DAILY WORK IS GOD'S IDEA

God is a worker. He loves work. In Genesis 1, we see God creating the heavens and the earth. The psalmist takes note of this creator God and declares, "I will extol the Lord with all my heart in the council of the upright and in the assembly. Great are the works of the Lord; they are pondered by all who delight in them. Glorious and majestic are his deeds, and his righteousness endures forever" (Psalm 111:1–3).

After God created Adam and Eve, He placed them in the garden of Eden, not to lounge eternally in perpetual paradise, but to work it and take care of it. This kind of work is obviously good and has nothing to do with sin. Eventually, sin would turn work into toil—backbreaking, painful, unproductive, and unfulfilling at times. Even so, work is a gift from God, a means by which we reflect His image, not a product of sin.

Work is a gift from God, a means by which we reflect His image, not a product of sin.

The apostle Paul knew the value of work, and he expected other Christians to be productive. He set a worthy example, writing, "Surely you remember, brothers, our toil and hardship; we worked night and day in order not to be a burden to anyone while we preached the gospel of God to you" (1 Thessalonians 2:9). Then he told the Thessalonians "to lead a quiet life, to mind your own business and to work with your hands, just as we told you" (1 Thessalonians 4:11). This has a practical application to the ministry of the church. No one will heed the testimony of people they do not respect, and those who do not work are not worthy of respect. And to make his point crystal clear, Paul regarded those who do not work as no better than thieves, writing, "He who has been stealing must steal no longer, but must work, doing something useful with his own hands, that he may have something to share with those in need" (Ephesians 4:28).

Honest daily labor is a reward unto itself. It has very little to do with the size of the paycheck, although that can be a worthy motivation. The reward is the God-given capacity to experience joy (Ecclesiastes 5:18–19).

Another reward comes when a Christian occupies a place of responsibility in his or her company. The *Journal of Leadership Studies* addressed the topic of "The Leader and Religious Faith." Extensive research concluded that Christian CEOs were a reward to their corporations. "Results support the premise that entrepreneurial Chief Executive Officers who 'always' consciously apply the teachings of their religion during the daily decision-making process, attain superior goal achievement results over those CEOs who never apply the teachings of their religion. CEOs of faith have more profitable companies and greater annual, personal net worth increases. They rank in the top quartile of questionnaire results that measure business acumen, leader performance and organizational goal achievement skills."[12]

The bottom line financial performance is a by-product of the CEO's faith-based production.

ATTITUDES TOWARD EMPLOYMENT

Howard Dayton is a very successful businessman who has committed all of his God-given talents and earthly resources to the Lord. Howard started Crown Ministries, a small group and financial-study organization. This was born out of a burden to see men and women understand the Biblical mandates for handling their finances, to pursue the goal of getting completely out of debt, and to freely experience the joy of productive labor that comes from a sense of God's calling.

Here's what he says on the subject of work, in the introductory notes in his workbook. "Over a fifty-year span, the average person spends 100,000 hours working. Most of an adult's life is involved in work, but often with the job comes some degree of dissatisfaction. Perhaps no statistic demonstrates the discontentment of Americans more than their job-hopping tendencies. A recent survey found that the average man changes jobs every four and one-half years, the average woman, every three years."[13]

Psychologists say that attitudes precipitate actions. A person can be dissatisfied with his or her work for many reasons. Often it is a result of not knowing what the Scriptures teach on the subject; not knowing his particular skills or gifts; not taking the time to figure out who is controlling his attitude; or failing to establish attainable goals for his life. Ultimately, we all have to take responsibility for our attitudes.

God says a good attitude concerning work begins with choosing the right motivation. No one wants to work for paycheck alone. The need for money may prompt you to keep working, but no one finds deep satisfaction in earned funds. Instead, the Scriptures say, "Whatever you do, work at it with all your heart, as working for the Lord, not for men, since you know that you will receive an inheritance from the Lord as a reward. It is the Lord Christ you are serving" (Colossians 3:23–24). You may receive your paycheck from your boss, but the Lord hands out the report card. Therefore, a Christian should be highly motivated and industrious, not unlike the tiny, yet mighty, ant. Ants don't require a supervisor to force them to work; they dutifully serve their colony to ensure provisions for the present and the future (Proverbs 6:6–8).

Consider also these work-related admonitions from God:

> "Whatever your hand finds to do, do it with all your might, for in the grave, where you are going, there is neither working nor planning nor knowledge nor wisdom" (Ecclesiastes 9:10). *Therefore, don't be halfhearted.*
> "Diligence is man's precious possession" (Proverbs 12:27, NKJV). *Therefore, don't be a quitter.*
> "One who is slack in his work is brother to one who destroys" (Proverbs 18:9).
> "If a man will not work, he shall not eat" (2 Thessalonians 3:10). *Therefore, don't be a freeloader.*

So much for sugarcoated spiritual clichés! Paul's liberality didn't cover the slothful.

HISTORICAL PERSPECTIVE

The concept of work has gone through various stages since the beginning of the Church. Whatever your attitude toward work today, you can look back in history and find its source and those who also held that view. For instance, the early church was greatly influenced by the thoughts of the Greeks and Romans. Work was, at best, a necessary evil and regarded as noble only when chosen freely. Otherwise, a person was a slave and lacked personal autonomy. These views spilled over into the teachings of the church where Augustine believed that the contemplative life had a higher value than the active life. This resulted in the idea that the highest calling of God was to move into a monastery with ample time for contemplation.

Along came the Reformers and the Puritans who rejected this "withdrawal from the world" approach. They developed four basic attitudes toward work that became the foundation for thought among nations that were distinctly influenced by the Christian viewpoint.

Attitude 1: The Sanctity of All Honorable Work

Those who held this view rejected a division between secular and sacred work. Martin Luther said clergymen were not engaged in more holy work than housewives and shopkeepers. "It looks like a small thing when a maid cooks and cleans and does other housework. But because God's command is there, even such a small work must be praised as a service of God far surpassing the holiness and asceticism of all monks and nuns."[14]

William Tyndale, who was burned at the stake for creating an English translation of the Bible, said, "There is no work better than another to please God: to pour water, to wash dishes, to be a cobbler, or an apostle, all is one; to wash dishes and to preach is all one, as touching the deed, to please God."[15]

These individuals believed that work—all work—was to be performed as an act of worship. No one said it more clearly that John Calvin: "Paul teaches that there is no part of our life or conduct, however insignificant, which should not be related to the glory of God, and that we must be concerned, in eating and drinking, to do all we can to promote it."[16]

Attitude 2: God Calls Every Person to His or Her Vocation

Some believe that only those who are called into full-time Christian work are strategically placed by God. Stanley Tam in his book, *God Owns My Business*, disagrees: "Although I believe in the application of good principles in business, I place far more confidence in the conviction that I have a call from God. I'm convinced that His purpose for me is in the business world. My business is my pulpit."[17] The practical result of this view is that it leads to contentment in our work. If a person really feels called to be a businessman, he no longer needs to feel like a second-class citizen in the kingdom. The Bible contains several principles regarding calling:

> **PRINCIPLE 1:** God calls certain persons to religious vocations while others are free to select any work. We see an example of this in Acts 13:2 where Paul and Barnabas were set aside by the Lord for special services.
>
> **PRINCIPLE 2:** God calls people to be Christians, but places of service depend on personal gifts and talents (1 Corinthians 12).
>
> **PRINCIPLE 3:** God calls people to be Christians, gives gifts to many for special Christian work, and calls a few to specific tasks. In the Old Testament, you have the example of God calling Abraham to leave Ur of the Chaldeans, or Moses to lead the children of Israel out of Egypt. In the New Testament, you have many examples of Christians being encouraged to use their talents and gifts as God gives opportunities (Romans 12:6–8; 1 Corinthians 12:4–10; Ephesians 4:11; 1 Peter 4:10–11).

Attitude 3: The Motivation and Goals of Work

If you were to ask the average businessperson in America what the primary goal of work is, he or she would probably answer, "To make money." Ben Franklin set this attitude in concrete when he declared, "Time is money," and "Early to bed, early to rise, makes a man healthy, wealthy, and wise." Although Ben may not have realized it, his thoughts downgraded the sanctity of the job itself, to say nothing of volunteer work. Taken to extremes, this view suggests that Bible study, family time, recreation, vacations, and other activities not affecting the bottom line of a financial statement are wasteful.

In the twentieth century, the age of technology carried Ben's thoughts even further. It concluded that economic survival depends not upon just the simple premise that time has to be well invested in productive work, but also that survival will only be assured to nations that move from the goal of economic necessity to economic freedom. In order to obtain this goal, we have to become relentlessly future-oriented. No company survives without an aggressive research and development department. But there is a price to be paid. The relentless and ruthless pursuit of profits robs employees of the satisfaction God intended us to receive from our labors.

As the Puritans looked at a pure motive for work, they concluded that it should meet six standards:

1. It should be useful to society.
2. It should glorify God.
3. It should be moral.
4. It should provide for the needs of the family.
5. It should use God-given talents.
6. It should provide a means to help the poor.

Attitude 4: A Sense of Moderation in Work

While laziness carries a stiffer social stigma than drunkenness, sexual immorality, and other taboos of past generations, our culture doesn't suffer an overabundance of slothful people. On the contrary, workaholism—addiction to work—threatens to tear society apart from the inside. The Biblical view is found somewhere between these two extremes. Martin Luther wrote,

> [I] refute those who tempt God, want to do nothing, and think God will give them whatever they desire without any work or diligence on their part. There is a fitting proverb for such people: "Sit still, and have faith; wait for the fried chicken to fly into your mouth." God wants no lazy idlers. Men should work diligently and faithfully, each according to his calling and profession, and then God will give blessing and success. This is intended also for those who presume to think that results will come because of their industry and labor, or their cleverness and skill, and care nothing about God. But here again the right balance is this: "Don't be lazy or idle, but don't rely solely on your own work and doings. Get busy and work, and yet expect everything from God alone."[18]

So we work and we work hard, but we keep things in perspective. We also know that Jesus said, "Seek first his kingdom and his righteousness, and all these things will be given to you as well" (Matthew 6:33). The Biblical approach is not to neglect the other priorities of life— our families, health, church, personal growth, and education. The Bible knows our frame, and it knows that if we have an inordinate lust for anything, then it will defile our spirit. The Lord gives a warning that everyone should heed, especially those who maintain a preoccupation with work: "In vain you rise early and stay up late, toiling for food to eat—for he grants sleep to those he loves" (Psalm 127:2).

A BIBLICAL PERSPECTIVE

> *"Unity does not mean uniformity - it means oneness of purpose. God created each of us unique. Be the you He made you to be."*
>
> —Dr. Tony Evans

Men and women are created in God's image; and because God is seen as One who makes, forms, builds, and plants, He has touched all of labor with dignity. Nowhere is this more plainly seen than when God selected a man named Bezalel, of the tribe of Judah, to carry out the construction of the tabernacle after the Israelites escaped slavery in Egypt. "And he has filled him with the Spirit of God, with skill, ability and knowledge in all kinds of crafts—to make artistic designs for work in gold, silver and bronze, to cut and set stones, to work in wood and to engage in all kinds of artistic craftsmanship" (Exodus 35:31–33).

Paul reminds the Ephesians (and all of us) to use our gifts as we unite together for God's purposes… doing our daily duties as unto Him. Paul writes:

> You have one Master, one faith, one baptism, one God and Father of all, who rules over all, works through all, and is present in all. Everything you are and think and do is permeated with Oneness.
>
> But that doesn't mean you should all look and speak and act the same. Out of the generosity of Christ, each of us is given his own gift…
>
> He handed out gifts above and below, filled heaven with his gifts, filled earth with his gifts. He handed out gifts of apostle, prophet, evangelist, and pastor-teacher to train Christ's followers in skilled servant work, working within Christ's body, the church, until we're all moving rhythmically and easily with each other, efficient and graceful in response to God's Son, fully mature adults, fully developed within and without, fully alive like Christ. (Ephesians 4:4-13 MSG)

Whether your gift comes through a trade, a skill, a talent or a service… do all that you do as unto the Lord.

A FINAL PERSPECTIVE

When Jesus ministered on earth, He came as a blue-collar worker and His parables related to matters like sowing seed, cultivating vineyards, harvesting crops, building houses, and tending livestock. This isn't a coincidence. He doesn't value one vocation over another; He honors service to others above all, and He expects no less than wise use of the talents He grants. According to the Scriptures, we will be rewarded or judged based on what we did with our gifts and how we responded to His created purpose for our lives.

TAKE ACTION

Read Colossians 3:23–25, 1 Thessalonians 4:11–12, 2 Thessalonians 3:10–15, Ephesians 4:28, which discuss the topic of work.
List your primary motivations for working in order of importance.

List, in order of importance, the motivations you believe the Bible teaches. How do they compare?

Explain how an honest day's work benefits these people:

- Yourself
- Your spouse or other significant person
- Your children or other people in your care
- Your friends
- Your coworkers
- Your community
- Your God

How can you honor the Lord more effectively at, and through, your work?

Be intentional: What are you going to do about what you've learned?

Be specific: What action will you take in the near future to begin applying what you've learned? When will you do it?

Be accountable: Pray it through. Share your plan with a friend and seek his/her prayer and counsel for your next step.

CHAPTER 27: CARING FOR THOSE WHO HURT

Scan here to watch the video!

Mother Teresa and Princess Diana were both cultural icons. Amazingly, both died the same week during the summer of 1997. But that's where the similarities end; the two women could not have been more different. One, dwarfed in stature and withered by age, lived among India's diseased and indigent poor. The other, tall and graceful, dwelt among the world's most beautiful and privileged elite. One died a pauper, the other a multimillionaire. Still Mother Teresa and Princess Diana shared one thing in common. Each of them was moved by compassion to reach out to the poor, the maimed, the ostracized, and the homeless. Both of them responded in love and stooped to touch the untouchables of society. No wonder the world grieved their sudden deaths with unprecedented adoration. Both women distinguished themselves as heroines because of their love for humanity. They serve as noteworthy examples for all of us.

A STOREFRONT MERCHANT OF CARE
Taylor Field is about as manly as they come. His 6'4" athletic frame towers over most people he passes on the streets of New York City. Although his name sounds like an upscale department store, Taylor has been the pastor of a storefront church on Manhattan's Lower East Side since 1986. This native of Enid, Oklahoma, entered Wake Forest College as a pre-law major, hoping to follow in the footsteps of his lawyer father, but God had other plans. After Taylor encountered Jesus Christ in a profoundly personal way, he decided to follow in the footsteps of the sandal-clad first-century carpenter.

At first, Taylor wasn't sure what that would mean. He received his divinity degree at Princeton Seminary and then earned a PhD at Golden Gate Seminary in California. His family and friends encouraged him to take a traditional pastorate in a comfortable suburb, but Taylor resisted. Deep in his heart, he knew he wanted to minister among the homeless and disadvantaged where he could express Christ's love in tangible ways. He couldn't fully explain it, but he cared for the down and out.

That inner desire found expression as Taylor moved with his wife and two small boys to a neighborhood of abandoned buildings ruled by a local drug lord. From a graffiti-covered storefront building, this thirty-two year old inner-city missionary began to love the unlovable and touch the untouchable. He brought the grace of Christ to that area in the form of literacy programs and soup kitchens, worship services and Bible studies. And he gave the gift of his friendship freely to prostitutes, drug addicts, alcoholics, single moms, and fatherless kids.

When the twin towers of the World Trade Center collapsed on September 11, 2001, Taylor watched in horror. His little church and outreach center stood only 5,000 feet from Ground Zero. In just a few hours, the dimensions of his call to care for hurting people grew exponentially.[19]

THE STANDARD OF COMPARISON

Not everyone who is moved with compassion toward the hurting and the hopeless is motivated by a desire to be like Jesus. But those who have invited the Savior to be their Lord can't easily dodge His agenda. Jesus lived with nonstop compassion toward people hurting physically, emotionally, relationally, or culturally. From the very beginning of His earthly life Jesus identified with the plight of those with deep hurts. Difficult circumstances and deep poverty forced Jesus' earthly mother and her betrothed husband to deliver her child in a stable. After Jesus was born, His parents were forced to take their newborn, flee their country, and live as refugees in Egypt. When it was safe for Joseph and his family to return to Israel, they settled in Nazareth, a town in rural Galilee, notorious as the brunt of demeaning jokes. Jesus knew what it was like to grow up among the poor, the outcasts, and the broken.

When Jesus began His public ministry, He wasted no time articulating why He had come to earth. One Sabbath, shortly after His baptism by John and His period of temptation in the wilderness, Jesus went to the synagogue in Nazareth:

> The scroll of the prophet Isaiah was handed to him. Unrolling it, he found the place where it is written: "The Spirit of the Lord is on me, because he has anointed me to preach good news to the poor. He has sent me to proclaim freedom for the prisoners and recovery of sight for the blind, to release the oppressed, to proclaim the year of the Lord's favor." Then he rolled up the scroll, gave it back to the attendant and sat down. The eyes of everyone in the synagogue were fastened on him, and he began by saying to them, "Today this scripture is fulfilled in your hearing." (Luke 4:17–21)

By claiming to be the subject of this age-old prophecy of Isaiah, Jesus not only identified Himself as Israel's long-awaited Messiah, He also announced the purpose of His earthly mission. Jesus' marching orders called Him to redeem the world from the tyranny of sin and evil, starting with the needs of those consistently overlooked by the current world system. Later, Jesus reiterated His mission: "For even the Son of Man did not come to be served, but to serve, and to give his life as a ransom for many" (Mark 10:45).

We see this consistently throughout the Gospels. Jesus befriended the Samaritan woman at Jacob's Well. He defended (and forgave) the adulterous woman about to be stoned. He was moved with compassion for the frantic leader of the synagogue whose little girl was dying. He raised Lazarus from the dead. He harnessed His last ounce of human strength to speak words of comfort to His mother as she watched Him die at the foot of His cross.

WWJD?

Not many people know the term, "Christian," means simply "little Christ." It began as an epithet in Antioch where pagans derided believers for their unswerving devotion to Christ. Of course, the followers of Jesus could think of no greater compliment, so they embraced the term. By adopting the designation, "Christian," we are asking the world to see Him in us. If that is true, isn't it fair to say that the passions that motivated Him should motivate us? When faced with real life situations where we see people trampled by injustice or bruised by neglect, we would do well to ask ourselves, "What would Jesus do in a situation like this?"

Jesus put the hurts and needs of others ahead of His own, and He calls us to do the same. He commissioned His followers to be His hands and feet and arms and heart until His inevitable return. We are the means by which He reaches out to touch, carry, hold, help, comfort, and love.

If that isn't enough motivation, here's an even more powerful concept. Before leaving His earthly mission in the hands of less-than-perfect disciples, He told them that they were to see Him in the faces of those who are bleeding physically or emotionally. In Matthew 25 Jesus underscored this point with a sobering revelation of our future.

> All the nations will be gathered before him, and he will separate the people one from another as a shepherd separates the sheep from the goats. He will put the sheep on his right and the goats on his left. Then the King will say to those on his right, "Come, you who are blessed by my Father; take your inheritance, the kingdom prepared for you since the creation of the world. For I was hungry and you gave me something to eat, I was thirsty and you gave me something to drink, I was a stranger and you invited me in, I needed clothes and you clothed me, I was sick and you looked after me, I was in prison and you came to visit me." Then the righteous will answer him, "Lord, when did we see you hungry and feed you, or thirsty and give you something to drink? When did we see you a stranger and invite you in, or needing clothes and clothe you? When did we see you sick or in prison and go to visit you?" The King will reply, "I tell you the truth, whatever you did for one of the least of these brothers of mine, you did for me." Then he will say to those on his left, "Depart from me, you who are cursed, into the eternal fire prepared for the devil and his angels. For I was hungry and you gave me nothing to eat, I was thirsty and you gave me nothing to drink, I was a stranger and you did

not invite me in, I needed clothes and you did not clothe me, I was sick and in prison and you did not look after me." (Matthew 25:32–43)

In other words, when we see those who are imprisoned behind bars or ravaged by poverty or debilitated by disease or injury, we must accept this as our opportunity to care for Jesus Himself. Singing worship songs and hearing biblical preaching in a church service may be comfortable ways to express devotion to the Lord, but He wants, most of all, to see His mission accomplished by those who claim His name.

According to some beautiful prose written by the apostle Paul in 1 Corinthians 13, our devotion to Jesus or other people can't be limited to careless routines or obligatory disciplines. Religious expression that doesn't include loving behavior and compassionate concern is empty and useless. The apostle James offered similar advice when he suggested that faith without works is dead (James 2:14-26). And if ever the world needed faith that is fully alive, it is today.

THE ABCS OF BEING A CAREGIVER

- Ask the Heavenly Father to give you Jesus' eyes that you can see the world around you as He does. Ask Him to break your heart with the things that break His. Begin each day by saying, "Lord, I'm available. Show me today who it is that I can best care for. Give me the courage to obey what You say."
- Be aware. Despite the temptation to close your eyes to the difficult people in your sphere of influence, try to look beyond the imperfect packaging that hides a broken heart or damaged emotions. Attempt to get your eyes off your own concerns (and often insignificant desires) in order to focus on people who are far worse off than you.
- Create a list of practical responses to those who need help. Invite that colleague who is battling depression to have coffee with you at the local Starbucks. Suggest to your Sunday school class that you take on a nursing home as a place to give encouragement. Offer to provide a hot meal for a single mom who works and whose kids are in day care. Sign your family up to work at a soup kitchen on a regular basis.
- Don't be too hard on yourself when you blow it. Chances are you will rationalize reasons why someone doesn't really need your help or doesn't deserve it. You will likely give in to selfish inclinations despite your best intentions. But don't beat yourself up. Ask God for forgiveness and look for the next opportunity to serve Him by serving others.
- Excuse those who don't seem to appreciate your overtures of friendship or compassion. No doubt some issues of pride will keep some who dearly want to be helped from publicly acknowledging their need. They may be embarrassed by what you do.

- Find time each month to help a widow in your neighborhood or church. Chances are she has the need for small household repairs. Bring her groceries. Cook her a meal. Take her out for ice cream with your children. Talk to her about her deceased husband. Look at family photo albums and encourage her to talk about some of her happiest memories.
- Grieve with those the Lord prompts you to care for. Risk lowering your guard in order to enter into the plight of this one who feels overwhelmed or underappreciated. Remember the old Swedish proverb, "A shared joy is a doubled joy. A shared sorrow is half a sorrow."
- Have a sense of your own well-being. In other words, know when to pull back and care for yourself. It is possible to be so preoccupied with helping others that your own mental health suffers. There is such a thing as compassion fatigue. Dietrich Bonhoeffer wrote in *Life Together*, his classic book on community, that there is a time to be with other people and there is a time when we need to pull back from them. Jesus Himself illustrated that spiritual reality in the first chapter of Mark's Gospel. Even though a seemingly unending line of people in Capernaum was coming to Him for healing, Jesus healed some but not all. Although the disciples assumed that Jesus would stay in the village to care for those with needs, He disappointed their expectations. He needed to get away by Himself.

TAKE ACTION

Read Matthew 25:32–43, which describes the Lord's expectations of His followers.
Describe your response to this scene. Does this future judgment fill you with confidence and hope or reduce you to fear and dread?

Jesus used several examples of people in need, but His list isn't exhaustive. What segment of your society appeals most to your sense of compassion? Why?

Personal involvement usually begins with a phone call to an organization. Which organization in your area helps the people you mentioned above? When will you make that call?

Be intentional: What are you going to do about what you've learned?

Be specific: What action will you take in the near future to begin applying what you've learned? When will you do it?

Be accountable: Pray it through. Share your plan with a friend and seek his/her prayer and counsel for your next step.

CHAPTER 28: BECOME A DISCIPLE-MAKER

Scan here to watch the video!

People sometimes say the most fascinating things before dying. Some of these departing declarations have become known as "famous last words." Here are some of the more interesting statements recorded by history.

> "I've never felt better." (Douglas Fairbanks, just before going to bed, never to wake up.)

> "I do not have to forgive my enemies. I have had them all shot." (Ramon Maria Narvaez, Spanish soldier and statesman in response to a priest's inquiry.)

> "They couldn't hit an elephant at this dist—." (General John Sedgwick, just before catching a Confederate sharpshooter's bullet in the face.)

> "I don't know which is more difficult in a Christian life—to live well or to die well." (Daniel Defoe, who died penniless and deeply in debt.)

> "Hi, Jules. It's Brian. I'm on a plane and we've been hijacked, and it doesn't look good. Hopefully, I'll talk to you again, but if not, please have fun and live your life the best you can. Know that I love you, and no matter what I'll see you again someday." (Brian Sweeney on United Flight 175, September 11, 2001.)

Last words are captivating because they often reveal the individual's nature, his values, his very self. They are especially memorable to loved ones left behind, many of whom find new purpose or direction in life. The widow of Todd Beamer wrote a best-selling book based on her husband's last words, "Let's roll," and donated the proceeds to charity. Today, on the campus of Wheaton College, a building bears his name.

Our culture regards a person's last words as virtually sacred; so much so that our laws consider final requests binding obligations for the living. Innumerable court cases have upheld the directives of people no longer living, despite the objections of those who remain. Someday, you will have the opportunity to make a dying request and you can be reasonably certain your wishes will be honored, and will even carry the force of law.

There are, perhaps, no more important last words than those spoken by Jesus Christ. As the most important man who ever lived, His words—His departing request—carries immense weight for those who follow Him. Just before departing the earth, never to be seen again until His eventual return, the Lord called His followers to a hillside overlooking Jerusalem, where He said,

> "All authority in heaven and on earth has been given to me. Therefore go and make disciples of all nations, baptizing them in the name of the Father and of the Son and of the Holy Spirit, and teaching them to obey everything I have commanded you. And surely I am with you always, to the very end of the age." (Matthew 28:18–20)

As we examine the final words of Jesus, we must bear in mind that this is more than a historical event worth studying. Other great men have delivered memorable speeches, some of which helped change the course of history. Abraham Lincoln's Gettysburg Address united a nation in the bloody aftermath of the war against slavery. Patrick Henry's closing line, "Give me liberty, or give me death," became the rally cry of the American Revolution. The radio addresses of Sir Winston Churchill gave courage to the citizens of Great Britain, who alone, stood against Hitler's Third Reich. Undoubtedly, you have in mind a historic speech or two that we should have included. But the final address of Jesus stands apart from these in one critical respect: He uttered these last words for *your* benefit.

While Jesus stood before a gathering of first-century followers, He addressed all of His followers, the great majority of whom had not yet been born. He spoke not only to the remaining eleven apostles and several dozen other faithful disciples; He directed His final words to all Jesus-followers throughout all time—twenty centuries and counting. This includes you! Not just preachers, evangelists, teachers, and other vocation ministers. YOU. From His lips to your ears, here's a closer look at what He said.

First, take note of His bold declaration, "All authority in heaven and on earth has been given to me." God the Father, the creator and ruler of the universe, has delegated His authority to govern the world to His Son. Jesus then, on the basis of this ruling authority, has commissioned you to accomplish an objective. Before we examine this "great commission," however, we need to appreciate the implications of this "authority" statement.

To illustrate, imagine a man in a dark suit and sunglasses were to knock on your front door and say, "You have been given the responsibility to contact all of your family, friends, and neighbors. You are instructed to tell them to appear in person at the local fire station, where they will receive a package and instructions."

Perhaps like me, you might respond, "Who me? This must be a joke! What if they refuse?"

"Compel them by any means necessary," the man replies.

"How am I supposed to do that?"

"Be creative," he says with a smile.

Then the man says something that changes everything: "I am here on direct orders from the President of the United States, and I now deputize you with the power of the Oval Office to carry out this mission. Here are your badge and credentials; all the resources of the United States government are at your disposal."

God did not give you a mission without first giving you the power and authority to carry it out. Let's face it; a mission without power and authority is doomed to failure. No one in his or her right mind should accept a mandate without sufficient resources. Jesus, on orders from His Father, the creator and ruler of the universe, has deputized you and has made the resources of heaven available to us, His people—not to make us healthy, wealthy, and comfortable—but to accomplish a mission.

Having deputized His followers, Jesus said, "Therefore . . ." This conjunction is crucial. Based on His power and authority, He issues a *command*: "Go and make disciples." We are to do this through evangelism and training. "Baptizing them . . ." refers to the process of sharing the good news and then welcoming new believers into our fellowship. Once a new believer has established a relationship with Christ and has become a part of our community, we must now complete the Lord's mandate, "teaching them to obey everything I have commanded you."

Historically, the church has done a reasonably good job with evangelism. But, let's face facts, of the two tasks—evangelism and training—evangelism is simpler. Evangelism brings about an event, a decision to accept Christ as Savior. Evangelism merely *begins* the disciple-making process; training truly *is* disciple-making. A single evangelist can influence masses of people to begin a relationship with Jesus Christ; he or she cannot, however, become an effective disciple-maker to more than a handful. That's where God wants you to play your part!

DISCIPLE-MAKER EXTRAORDINAIRE

The apostle Paul obviously took the Lord's final address to heart! He made "making disciples" his personal mandate, becoming perhaps the most productive follower of Jesus Christ in history. He traveled the Roman Empire between Jerusalem and Rome, logging an estimated 15,000 miles over land and sea, preaching the gospel, teaching new believers, and establishing churches. But he didn't accomplish all of this alone. He understood the value of collaboration. He also knew that his impact for the gospel would begin to fade soon after his passing away. To make the most of his time and to safeguard all he had built, Paul became a discipler to a selection of men. Throughout his fifteen-plus years of active service, he invited certain men to follow him, to observe him in action, to learn from his successes and failures.

A survey of the New Testament reveals an impressive list of people Paul invited to learn from him, people in whom he invested time and energy.

God did not give you a mission without first giving you the power and authority to carry it out.

We are fairly good at reproducing spiritual babies, but not so good at raising them!

JOHN MARK	Acts 13:2, 4; 2 Timothy 4:11
SILAS	Acts 15:40–41
TIMOTHY	Acts 16:1-3; 1 Timothy; 2 Timothy
TITUS	Titus; 2 Corinthians 2:13; 7:6, 13; 12:18; 2 Timothy 4:10
LUKE	Acts 27:1–28:16; Colossians 4:14; Philemon 24; 2 Timothy 4:11
AQUILA AND PRISCILLA	Acts 18:18
DEMAS	Colossians 4:14; Philemon 24; 2 Timothy 4:10
ERASTUS	Acts 19:22, 29
GAIUS	Acts 19:22, 29
ARISTARCHUS	Acts 19:22, 29; 20:4
SOPATER	Acts 20:4
SECUNDUS	Acts 20:4
TYCHICUS	Acts 20:4
TROPHIMUS	Acts 20:4
EPAPHRODITUS	Acts 28:16; Philippians 2:25; Colossians 4:12; Philemon 23
CRESCENS	2 Timothy 4:10
ONESIMUS	Philemon 10-12

Paul not only evangelized; he made disciples. He spread the good news far and wide, but he also invested himself in a select few. When Jesus said, "teach *them* to obey everything I have commanded *you*" (2 Timothy 2:2, emphasis mine), Paul understood that Jesus wanted His followers to recruit and train others, who would in turn recruit and train the next generation. Consequently, Paul urged others to "follow his example" and to "be imitators of me" (1 Corinthians 4:16; 11:1; Philippians 3:17; 4:9), not because he believed himself to be perfect. Far from it! He merely encouraged others to pursue Christ as he had, and to use his footprints as a guide.

Now, let's face facts. Paul's example is awe-inspiring, but less than motivational. Who could possibly fill the shoes of a man like Paul? You might be saying to yourself, "I am certainly no Paul! If that's what it means to be a disciple-maker, forget it; I'm not right for the job!" But, the truth is you are the right person for the job because Jesus never commands us to do anything that He does not equip and empower us to do. Futhermore, do you really want to risk missing out on the great adventure of changing the planet?

CHANGING THE PLANET BY MULTIPLYING DISCIPLES

So what was Jesus' strategy to change the planet? He picked twelve men (Mark 3:13-19), spent three years building into them, and then charged them to go out into the world and do the same. *That's it? That was His strategy to change the planet?* Yes. Jesus' strategy was either STUPID or it was SUPERNATURAL!

Jesus set a *movement in motion*. He died to make that movement happen. He was buried. He was raised from the dead. He went to Galilee and uttered His famous last words, "Go… and make disciples!" (Matthew 28:16-20). Jesus expects you, as His follower, to join His movement and change the planet.

C'mon, really? Change the planet? Me? Good question. The answer is "Yes! You can!" Jesus' method works. If we do what He asks of us, we have the potential to see thousands and hundreds of thousands reached for Jesus. "I tell you the truth, anyone who has faith in me will do what I have been doing. He will do *even greater things than these*, because I am going to the Father" (John 14:12, emphasis mine).

Greg Ogden, in his book *Transforming Discipleship*, shares an illustration we've used time and again to show the potential of discipleship by multiplication. Ogden writes, "Let us suppose an evangelist operated out of an addition strategy. If an evangelist won one person a day to Christ for the next sixteen years (365 per year) there would be 5,840 decisions for Christ." In contrast, the disciple-maker "would win one person per year and spend the year discipling that person to maturity in Christ, which includes reproduction. At the end of that first year the same disciple would win another person and follow

EVANGELISTIC ADDITION vs. DISCIPLESHIP MULTIPLICATION

YEAR	EVANGELIST	DISCIPLE-MAKER
1	365	2
2	730	4
3	1,095	8
4	1,460	16
5	1,825	32
6	2,190	64
7	2,555	128
8	2,920	256
9	3,285	512
10	3,650	1,024
11	4,015	2,048
12	4,380	4,096
13	4,745	8,192
14	5,110	16,384
15	5,475	32,768
16	5,840	65,536

the same process. The multiplication occurs when the person discipled during the first year is also able to bring another to Christ and walk with him or her so that the new convert is capable of reproducing as well. The addition approach makes it the responsibility of the lone evangelist to win and nurture. Follow-up, or grounding the new believers in this model, becomes a numerical impossibility, whereas with the multiplication model, follow-up is built in."[20] While the potential is obvious, Ogden and I both agree that these numbers shouldn't be the focus. It's likely you may never meet (until you enter Heaven) the 65,000+ who would be impacted by you beginning one discipleship relationship. Don't focus on the numbers. Just start with one!

WHAT DOES IT MEAN TO MAKE DISCIPLES?

The great coach of the Green Bay Packers, Vince Lombardi, would stand before his team at the start of every season, holding a football, and say, "Gentlemen, this is a football." The point was if you don't know where it all starts and what the game is all about, you will not succeed!

Return to the Introduction for a brief review of the characteristics of a disciple: Learner, Follower, and Reproducer.

The same is true for making disciples. The word "disciple" is mentioned approximately 269 times in the New Testament. The word "Christian" is mentioned only three times. If you take all the instances of "disciple" and study each meaning, you will discover that a disciple is one concept with three phases:

> A disciple is a:
> Phase 1: Learner
> Phase 2: Follower
> Phase 3: Reproducer

All three phases are an assignment as a follower of Jesus. To be a fully functioning disciple we need to engage in all three; but most disciples of Jesus fade out in the Reproducing phase.

Being a maturing, reproducing disciple should mark our lifestyle. In 2 Timothy 2:2, Jesus tells us *(in the John Tolson paraphrase)*, "I want you to allow me to build a foundation of faith in you, so you can build a foundation of faith in others, who in turn will do the same."

WHO SHOULD MAKE DISCIPLES?

All followers of Jesus have been commanded to make disciples who in turn will make disciples.

WHAT ARE SOME OBJECTIONS TO DISCIPLE-MAKING?

1. I'm too busy!
Really? So you are going to stand before the Lord someday and say to Him, "Sorry I didn't get around to doing what You asked...because I was busy." When you realign your life with the biblical priorities laid out in this book,

the result is more time available and you'll find you have the time to disciple others.

2. I'm not called to disciple!
No one is *called* to disciple. We are *commanded* by Jesus to make disciples.

3. Disciple-making is meant for "professional" Christians.
Sorry, wrong again! Jesus didn't say, "Now go find your Pastors and Church Staff and tell them to make disciples." Nope. He said to you, "Go…and make disciples!"

4. I don't know enough.
You have the ultimate resource in the Bible. You've read and worked through *The Four Priorities*. You know enough. Take your Bible and a copy of *The Four Priorities*, get a copy for your disciple, and work through it again. It's that easy.

HOW DO I GET STARTED?

1. Get familiar with the principles of *The Four Priorities*.

2. Commit to living out the applications of *The Four Priorities*.

3. Look for one or two other persons (men with men, women with women, married couples with couples) who demonstrate:

- A love for Jesus
- A commitment to follow His Word
- A willingness to be prepared to make disciples

4. Meet with these candidates and share with them what a discipleship relationship is and why it is important. Invite them to consider going through *The Four Priorities* with you in preparation for them to disciple others.

5. Clearly convey the expectations of a discipleship relationship. (See next page for expectations.)

6. After completing Priority 1 and 2, give your disciple an opportunity to lead the meeting. This will aid in building confidence and skills in their training to become disciple-makers.

7. Remember, *The Four Priorities* is a "tool" for training you to become a fully functioning disciple…and training others to become fully functioning (reproducing) disciples. Throughout your reading and study as a group, you should continually encourage your disciples to prayerfully look for those whom they will disciple.

8. After your disciples complete *The Four Priorities*, set them loose to start their own discipleship relationships. Then you start again with another disciple.

FINAL CHARGE

Our lives are busy, hectic and hurried. There never seem to be enough hours in our day as it is. Reading, "Go ... and make disciples" can make some feel like, *Really? One more thing to add to my to-do list!*

If that's you, let's pause a moment. *The Four Priorities* is a "tool" to help you realign your lifestyle to biblical priorities...the priorities that Jesus Himself modeled out for us in the Gospels, and the very priorities that enable us to live the "abundant life"...the full and effective life that God has called us to (John 10:10). We began this book with a quote from John Tolson, "True learning doesn't take place until it *changes the way you live.*" Maybe, in the reading of this book, you've discovered some of your priorities are out of alignment... adjustments need to be made or activities may need to be removed.

Our time on earth is short. James reminds us, "Why, you do not even know what will happen tomorrow. What is your life? You are a mist that appears for a little while and then vanishes" (James 4:14). In the original Greek, the word for mist means a *vapor*—something that evaporates quickly. All to say life is, indeed, short in terms of God's timeline. But, don't mistake that for meaning that your life is in any way insignificant. Not at all! Your life is *crucial*

WHAT ARE THE EXPECTATIONS IN A DISCIPLESHIP RELATIONSHIP?

A. Intentional Participants. Each disciple should have a willingness to commit on the front end to disciple two people per year. As a disciple-maker, your time is valuable. If you invest your time into another person, that person should be willing to make the same commitment to others (and request the same commitment from those they disciple).

B. Meet weekly. Frequency in meeting helps with accountability and follow-through.

C. Come prepared. The discipleship relationship is a mutually transforming relationship. The disciple-maker and the disciple should arrive having read the chapter and be ready to actively discuss the insights gained through the study and application of the material.

D. Consistent Application. Both the disciple and the disciple-maker should leave the meeting time committed to applying the lessons learned in each chapter.

to the time and generation in which you were chosen to live, and God has intentionally planned and purposed you to live a *profoundly effective* life, a life of *high impact*, during your watch on planet Earth!

We all want to leave our mark on this world in some way. In the poetical book of Ecclesiastes, King Solomon expounds on this truth and the brevity of life, saying, "God…has set eternity in the hearts of men…" (Ecclesiastes 3:11b). We are hardwired by our Creator to make the kind of difference in this world that will have a lasting impact…to accomplish something for which we will be remembered long after we're gone.

My friends and fellow disciple-makers, I am here to tell you that the most profoundly effective thing you could possibly invest your life in is the eternal work of following Jesus Christ and making disciples for Him. There is no greater cause than the cause of Christ: Knowing Him, loving Him and reproducing your life in the lives of others…for His sake and His glory alone. That, my friend, is the Great Adventure!

So the question remains: *What do you want your life to count for?*

One day we will stand before our Creator and give an account of how we spent our time and the opportunities He gave us while on earth. While the Scriptures tell us that there will be no condemnation for those who are in Christ, we will have to speak about the "eternal fruit" of our lives (Romans 8:1). I believe that on that day the Lord will smile on us with great delight as He asks all those assembled, "Now, which of My followers came to know Me, love Me and follow Me because ____(insert your name)____ helped you along the way? Please step forward and line up behind him/her!" *Who will line up behind you?*

At the end of the day, this poignant thought will ring true:

Only one life, 'twill soon be past,
Only what's done for Christ will last.
–C. T. Sudd

God bless you and be with you as you follow Him, making disciples for Jesus Christ…all the days of your life!

TAKE ACTION

Read Matthew 28:18–20. How does the empowerment of God impact your view of discipleship and your potential as a disciple-maker?

Make a list of potential individuals for either one-to-one or one-to-two discipleship relationships. Keep the list handy and begin praying for courage and direction.

When you are ready to invite others, meet with them and explain the importance of discipleship and your desire to engage with them using *The Four Priorities*. Ask them to prayerfully consider making this commitment.

Contact us. Ask questions. Let us know how we can help you.

Be intentional: What are you going to do about what you've learned?

Be specific: What action will you take in the near future to begin applying what you've learned? When will you do it?

Be accountable: Pray it through. Share your plan with a friend and seek his/her prayer and counsel for your next step.

SCAN THE QR CODE FOR A FINAL MESSAGE AND CHALLENGE FROM THE AUTHOR, DR. JOHN TOLSON!

Congratulations on completing *The Four Priorities!* I am so proud of your commitment to being discipled. The "baton" has now been passed to you— and I'm praying for you as you go out and fulfill the Great Commission, that your impact for the Kingdom will multiply.

May the Lord bless you as you continue in this new way of life, making disciples of Jesus Christ. And remember— Jesus is with you all the way (Matthew 28:20).

John

RESOURCE APPENDIX

HOW TO BEGIN A RELATIONSHIP WITH JESUS CHRIST

The Bible states that, in the beginning, God made humanity flawless. The first people were morally perfect, living in complete harmony with God and the rest of creation. But it wasn't a forced obedience. He gave them the gift of autonomy, self-determination, the privilege of making choices and the dignity of living by the consequences of those choices. The first people were free to either obey God or disobey Him. He said, "You are free to eat from any tree in the garden; but you must not eat from the tree of the knowledge of good and evil, for when you eat of it you will surely die" (Genesis 2:16–17). After all, God didn't want the love of robots; He created people to enjoy a relationship based on freely given love and complete trust in Him.

The first people obeyed for a time, and then did the unthinkable. They chose to disobey. They chose to go their own way rather than live God's way. And they brought upon the world four lingering consequences that impacted them, and continue to impact us today.

FIRST, we are cut off from God.
Our relationship with Him is broken, and we are spiritually disconnected from Him. When I unplug a lamp, the light goes out. The same has happened to us. We are cut off from the One who made us, gives us life, provides for our needs, and gives us purpose. We might fill our lives with things to make us feel alive, feel meaningful, or feel hopeful, but it's nothing that will ever replace what we're missing from the Life-giver.

SECOND, we are cut off from ourselves.
There's nobody on the planet who has it all together. Emotionally. Psychologically. Mentally. Physically. All of us are born out-of-kilter. All of us have wounds and deficiencies that go back further than we can remember. When a man is unplugged from God, it has a devastating effect on how he views himself. The same is true of a woman. And our society bears that out. This futile search for significance has spawned an endless variety of vices, and addictions, and psychological problems, and coping mechanisms.

THIRD, we are cut off from each other.
Soon after the first man and woman disobeyed God, they started pointing the finger at one another, and we've been throwing each other under the bus ever since. The national divorce rate is nearly fifty percent. People don't live in peace, so we have police, attorneys, judges, and jails to contain crime.

They don't keep their word, so we have a civil code that takes people years to understand. Countries covet the territories of their neighbors, so all of them train soldiers in the science of killing and destroying. The world is now defined by conflict.

FOURTH, everything in the created world has been affected.
To put it simply, there's something terribly wrong with everything. Nothing in the world remains unaffected by the evil humanity first introduced through one disobedient act. And each of us continues to make the problem of evil worse by adding our own wrongdoings to the chaos. All of us are guilty; none of us can claim moral perfection. All we can do is point to the next guy and try to prove that his sins are worse than our own.

According to the Bible, God is one-hundred-percent perfect, and He will tolerate nothing less than one-hundred-percent moral perfection in His presence. To violate any portion of His moral code is to reject Him personally. Deep in the core of His nature is justice, so all wrongdoing must be punished. So even the most moral person in the world cannot meet God's standard of goodness if he or she bears the guilt of just one, single, solitary sin.

That's the bad news. We are hopelessly lost if the task of restoring the relationship is our responsibility. Fortunately, there's good news! If a restored relationship with God is the goal line, there are four "downs" we must consider:

FIRST DOWN: God looked down.
The Lord could have said, "Well, you blew it. You had your chance. I gave you everything you needed to be happy, healthy, whole, and fulfilled, but you had to do it your own way. You made this mess, now live with it. In fact, the just penalty of your rebellion is death (Romans 6:23), so I'm going to let justice take its course."

But He didn't say that. Instead, "God so loved the world that He gave His one and only Son so that whoever believes in Him shall not perish, but have eternal life" (John 3:16). He didn't love what people did to disconnect themselves from Him, but He loved people. He loved us and had compassion for us. But He didn't stop there.

SECOND DOWN: God came down.
While God hates evil, He loves people. But that causes a dilemma. You see, the problem isn't merely the bad things we have done; we are infected with what might be called the disease of sin. We are entirely corrupted with a moral cancer called "sin." And until the disease of sin is eradicated from within, we cannot avoid future wrongdoing. That's why willpower is never enough. As hard as you try, you cannot keep from sinning because you are sinful all the way down to your DNA. Consequently, it's going to take something miraculous to cure us of this moral disease.

The cure came to earth when God became a man in the person of Jesus

Christ. Fully human, so He could represent us. Morally perfect, so He was qualified to bear the penalty of others. And fully God, so that He could not only die the death owed by all people, but rise again to conquer death and live on. Jesus Christ, God in human flesh, was born and then lived as people ought to live. And for thirty-plus years, He lived an incredible life. When He spoke, people listened. When He touched people, their diseases were healed. When He confronted evil, it shrank from His presence. But through it all, He knew He had a mission.

THIRD DOWN: Christ laid down.
Jesus came to earth to become our substitute, to pay the penalty of death that we owe for all the bad things we have done. He came as the perfect representation of good on earth, which drew the wrath of evil. As Jesus, Himself, stated, "Light has come into the world, but men loved darkness instead of light because their deeds were evil" (John 3:19). Rather than accept Jesus as their king, evil people rejected Him, beat Him to a bloody pulp, and executed Him on a cross to get rid of Him.

Evil put the Son of God down, but He didn't stay down. Evil put Jesus to death, but He didn't stay dead. Having paid the penalty of sin on behalf of all people, He rose from the dead—literally, not just figuratively or spiritually. He left behind an empty tomb, having risen to a new kind of life. And now He offers this new kind of life to all who will receive His gift.

FOURTH DOWN: Every knee must bow down.
From the beginning, God said that the just penalty for rebelling against Him is death (Genesis 2:16–17; Romans 6:23). Not just the demise of the physical body, but spiritual death (Revelation 20:14–15), which is eternal torment in hell. That's not a pleasant thought, but it is nonetheless true. While Jesus bore the penalty on behalf of all humanity, He didn't set aside the gift of autonomy originally given to people back in Genesis. We are not automatically saved from sin whether we want it or not. We still possess the gift of choice and the dignity of living with the consequences of our choices. And so it is with the gift of Christ's death on our behalf.

The penalty of sin is death, and you have a choice as to how that debt will be paid. You can reject Christ's sacrificial gift and pay it yourself by choosing hell, or you can let His death satisfy your debt.

To accept His gift, you merely admit you cannot overcome the internal problem of evil on your own. You admit you are powerless to save yourself or even clean up your own act. And in that realization of helplessness, you ask for Christ to accomplish for you, and within you, what you cannot do yourself. You say, "Lord, I bow down. I give You everything. I want You to come into my life, rid me of the disease of sin, clean up my mess, make me the person You created me to be, and someday welcome me into Your eternal presence when my physical life ends."

If you're at the place right now where you would like to bow your knee and accept this gift of healing from the disease of sin and the promise of eternal life, you simply pray something like the following. This is just an example prayer; there are no magic words. This is not about saying or doing the right thing. All you're doing is admitting you need God to save you, believing His promise to welcome you, and accepting His free gift of Himself in your life.

Dear Lord,

I admit that I am helpless to overcome my shortcomings to be the man/woman You want me to be. I also admit that the things I have done and the disease of sin within me have disconnected me from You, and that I deserve eternal death as a penalty for my sin. Thank You for sending Your Son, Jesus, to die in my place. I trust in Him alone to pay the penalty of my sins and to grant me forgiveness. I accept His gift of eternal life, and I ask Jesus to be the Lord of my life. Thank You.

In Jesus' name,
Amen.

If that prayer expresses your thoughts, then you have received a wonderful gift. Your life will never be the same. Moreover, you have joined an extended family of believers. So let me be the first to say, *Welcome to the family of God!*

You have begun a new journey, but you don't have to walk alone. You have many brothers and sisters who would count it a privilege to help you know what comes next. We would love to hear from you and help put you in touch with other men and women who have walked the path you have begun. Please contact us at:

thetolsongroup.com

HOW TO MAKE A DIFFERENCE FOR CHRIST USING THIS BOOK

Clearly, we must *become* disciples and Jesus has commanded us to *make* disciples. The question is "How?" By using *The Four Priorities*, you will help others discover how to make a difference for Christ in the world.

There's no one "right" way to use this book. There are churches using this book as curriculum in small discipleship groups, in Sunday School, and in life or home groups. Outside the church, men are discipling men, women with women, couples with couples – the possibilities are endless. Fathers are discipling sons home from school during summer months, hometown missionaries are reaching international students, and so on.

WHAT QUALIFICATIONS DOES A DISCIPLE-MAKER NEED?

Whatever your situation, disciple-makers should be men and women who:

- commit themselves to following Christ by living as He wants in every area of life.
- implement the principles described in *The Four Priorities*.
- desire to help others understand and apply the Four Priorities.
- want to reproduce reproducers by developing other disciple-makers.

Disciple-makers don't have to be "super Christians" or first become dynamic or charismatic communicators. They just need to be men and women who live for Jesus and want to help others do the same—*someone like you*.

This book and the study works well in small group settings as well as one-on-one or one-on-two personal discipleship relationships.

DO YOU HAVE A RECOMMENDED AGENDA FOR EACH WEEKLY MEETING?

We recommend that the group members plan on meeting for about an hour or more each week. There are two sample agendas to share with you, but we greatly encourage you to customize your agenda that works for the time, ages, and location for your meetings:

Example #1:
- Share a brief prayer to open the meeting.
- Encourage everyone to share observations and comments from *The Four Priorities* chapter studied.

- Challenge your group members to find at least one application they will live out from each study.
- Share briefly your schedules (key events) for the week. Briefly share the status of your relationships. Share briefly where you are now (stress points, good points, etc.).
- Close in prayer. Have one person pray or open it for all to pray (if people are ready). Pray about those matters that people shared in the time you have been together.

Example #2:
- Warm up with small talk about sports/news/personal matters over a cup of coffee.
- Open in prayer and review the chapter theme for the day.
- Go over statements in the chapter that created personal interest. Let the group chase a few rabbits (tangential subjects) but rein in the discussion fairly quickly each time. Read appropriate passages from Scripture and discuss how they apply.
- Review the "Take Action" questions for everyone to process and share their thoughts. If it is obvious participants have not been consistently answering the questions at the end of the chapters, they need to be challenged to get in the game to make the experience worthwhile.
- Ask for prayer requests. Then pray and wrap up.

Here are some lessons gleaned from the experience of many groups and group leaders.

1. If the men or women know up front that they are expected to start their own groups at some point, they will be far more attentive, take copious notes, and engage more enthusiastically in the discussion. If you have flexibility with the location, look for a room that is easily accessible, has a feeling of warmth, and is comfortable to sit, talk, and pray.
2. If you get questions you can't answer, say that you'll have a response at your next meeting.
3. As the Boy Scouts say, "Be prepared!" Be sure to study the chapter well in advance of the meeting, reviewing all the Scripture mentioned and preparing a few key points that personally resonated with you during your study.
4. You are developing friendships—so be a friend!
5. Almost all of the participants feel inadequate to lead a group. This is one more reason for having a co-leader to help boost the discussion. Give your leaders resources to help

them lead and answer questions. For example, the *Holman Personal Evangelism New Testament or Share Jesus Without Fear* includes thirty-six answers for the most common objections to receiving Christ and can help build confidence that the facilitators can anticipate in advance the answers to tough questions.

6. Add personal stories to the discussion or other sources of information regarding the subject matter. Also write in the margins of your book the comments that will be worth remembering and sharing in future group studies.

7. Plan social events where the group can get together outside of the study. You could go out to dinner, go to a ball game, play golf, or something similar. The purpose of *The Four Priorities* group is not just to process information but to become a living, vital experience of what is being taught in the material. As you get into Priority Four, the group should be discussing how each individual is going to live out that priority. How will they be involved in evangelism, caring for those who hurt, and living out their calling?

8. Some of the chapters will hit close to home and may make certain individuals feel uncomfortable. The topic might be bitterness, depression, marriage, parenting, stewardship, or something else. The facilitator should explain that no one escapes the feeling of being in the bull's-eye and to listen to the conversation without feeling everyone is looking at him or her. At this point, remind the group that everyone has "enemy held territory" that is a part of their journey.

9. This study will uncover a wide divergence in theological opinions. Encourage expression without being judgmental. Maturity will come in time if everyone is kind to one another and no one is put down for holding a contrary view.

HOW TO STUDY THE BIBLE

1. PICK A TIME, HAVE A PLACE, AND BE PREPARED
Your study time is more likely to happen if you have a regular time and place to meet with the Lord for study and prayer.

2. PRAY FOR THE HOLY SPIRIT'S GUIDANCE
Bible study is more than just gaining knowledge of God's Word, it's developing a relationship with God's Son.

Begin by asking the Lord to help you understand His Word. Use your own words, or pray what the Scriptures themselves say:

> *"Lord, thank You for Your Word so that I may know You and what You desire for my life. Now I ask You, please, to give me the Spirit of wisdom and revelation to know you better" (Ephesians 1:17). Lord, open my eyes that I may see wonderful things in your law" (Psalm 119:18); open my mind to understand the Scriptures" (Luke 24:45), and to do what You want me to do."*

3. READ AND RE-READ THE SCRIPTURES
There is no other book like the Bible! It is the most important book you will ever read; a message from the God who created you, who loves you and who wants to have a relationship with you. Train you ear to listen to your Shepherd's voice as you prayerfully, purposefully, thoughtfully, inquiringly… and slowly read and re-read His love-letter to you.

4. STUDY THE SCRIPTURES
The goal of Bible study is *transformation*: A changed life, and that requires good interpretation as well as application of the Scripture. The method of "Inductive Study" teaches us how to think and to correctly apply the Word of God by following these 4 steps:

Observation ~ Interpretation ~ Application ~ Response

USING THE INDUCTIVE BIBLE STUDY METHOD

STEP 1) OBSERVATION

<u>Observation</u> answers the question: *What does God's Word say?* (Not what you *think* it says…but what does it *actually* say?) What do you see in the actual content in the text?

Before we consider what the text means, we must ask what it says. This means *reading and re-reading* a text until we become acquainted with it. Observation is the process of seeing and taking notice of things as they really are in the passage you're studying. You want to look for facts like a detective uncovering clues by asking good questions of the Scripture using "who, what, when, where, why, and how" questions. Soak up as much as you can and write down your observations and facts; this takes time, so look carefully and don't rush through it.

Consider who, what, when, where, why and how…

- Who is writing? To whom are they writing? Who are the people involved in this scene?
- What is happening in this scene? What's being said? Is there a lesson to learn? Is there a command to obey? Is there a promise to claim? Is there a sin to avoid? Is there a blessing to enjoy? Is there an exhortation, a rebuke, a question, an answer, a prayer, a quotation of another passage of Scripture? What's the main point? What key words or phrases are used? What's the context? What literary style is being used? Is it narrative, conversation, parable, prophecy, poetry, a letter, or a sermon?
- When? Are there any references to time or date; any words related to the past or future? Look for words like after, until, then…
- Where? Are there any locations mentioned—towns, roads, rivers, mountains, regions, or other landmarks?
- Why? Are there any clues about why things are being said or done?
- How? Is there an explanation about how things are done or a process or any cause-and-effect statements? How is Jesus reflected in this passage?

STEP 2) INTERPRETATION

<u>Interpretation</u> answers the questions: *What does God's Word mean? What did*

God mean by what He said?

Our goal is to discover the original intent and meaning of the author. Paul writes, "Do your best to present yourself to God as one approved, a workman who does not need to be ashamed and who correctly handles the word of truth" (2 Timothy 2:15). In the original Greek language, "correctly handles" literally means "cutting a straight line". As in cutting material in a straight line in order to make a garment or a tent, our interpretation of Scripture needs to be precise and accurate so that it will all fit together without contradiction.

- Don't overanalyze the "main things and the plain things"
- A golden rule of interpretation: *"If the plain sense makes good sense, seek no other sense or it will result in nonsense."* D. Cooper, Biblical Research Society

STEP 3) APPLICATION

<u>Application</u> answers the question: *What does it mean to me?*

Bible study doesn't end with interpretation; it continues to the question, *So what?* The goal of studying the Bible is not only to gain information but also to **experience transformation**: A changed life!

Once we've completed the observation and interpretation steps, we can now apply the lessons from the passage and put God's Word into practice in our life. The benefit of Bible study comes in *obeying the voice of God*—receiving what He has said and putting it into practice. These questions in the form of an acronym can help you apply the Word to your life:

S – Is there a **sin** for me to avoid?
P – Is there a **promise** from God for me to claim?
E – Is there an **example** for me to follow?
C – Is there a **command** for me to obey?
K – How can this passage help me to **know** God or Jesus Christ better?

STEP 4) RESPONSE

<u>Response</u> answers the question: *How will I apply God's Word to my life?*

Here's where we get very specific and give some feet and legs to our lesson. Remember that you're not simply filling in the blanks on a lesson page or making note of another great lesson. You're responding to God, and your response should be motivated by the fact that God loves you, and your desire to please and glorify Him.

Be <u>specific</u> in your personal response to the Scripture: *When will I apply this to my life? How will I apply this to my life and in what area of my life? With whom?* You may also want to date your response and have someone hold you accountable to follow through with it.

"Biblically speaking, true learning only takes place when it changes the way you live!" ~ *John Tolson*

Inductive Bible Study Methods adapted from writings of Kay Arthur, Howard Hendricks, Robert M. West, Anne Graham Lotz, The Navigators Bible Study Handbook, and Dr. John F. Tolson.

BIBLE STUDY TOOLS

BIBLE TRANSLATIONS:
Modern-day Bibles have been translated from the original Greek and Hebrew texts that were recorded in Jesus' time. Translations will vary depending on whether they are:

- *Literal* ("word-for-word" translation that conveys the exact meaning of the original words)
- *Paraphrase* (usually translated in contemporary language for easy reading, it conveys the thought or intent of the original words).

There are varying degrees of each type of translations and both types of translations are good for reading through the Word. But for going deeper in learning to study the Bible, it's best to use "literal" translations that will most closely convey the original meaning of the Greek or Hebrew text.

BIBLE TRANSLATIONS RECOMMENDED FOR STUDY:
These Study Bibles are "literal" translations that contain notes and commentary pertaining to the Scriptures.

If you decide to purchase a study Bible, look for these things: wide margins, Scripture cross-references, and an adequate concordance in the back. The translations we find best for studying are:

- English Standard Version (ESV)
    - ESV Study Bible (Crossway Books)
    - The Reformation Study Bible
      (R.C. Sproul/Ligonier Ministries)

- New International Version (NIV)
    - 1984 Edition

- New King James Version (NKJV)
    - MacArthur Study Bible (Thomas Nelson Publishers)

- Life Application Study Bible (NIV 1984 edition; Tyndale House Publishers)
    - GREAT for those who are new to studying the Word!
    - Has an extensive concordance, topical references, and commentary.

- Word of caution: Don't get too dependent on the commentary and application notes. Stick to the Scriptures themselves for your interpretation.

- Hebrew-Greek Key Word Study Bible (NIV 1984 edition; AMG Publishers)
    - Includes word studies and lexical aids.

BIBLE TRANSLATIONS RECOMMENDED FOR READING:

These Bibles are "paraphrase" translations. Use the paraphrase translations to re-read the passage of Scripture you're studying to get another perspective. But do keep in mind that since these are paraphrased they do not generally convey the original meaning of the word.

- New Living Translation (NLT)
    - We highly recommend *The Swindoll Study Bible* by Charles R. Swindoll in the NLT translation for reading and study.
- New English Translation (NET)
- The Message (MSG)
- Amplified Bible (AMP)

ONLINE BIBLE STUDY RESOURCES:

These web sites feature various translations of the Bible, concordances, commentaries, lexical aids and dictionaries.

- MyStudyBible.com
- BibleStudyTools.com
- BibleGateway.com
- BlueLetterBible.org
- NetBible.org
- Dictionary.com

CONCORDANCES, DICTIONARIES, AND OTHER TOOLS:
- Strong's Concordance
- Vine's Expository Dictionary
- What the Bible is All About – Bible Handbook (H. Mears; Regal Books)
- The Complete Word Study – Old Testament (Baker/Carpenter; AMG Publishers)
- The Complete Word Study – New Testament (Zodhiates; AMG Publishers)
- The Navigators Bible Studies Handbook (NavPress)

PREPARING A PRAYER NOTEBOOK

1. Pray. Ask God to honor and bring fruit to what you are setting out to do.
2. Refer to page 57 to review verses which relate to the following four "ACTS" of prayer:
   - Adoration (Praise)
   - Confession (Repentance)
   - Thanksgiving (Gratefulness)
   - Supplication (Ask/Petition)
3. Prepare the first 4 pages of your notebook. Page 1 should have "Adoration" written at the top as the title. Under the title, write the verses and the references you found. Repeat for Confession, Thanksgiving, and Supplication.
4. On a new sheet of *scratch* paper (not in your notebook), prepare a list of **people and people groups** for whom you'd like to pray for regularly. Think of all the "people groups" you are part of – your family, your work, and friends in your social settings, etc. You can pray for these people individually, or as a group.
5. Add to this list the **events** for which you'd like to pray – your Bible study meeting, worship service, small groups, etc. Be sure to include one-time events also, like a big project coming up at work, or a wedding or graduation, etc. (Psalm 37:23).
6. Add to this list the **organizations** for which you'd like to pray – these are ministries you support and causes you support. For example, pray for The Tolson Group, The Gathering/USA, your local church, and other ministry groups doing the work of the Lord (feeding starving children, building water wells, serving the poor, etc.).
7. Add to this list other **countries** that are close to your heart, or that God has placed on your heart and mind, so your prayer life will not be limited to where you live (Acts 1:8).
8. Take this long list of prayer subjects (created in steps 4 – 7) and subdivide each list into 7 pages in your notebook. When finished, you will have 7 small lists representing each day of the week. It's helpful to have a mixture of people, organizations or ministries, a country, and at least one event on each day.
   - Remember, as you move forward with this notebook your lists will change and fluctuate. It's ok to add and remove people, places and events from your prayer notebook as time goes on.
9. Title each of the subdivided lists with the days of the week, "Monday", "Tuesday", etc. These daily lists will now serve as the "Table of Contents" for each day of the week in your notebook. If you like, use divider tabs to

help you easily find these days in your notebook.
10. To go even deeper and record your requests and answered prayers, you can create individual pages for each subject on your daily "Table of Contents." To do this, use a new sheet of paper and draw 3 columns. The title for the page is the individual item, and the titles for the 3 columns are Date > Request > Answer.
   - For example, if your "Sunday" list has your church, your mom, and a ministry, you will then prepare 3 new sheets of paper – 1 each for church, mom, and ministry. These sheets for individual items will be placed behind the "Sunday" table of contents in your notebook.
11. You can customize this notebook however you'd like. Using a prayer notebook will help focus your prayers and see God answering them! For more options, you can add a "daily" prayer sheet to the beginning of your notebook for people you want to pray for every day. Also add a monthly calendar if you like. Place all these sheets in a 3-ring binder that will last. Rejoice and ask God to make you a faithful person at prayer!

RECOMMENDED READING

BY THE AUTHORS OF *THE FOUR PRIORITIES*:
Take a Knee by Dr. John Tolson
Search and Rescue: This Time for the Children by Larry Kreider

SUPPORTING THEMES IN *THE FOUR PRIORITIES*:
Intimacy with the Almighty by Charles R. Swindoll
More Than a Carpenter by Josh McDowell
Know What You Believe by Paul E. Little
Know Why You Believe by Paul E. Little
The Training of the Twelve by A. B. Bruce
Living By The Book by Howard G. Hendricks and William D. Hendricks
The Great Omission by Dallas Williard
Don't Waste Your Life by John Piper
Margin by Richard A. Swenson, M.D.
7 Basic Steps to Successful Fasting and Prayer by Bill Bright
Basic Christianity by John Stott
The Blessed Life by Robert Morris
Boundaries by Dr. Henry Cloud and Dr. John Townsend
The Call: Finding and Fulfilling the Central Purpose of Your Life
    by Os Guinness
Celebration of Discipline by Richard J. Foster
Concise Theology by J. I. Packer
Essential Truths of the Christian Faith by R. C. Sproul
Growing Deep: Exploring the Roots of Our Faith by Charles R. Swindoll
The Power of Who by Bob Beaudine
The Practice of the Presence of God, and the Spiritual Maxims
    by Brother Lawrence
The Spirit of the Disciplines by Dallas Willard
Think Differently Live Differently by Bob Hamp
Management Waste by Larry O'Donnell, III
The Treasure Principle by Randy Alcorn
Out of the Salt Shaker and into the World by Rebecca Manley Pippert

ABOUT THE AUTHORS

DR. JOHN TOLSON OF THE TOLSON GROUP

Dr. John Tolson's calling in life is to "make disciples" (Matthew 28:19), and he pursues that calling with fierce determination and unparalleled tenacity. To that end, John began The Gathering movement more than thirty years ago. The organization was officially formed in 1987 in Orlando, Florida, when Larry Kreider came on board as the President. As a relevant and effective discipleship and outreach ministry to men, The Gathering has spread across the country to reach more than one million men with the resources and motivation to disciple one another in Christ.

In 2006, John and his wife Punky Leonard Tolson began to extend the work of The Gathering through a new discipleship ministry called The Tolson Group based in Dallas, Texas. Designed to equip men and women to become and mentor disciples of Jesus Christ, John speaks, teaches, and consults at organizations across the country. John's passion for The Tolson Group is to see men and women so transformed by Biblical discipleship that every believer embraces the work of going and making disciples of Jesus Christ.

As an avid basketball player and fan—holding a personal best record of 127 straight free throws—John serves as a spiritual coach for some of the nation's leading executives, celebrities, and athletes. John started one of the first team chaplain programs in the NBA, and he has served multiple sports teams, including the Houston Rockets, Houston Astros, Houston Oilers, Orlando Magic and the Dallas Cowboys.

Married to "Punky" Leonard Tolson since 2001, John is the father of two grown children with his late wife Ruth Anne and has three adorable granddaughters. To schedule John for a ministry retreat, church conference, or disciple-making summit, please visit thetolsongroup.com.

LARRY KREIDER OF THE GATHERING/USA, INC.

Larry Kreider is a native of Colorado and has lived in the Orlando area since joining The Gathering as their President in 1987. He and his wife, Susan, have two grown children, Brett and Erica and six grandchildren. Larry authored two additional books, *Bottom Line Faith* and *Search and Rescue: This Time for the Children*.

The Gathering/USA, celebrating their 25th anniversary in 2012, was formed as a ministry of evangelism and discipleship for the men of our country. It has since spread to twenty communities, some groups led by volunteers and other groups led by full-time staff. The Gathering's main event is an annual or semi-annual outreach breakfast. Over the years, the attendance for these events has been from 300 to 3,000, and many men have found Christ by hearing some of the nation's most gifted communicators of the Gospel.

Each city has its own delivery system for discipling, including small group studies, large weekly Bible studies, mentoring and coaching programs, and individual counseling. In Orlando, Florida, the headquarters for The Gathering, there is a similar ministry for women.

The Gathering also has a mission emphasis in the Dominican Republic under the name of Mission Emanuel. Numerous teams of men, women, and children have gone to help build churches, schools, and medical clinics, and to sponsor the 500 children now receiving an education.

The Four Priorities is the main strategy for connecting men and women with the Biblical model for the Christian life. If you are interested in learning more about The Gathering, view them online at thegathering.org.

of these five stages.

12 Frank Toney and Merrill Oster, "The Leader and Religious Faith," *Journal of Leadership Studies* Vol. 5, No. 1: 135–147.

13 Howard Dayton, *Discovering God's Way of Handling Money: Course Workbook* (Crown Financial Ministries, 2001).

14 Martin Luther, commentary on Genesis 13:13, in *Luther's Works*, ed. Jaroslav Pelikan (St. Louis: Concordia, 1960), 2:349.

15 William Tyndale, *Doctrinal Treatises and Introductions to Different Portions of the Holy Scriptures*, ed. Henry Walter (Cambridge: The University Press, 1848), 102.

16 John Calvin, *The First Epistle of Paul the Apostle to the Corinthians*, transl. Oliver and Boyd Ltd. (Grand Rapids: Wm. B. Eerdmans Publishing Co., 1996), 224.

17 Stanley Tam, *God Owns My Business* (Camp Hill: WingSpread Publishers, 2008), 62.

18 Martin Luther, *Luther's Works*, Vol. 14, ed. Jaroslav Pelikan (St. Louis: Concordia Publishing House, 1958), 115.

19 Visit the East 7th Street Baptist Church (known as Graffiti Church) online at GraffitiChurch.org

20 Greg Oden, Transforming Discipleship (Downers Grove: InterVarsity Press, 2003) 137-138.

9   TheFatherlessGeneration.wordpress.com/statistics

10   Chuck Aycock and Dave Veerman, *From Dad with Love: Gifts for Kids That Money Can't Buy* (Wheaton: Tyndale, 1994), 2-74.

11   John Wooden, quoted in *Beyond Success: The 15 Secrets to Effective Leadership and Life Based on Legendary Coach John Wooden's Pyramid of Success*, by Brian D. Biro (New York: The Berkley Publishing Group, 1997), 38.

12   Chuck Aycock and Dave Veerman, *From Dad with Love: Gifts for Kids That Money Can't Buy* (Wheaton: Tyndale, 1994), 75-132.

13   Gary Chapman, *The Five Love Languages: How to Express Heartfelt Commitment to Your Mate* (Chicago: Northfield Publishing), 39–40, 55-56, 74-75, 87-88, 103.

14   Charles R. Swindoll, *Parenting: From Surviving to Thriving* (Nashville: Thomas Nelson Publishers, 2006), 37.

15   *Merriam-Webster's Collegiate Dictionary*, Eleventh ed. (Springfield: Merriam-Webster, Inc., 2003), s.v. "confidence."

16   Chuck Aycock and Dave Veerman, *From Dad with Love: Gifts for Kids That Money Can't Buy* (Wheaton: Tyndale, 1994), 133-158.

17   Visit MontyRoberts.com for more information about Join-Up®

18   David Aikman, *Jesus in Beijing: How Christianity Is Transforming China and Changing the Global Balance of Power* (Washington, D.C.: Regnery Publishing, Inc., 2003), 287.

PRIORITY FOUR

1   George Barna, *Think Like Jesus: Make the Right Decision Every Time* (Brentwood: Integrity Publishers, 2003), 19.

2   George Barna, *Think Like Jesus: Make the Right Decision Every Time* (Brentwood: Integrity Publishers, 2003), 21.

3   Information condensed from George Barna, *Think Like Jesus: Make the Right Decision Every Time* (Brentwood: Integrity Publishers, 2003), chapter 2.

4   Dio Chrysostom, *Orations* 11:1–2, LCL.

5   Francis Schaeffer, *Death in the City*, (Wheaton: Crossway Books, 2002), 87.

6   Dr. Alan Bloom, *The Closing of the American Mind* (New York: Touchstone, 1988), 25.

7   A fairy tale written by Ron Peri.

8   Bill Bright, 1998

9   This is not to say that *all* parents who home-school or send their children to private institutions have this as their motive. Only that some do.

10   Os Guinness, *The Call: Finding and Fulfilling the Central Purpose of Your Life* (Thomas Nelson Publishers, 2003), 29.

11   In order to find the role you are best suited to fill and to enjoy long-term success, a five-step process will help to eliminate years of trial and error. For more information, visit BobbBiehl.com and look for a copy of Team Profile, which offers an in-depth explanation

18   mayoclinic.com

19   Charles Stanley, *The Gift of Forgiveness* (Nashville: Thomas Nelson, Inc.), 141.

20   Bob Hamp, "Freedom Through Forgiveness - Part 5," bobhamp.com, October 1, 2009.

21   Points A-C from Bob Hamp, "Freedom Through Forgiveness - Part 5," bobhamp.com, October 1, 2009

22   Bob Hamp, "Freedom Through Forgiveness - Part 6," bobhamp.com, October 2, 2009

23   Dr. Archibald Hart, *Unmasking Male Depression: Recognizing the Root Cause to Many Problem Behaviors Such as Anger, Resentment, Abusiveness, Silence, Addictions, and Sexual Compulsiveness* (Nashville: Thomas Nelson Publishing, 2001)

24   Philip Zimbardo, "The Age of Indifference," *Psychology Today* (August 1980): 72.

25   Millicent Fenwick, quoted in *Words of Wisdom*, ed. William Safire and Leonard Safire (New York: Simon & Schuster, 1989), 261.

26   Abraham Lincoln, quoted in *Lincoln's Melancholy: How Depression Challenged a President and Fueled His Greatness* by Joshua Wolf Shenk (New York: Mariner Books, 2005), 62.

27   George S. Patton, Jr., *War As I Knew It* (New York: Mariner Books, 1995), 402.

28   Abraham Lincoln, quoted in *Abraham Lincoln: A History*, vol. 6, by John G. Nicolay and John Hay (New York: The Century Co., 1909), 328.

29   John 4

30   Onesimus is found in the New Testament book, Philemon

PRIORITY THREE

1   Ann Voskamp, "How to Live the Really Best Bucket List," aholyexperience.com, August 28, 2012

2   David W. Smith, *The Friendless American Male* (Ventura: Regal Books, 1983), 22.

3   John Powell, *Why Am I Afraid to Tell You Who I Am?* (Grand Rapids: Zondervan, 19xx), 30–35.

4   J. B. Phillips, *The New Testament in Modern English for Schools* (London and Glasgow: Collins, 1972), 412.

5   The name Stradivarius is associated with violins and cellos built by members of the Stradivari family. The name "Stradivarius" has become a superlative often associated with excellence; to be called "the Stradivari" of any field is to be deemed the finest there is. A Stradivarius made in the late 1600s to early 1700s is often worth several million U.S. dollars at today's prices. (Wikipedia.com)

6   *Merriam-Webster's Collegiate Dictionary.*, Eleventh ed. (Springfield: Merriam-Webster, Inc., 2003), s.v. "concerted."

7   J. B. Phillips, *The New Testament in Modern English for Schools* (London and Glasgow: Collins, 1972), 412.

8   Chuck Aycock and Dave Veerman, *From Dad with Love: Gifts for Kids That Money Can't Buy* (Wheaton: Tyndale, 1994).

FOOTNOTES

32   Randy Alcorn, *The Treasure Principle* (Colorado Springs: Multnomah, 2001), 60.

33   Randy Alcorn, *The Treasure Principle* (Colorado Springs: Multnomah, 2001), 60.

34   Randy Alcorn, *The Treasure Principle* (Colorado Springs: Multnomah, 2001), 27.

35   Exodus 23:19, Numbers 18:20-21, Proverbs 3:9-10, Malachi 3:10, Matthew 23:23, 1 Corinthians 9:13-14, Galatians 6:6, James 1:27.

PRIORITY TWO

1   Dr. Finn R. Amble, M.D., received his training at the Mayo Clinic and has provided invaluable insight while preparing this chapter.

2   According to studies by David Lamb, *Physiology of Exercise: Responses and Adoptions*, MacMillan Publishing Co., 1984

3   Dr. Andrew Weil, *The Healthy Kitchen: Recipes for a Better Body* (Borzoi Books, 2003), xi–xii.

4   Institute of Medicine, *Accelerating Progress in Obesity Prevention: Solving the Weight of the Nation* (iom.edu, 2012)

5   Institute of Medicine, *Accelerating Progress in Obesity Prevention: Solving the Weight of a Nation* (iom.edu, 2012)

6   Institute of Medicine, *Accelerating Progress in Obesity Prevention: Solving the Weight of a Nation* (iom.edu, 2012)

7   Richard H. Carmona, M.D., M.P.H, F.A.C.S., Surgeon General, as cited in the testimony before the U.S. House of Representatives, July 16, 2003

8   Institute of Medicine, *Accelerating Progress in Obesity Prevention: Solving the Weight of the Nation* (iom.edu, 2012)

9   Institute of Medicine, *Accelerating Progress in Obesity Prevention: Solving the Weight of a Nation* (iom.edu, 2012)

10   Frederick Buechner, *Godric* (New York: HarperCollins Publishers, 1980), 153.

11   Martin Luther, quoted in *The Wit of Martin Luther*, Eric W. Gritch (Minneapolis: Augsburg Fortress, 2006), 53.

12   Lord Palmerston, quoted in *Littell's Living Age*, Vol. 22 (Boston: E. Littell & Company, 1849), 477.

13   Andy Andrews, *How Do You Kill 11 Million People: Why The Truth Matters More Than You Think* (Nashville: Thomas Nelson, 2011), 11.

14   For a complete listing of the Beatitudes, see Matthew 5:3-12.

15   According to research from the Health Emotions Research Institute at the University of Wisconsin.

16   Also taken from Brenda Polk.

17   Herb Kelleher, quoted in *The Levity Effect: Why it Pays to Lighten Up*, Adrian Gostick and Scott Christopher (Hoboken: John Wiley & Sons, Inc.), 92.

16; 2 Peter 3:13; Revelation 21:1; Ephesians 1:3, 20; 2:6; 3:10, and 6:12; 2 Corinthians 5: 1-8, 1John 3:2; Revelation 21:1-4; Daniel 7:18 See more on Hell: Matthew 10:28; 13: 40-42; Mark 9:43-44; Matthew 8:12; Revelation 20:12-15; Matthew 13:40-42; 13:50; 22:13; 24:51; 25:30; Luke 13:28

10   Howard Hendricks, in Kenneth Boa, *Conformed to His Image* (Grand Rapids: Zondervan, 2001), 78.

11   J.I. Packer, *Concise Theology* (Wheaton: Tyndale House Publishers, 1993), 143.

12   J.I. Packer, *Concise Theology* (Wheaton: Tyndale House Publishers, 1993) 69-70. See also 1 Chronicles 21:1; Job 1-2; Zechariah 3:1-2; John 12:31, 14:30, 16:11; Matthew 4:3; 2 Corinthians 4:4; cf. Ephesians 2:2; 1 Thessalonians 3:5; 1 John 5:19; Revelation 12: 9-11, 20:2.

13   Wayne A. Grudem, *Christian Beliefs* (Grand Rapids: Zondervan, 2005), 55.

14   J.I. Packer, *Concise Theology* (Wheaton: Tyndale House Publishers, 1993) 69-70.

15   Dietrich Bonhoeffer, in Eric Metaxis, *Bonhoeffer: Pastor, Martyr, Prophet, Spy* (Nashville: Thomas Nelson Publishers, 2010), 540.

16   Oswald Chambers, *My Utmost for His Highest: Selections for the Year* (Grand Rapids: Discovery House Publishers, 1993), Aug. 28th.

17   Oswald Chambers, *My Utmost for His Highest: Selections for the Year* (Grand Rapids: Discovery House Publishers, 1993), Sept. 16th.

18   Brother Lawrence, *The Practice of the Presence of God, and the Spiritual Maxims* (New York: Cosimo, Inc., 2006), 72.

19   www.businessofprayer.com/ACTSprayermodel

20   Richard J. Foster, *Celebration of Discipline* (New York: Harper and Row, 1988) 48-49.

21   Elmer L. Towns, *Fasting for Spiritual Breakthrough* (New York: Regal Books 1996), 17–18.

22   Dallas Willard, *The Spirit of the Disciplines* (San Francisco: Harper San Francisco, 1988), 166.

23   Helen H. Lemmel, 1922, Hebrews 12:2

24   Dr. Larry Crabb, *The Papa Prayer: The Prayer You've Never Prayed* (Nashville: Thomas Nelson, 2006), Kindle Edition pp. 22-23.

25   Vineyardmusic.com

26   Gordon Dahl, *Work, Play, and Worship in a Leisure-Oriented Society* (Minneapolis: Augsburg, 1972), 12.

27   Robert Morris, *The Blessed Life* (Ventura: Regal Books, 2004), 48-49.

28   Robert Morris, *The Blessed Life* (Ventura: Regal Books, 2004), 51.

29   Randy Alcorn, *The Treasure Principle* (Colorado Springs: Multnomah, 2001), 62.

30   Randy Alcorn, *The Treasure Principle* (Colorado Springs: Multnomah, 2001), 62.

31   Robert Morris, *The Blessed Life* (Ventura: Regal Books, 2004), 47.

FOOTNOTES

INTRODUCTION

1 Allen Saunders, quoted in *The Quote Verifier: Who Said What, Where, and When*, ed. Ralph Keyes (New York: St. Martins Griffin, 2006), 123–124.

2 Followers of Jesus Christ were first called "Christians" at Antioch (Acts 11:26)

3 Bill Hull, *Jesus Christ, Disciplemaker: 20th Anniversary Edition* (Grand Rapids: Baker Books, 2004), 136.

4 "Street Level Evangelism, Where is the Space for the Local Evangelist," by Michael Parrott, Acts Evangelism, Spokane, WA, 1993, pp. 9-11, via http://bible.org/illustration/evangelism-statistics

5 "Street Level Evangelism, Where is the Space for the Local Evangelist," by Michael Parrott, Acts Evangelism, Spokane, WA, 1993, pp. 9-11, via http://bible.org/illustration/evangelism-statistics

6 See "How to Make a Difference for Christ Using this Book" in the Appendix

PRIORITY ONE

1 B.C. refers to the time period "before Christ." If a year is represented, as in 30 B.C., it refers to 30 years before Jesus Christ. Anno Domini, or A.D., refers to the years after the death of Jesus Christ.

2 Keynote at Exodus 3:14 in *The Hebrew-Greek Key Word Study Bible*, as quoted by Sylvia Gunter, *Prayer Portions* (Birmingham: The Father's Business, 1995), 28. See also: Exodus 3:14, Revelation 1:4, Hebrews 13:8

3 Adapted from the sermon, "The Absolute Power of Jesus Our Lord," given by Charles R. Swindoll on Feb. 7, 1999, at Stonebriar Community Church in Frisco, Texas.

4 Excerpted from John Stott, *Basic Christianity* (Downers Grove: InterVarsity Press, 2006), 80-81. See also: Sin - Romans 3:22-23, 1 John 1:8, 10; Biblical Standard - Exodus 20:1-17, Matthew 22:36-40

5 RC Sproul, *Essential Truths of the Christian Faith* (Carol Stream: Tyndale House Publishers, 1992), 195. See also: John 15:1-8; Romans 4:1-8; Romans 5:1-5; 2 Corinthians 5:17-19; Titus 3:4-7

6 AB Simpson.

7 Charles R. Swindoll, *Growing Deep: Exploring the Roots of Our Faith* (Portland: Multnomah Press, 1986), 416.

8 John Stott, *Basic Christianity* (Downers Grove: InterVarsity Press, 2006), 105-107. See also: Mark 8:31, Luke 12:50, John 17:1, 12:27-28, 18:11, Matthew 26:53-54

9 Randy Alcorn, *Heaven*, (Carol Stream: Tyndale House Publishers, 2004), 23. See more on Heaven: John 14:1-3; Philippians 1:23; Psalm 33:13-14; Matthew 6:9; Psalm 2:4; Acts 1:11; Hebrews 12:22-25; John 17:5, 24; 1 Thessalonians 4:16-17, Hebrews 11:10,